# BLANK MINDS and STICKY MOMENTS in COUNSELLING

## PRACTICAL STRATEGIES and PROVOCATIVE THEMES

# BLANK MINDS and STICKY MOMENTS in COUNSELLING

## PRACTICAL STRATEGIES and PROVOCATIVE THEMES

SECOND EDITION

Janice russell and graham dexter

Los Angeles • London • New Delhi • Singapore

First edition published by Insight Press, York in 1997
This second edition published 2008

SAGE Publications Ltd
1 Oliver's Yard
55 City Road
London EC1Y 1SP

SAGE Publications Inc.
2455 Teller Road
Thousand Oaks, California 91320

SAGE Publications India Pvt Ltd
B 1/I 1 Mohan Cooperative Industrial Area
Mathura Road
New Delhi 110 044

SAGE Publications Asia-Pacific Pte Ltd
33 Pekin Street #02-01
Far East Square
Singapore 048763

**Library of Congress Control Number: 2001012345**

**British Library Cataloguing in Publication data**

A catalogue record for this book is available from the British Library

ISBN 978-1-4129-4576-9
ISBN 978-1-4129-4577-6 (pbk)

Typeset by CEPHA Imaging Pvt. Ltd., Bangalore, India
Printed in India at Replika Press Pvt Ltd
Printed on paper from sustainable resources

#165409965

# contents

# 1

# welcome to the concepts: introduction and overview

**Abstract:** In this chapter, we overview the rationale for the book, and introduce the second edition. We offer some examples of what kind of instances present as blank minds or sticky moments, and provide the reader with a map to guide them through the rest of the book.

## Welcome

Welcome to the second edition of *Blank Minds and Sticky Moments*. In the first edition of this book, we invited you to be open to stimulation, to have an interest in what makes counselling tick, and to be willing to be entertained. We suggested that if we could achieve this, and if you could glean or reinforce some educative principles to boot, then your money was well spent.

Feedback suggested that we achieved our aims. The book was appraised as highly pragmatic as well as having a 'can't put it down' flavour. A second edition was called for, so here we are, offering another opportunity for you to evaluate and challenge the myths and false expectations that litter the world of counselling, while focusing on successes, pragmatic approaches and provocative lines of thought.

## Who are we?

Our names are Janice Russell and Graham Dexter, and we have worked in counselling and communications over a 30-year span. We bring personal experience and influence, with all that this entails, to our work and our lives. Even now that we are of an age to qualify for SAGA car insurance, we still indulge ourselves when some infantile-based response rears its cheeky head. We try and resist the concept of having self-developed to a point of 'getting there'. Having five children between us, and two grandchildren, we run a gamut of life experiences. Our family brings us a great deal of joy, pleasure and pride: equally, we know loss, frustration, fear and uncertainty. We do our very best whilst not having all the answers, weaving our way through our personal journeys, using survival techniques and the resources that we have at the time. We're two ordinary people who from time to time do extraordinary things, just like you.

As we explained in the first edition, we both chose 'helping' professions at an early age, Jan training in social work, Graham in psychiatric nursing. We both fell into counselling in the early 1980s as much by accident as deliberate intent, and undertook a wide range of ventures to learn and practise our art. One of those ventures was to return to higher education as mature students; we believe that this experience helps us now to teach in an understanding and creative manner. We began to critique that which we had learned, and we encourage our own students to do likewise. So now we counsel, supervise, train, consult, research, read, write, travel; we go to the cinema, go walking, keep pigeons, still keep on trying to learn new things (currently dancing and Portuguese), and we value what we have.

## What's changed since the first edition?

Since the last edition, we have moved to Portugal, enjoying the laid-back culture and the sunnier climes, and discovering different challenges. Specifically, it's interesting to be an immigrant, to experience cultural difference from a particular perspective, to try to learn a new language, and to set up a livelihood when you are an incomer.

The counselling world has moved too, as the steady 'drip drip' of professionalisation has continued. Definitions of counselling have altered, and there is a greater mergence between counselling and psychotherapy than 10 years ago; there are still no absolute measures of the 'success' of counselling. The profession is still messy around the edges, with a tendency to mysticism here and there.

When we wrote the first edition, there were moves to make a register of counsellors, and we suggested that it would be interesting to see how this is policed, given that counselling depends upon human interactive skills and activities – would helping people problem-solve over dinner parties be illegal? Could people be outlawed for empathising during pillow talk, on the grounds that it has elicited self-disclosure beyond that which the partner had wanted to engage in (but of course only realised this retrospectively)? The current quality of efforts to police the profession is the subject of some disappointment, wherein criteria for 'good character' and 'fitness to practise' are at best inconsistent and at worst simply non-establishable (Department of Health, 2006).

Despite a continued fuzziness, BACP (British Association for Counselling and Psychotherapy) accreditation has become much more formally recognised now in the UK, and many organisations demand it when recruiting counsellors. Online counselling has developed, with a number of delightful paradoxes which invite new perspectives on received wisdoms and definitions, some of which create dilemmas for practitioners.

We commented in the first edition that a degree of uncertainty has always facilitated innovation within counselling: yet we had noticed an increasing shift away from the pioneer approach of what *could* be done in counselling being replaced by an insistence on what *should* be done. The pendulum has shifted a little, and we observe new spirits of adventure and discovery emerging with new technologies and ways of thinking. At the same time, the urge to regulate is stronger than ever. Notions of success and failure continue to haunt even the most experienced practitioners.

In Portugal, regulations are way behind those in the UK, painting a different picture altogether. In the indigenous culture, there is a split between 'psychologists' and counsellors. Psychologists are the practitioners most likely to be officially assimilated within government health initiatives such as community addiction teams. Counselling tends to be offered by those who have moved here, and often offered with innovation and little regulation – such as counselling while clifftop walking. In many ways, the situation reminds us of how things once were in the UK.

## Why the book?

We still carry the conviction that counselling draws on ordinary, non-mystical activity and skills in a principled manner. At the end of the day, we believe that counselling is about a purpose, and an attitude. The adoption of each results in the construction of a number of skills and techniques which achieve the desired outcome. However, such skills and techniques are merely principled footprints made on the road to fulfil the purpose; just because one person walked this way, we don't all have to. There is no one right way to do it, and there is no proficiency in technique without the attitude and approach of inquiry. We essentially understand counselling to be a dynamic process of negotiation which purports to create opportunities for self-determined change for the client.

The overall purpose of this book, then, is to address the principles and issues associated with the complexities of counselling, whether for the 'pure' counsellor, the student counsellor, or for workers who use counselling as one part of their job, e.g. mental health workers, psychiatric social workers. We recognise that people arrive at the role of counsellor through different routes, some through academic courses, others through practice-based learning. Some deliberately work towards counselling as a career, some 'fall' into it through their life's journey. How often do we hear people say that 'I always ended up listening to people's problems anyway, so I thought I might as well train'. We want this book to be accessible to a varied audience, to have academic credibility and to be non-exclusive. In other words, we want to reach the practitioner, whatever their background.

The idea for the book began from our own practice in counselling, training and our supervision of practitioners. It had become apparent that whatever their level of training and experience, when counsellors feel stuck, certain themes, issues or 'skill gaps' emerged consistently. At such times, counsellors either don't know what to do, do not have the confidence to try out their own ideas, or suspect that they may be about to infringe some taboo or other. We wanted a book which would address these areas in detail, with reference to pragmatic experience and reference to relevant literature.

In our experience as trainers, we had found that the 'blank minds' and 'sticky moments' to which we refer are often not fully addressed in training courses or supervision, despite there being a strong call from practitioners that they should be. There is a dearth of literature which is bold enough to present both pragmatic and academic issues as integral to each other and to the profession of counselling rather than as separate and specialised subjects. Having identified some of the common issues or scenarios which seem to confuse or baffle counsellors, we suggest a range of intervention techniques to help deal with them. We acknowledge some of the deeper intra- and interpersonal issues which may occur within the counselling relationship, while examining theoretical underpinnings which might influence them.

The philosophy of the book is very much concerned with empowering the counsellor to free themselves up to be imaginative, creative and flexible. Much counselling literature has been caught up with what *should* be done, whereas the intention of this book is to encourage counsellors to think of what *could* be done within a framework of purposeful and ethical practice. We adopt a somewhat realist and relativist view that while psychological theories are a useful adjunct to counselling, in the end they are merely informed speculations: we need to beware the trap of accepting metaphors as gospel. Ask yourself – who said that the self is like a layered onion? Where does the idea of 'real' experience, or the notion of the self having a 'core', come from? How can we measure the *depth* of emotion? We are interested to demystify some of the more 'precious' aspects of counselling which can be inhibiting to the counsellor, or which might diminish their trust in the client. It is important to regain some humility for a profession which assumes and theorises so much about human nature.

The inception of this book lies in strong personal views, experiences and philosophy. We made the original proposal to our publishers in 1995: their readers expressed severe reservations. One was that the subject matter was not appropriate to be treated humorously, while another was that it seemed a very pragmatic and eclectic approach which was not currently in vogue. We believed that counselling needs to be developed towards the interests of the client first. We depend on the pragmatic, wanted to be light-hearted here and there, and so decided to publish ourselves.

Since then, ties have been loosened a little. Works such as *Counselling for Toads* (de Board, 1998) and *Tigger on the Couch* (James, 2007) appeared on the market, with deserved success, marrying serious theory with entertainment and wry humour. Now we are delighted that SAGE have chosen to commission the second edition. We trust that you will find it both helpful and provocative, and a contribution to the rich debate of counselling.

The book progresses through inherently interdependent sections, focusing first on pragmatic issues, presenting ideas, approaches, principles and skills, moving toward exploration of the more general context of counselling and some of the theoretical issues and arguments. We believe that both need to be considered by every single person who is offering someone else theory-based psychological help.

The remainder of this chapter will guide you through the structure and spirit of the book, painting a picture of the kind of blank minds or sticky moments which seem to be common, directing you to the relevant chapter for each. We might add that some of our personal worst moments in counselling have taught us best, and we can now look back at these with a good dose of humility and sometimes with humour. They are many and varied, some more ridiculous than others, some more dramatic, some more serious; we learned from them all. We hope that as you read on, you will dare to feel reassured, amused, even, engaged, and perhaps a little freed up.

## Excuse me, I believe I was here first

Chapter 2 explores 'intrapersonal issues'. We refer here to those kinds of moments when whatever is going on for the counsellor as a direct result of the work influences either their lives or their professionally intentioned interventions.

For example, the guru effect. Most of us have moments where a client says something like:

> Jan, this has been so useful. I don't know what you've done, but whatever it was, it was wonderful. You have helped me more than anybody ever. I don't know what I'd have done without you. I shall recommend you to my friends, and if ever I'm stuck I know where to come!

When this did first happen for Janice, she went home with a rosy glow, pleased that the counselling had 'worked'. And lo! to be so marvellous into the bargain: to have been so indispensable, so magical: to have such powers.

Over a period of time, niggles entered the process of self-satisfied reflection: it was those small statements: 'I don't know what you've done', and 'I don't know what I'd have done without you'. Questions arose – who had done what, to whom, and what had been learned? Maybe, just maybe, Janice's need to be 'the helper' had been a bit too strong.

Of course, time then generated opportunities for somewhat humbler and more gratified feelings. Helping someone work through a complicated bereavement where reviewing the process enabled a client to go away with a method for coping with future problems and concerns, brought a new understanding regarding the educational and equal aspects of counselling. This was a delightful outcome and good learning. To achieve it, we need to hang up the magician's hat and be comfortable in the role of sorcerer's apprentice. It's very easy to be seduced or even motivated by the thought of being somehow 'special' in 'helping' others.

'I know just how you feel' is another little gem which falls within intrapersonal issues, and which most will recognise. People do it all the time. When Janice had breast cancer, many people claimed to know just how she felt because they had once had a suspicious lump on their back (which had turned out to be a cyst), a pain in their breast (muscle strain), a painful growth on their foot (a verruca). Even the breast nurse knew just how Janice felt, so inaccurately and pompously that Janice wanted to slap her (Russell, 1998).

In the counselling situation, this tendency (identification – not the urge to slap!) is an easy temptation. Maybe you are working with

6

someone who has experienced a loss that seems similar to your own experience: you may think you know how the client feels. Again, very common, very easy to do.

Intrapersonal certainty can also creep into situations you have never experienced, where the counsellor can *imagine* how you must feel. Some years ago on a training tape we heard the following, where a woman was talking about the death of her husband. The dialogue went something like.

> *Client*: I've got these really strong feelings and I don't know how I'm going to get through them. I feel so guilty.
> *Counsellor*: It's normal to feel guilty when someone dies. You loved your husband and you feel there's more you could have done or said. It's normal to feel guilty because you are still alive.
> *Client* (animatedly): But that's just it. I feel guilty because I feel so free. He was a miserable old bastard and I'm glad to be rid of him. And now you're like all the rest, making me feel bad for not having normal feelings.
> [15-second gap on tape.]
> *Counsellor*: Oh. I see.

Beware the power of the theory-led imagination! All of these are examples of how what is going on for us might intrude into what is going on for the client.

An addition to this chapter in this revised edition is an exploration of what might happen intrapersonally for counsellors in training, when their lamp is burning brightly, and they are keen to 'try this at home'. We suggest that counselling training should perhaps carry a government health warning (Dexter, 1997), and we invite the reader to look closely at the possible personal cost of such undertaking.

## Knowing me, knowing you – aha!

In Chapter 3 we will look at interpersonal issues, employing four key headings of intimacy, sexuality, friendship and culture. The focus is on what goes on, and what affects, the relationship between counsellor and client. We look at complications which might arise through unconscious motivation, e.g. that which Freud coined transference and countertransference. These are quite simple concepts to describe a process which might occur in any relationship, where, quite literally, feelings which were evoked in a previous relationship are 'transferred' to the current situation.

For example, Graham once counselled a woman who was the same age as his mother, with offspring the same age as him. She presented herself as something of a victim in the family, coming over as martyrish, often performing tasks which she didn't want to, and then bemoaning the family for taking her for granted. Graham soon got irritated with her, just as he had with his own mother, who also had a tendency to behave in this way. Once identified, he could use this realisation constructively to both better understand and to challenge the client into new understandings. Not rocket science, but something to be aware of.

Counsellors can also be seduced by letting the client pull their strings. The client may brings a certain way of relating into the counselling relationship. An individual who is used to being related to sexually might act in a way which is sexually provocative, and this may evoke a sexual response from the counsellor: a client who is used to people being irritated by them might have developed a whiny or apologetic interpersonal style, which the counsellor becomes irritated with. Before they know it, the counsellor might actively internalise the proffered role, and begin to behave accordingly.

Simplistically, this can create a form of self-fulfilling prophecy, and unspotted, can lead the way for some very unhelpful and at times exploitative or destructive practice. The chapter explores principles for monitoring and avoiding unhelpful responses.

And then there is the thorny issue of friendship. Most of us, in the process of being empathic, challenging, creative and caring, will meet clients with whom we have a 'natural' rapport: had we met in other circumstances, perhaps friendship might have ensued. It's easy to think, as a colleague of ours put it, 'Oh sod the counselling, let's go down the pub'. And what if we had met in other circumstances – how would it have worked? The answer, of course, is that we'll never know: some of the clients you meet might indeed have developed into friends.[1] Some might not have, and it seems pragmatic to us to have a perspective which recognises our different roles within the relationship,[2] a perspective which we present throughout the chapter.

## Clients turning the table: how the heck do I challenge them?

Chapter 4 offers a dynamic approach to skills and attitudes of challenging clients into leaving behind their own blank minds and sticky moments for ever. If a client is telling us that we don't do this enough, then we need to listen carefully. Client feedback is usually, and theoretically, a useful event. Without it, how many of us would know if our counselling relationships are productive? On occasion, however, the client might use their feedback, wittingly or otherwise, as a means of gaining control. This can only happen really if the counsellor is not challenging the client.

For example, Vesna, a newly qualified counsellor, is counselling Maria. Maria is a lonely single parent with a history of abuse. Her cohabitee frequently threatens her, and sometimes hits her. Maria is frustrated. What is more, she feels so isolated that when she has the opportunity to talk about her problems, she 'gushes' the story with emotion.

Vesna is more than sympathetic. She was at one time in a similar situation and is keen to show her understanding. What is more, she is apprehensive of taking control of the process and interrupting her client 'in full flow': inexperience leads her to believe that this would be disrespectful. Thus she is not as challenging as she might be to Maria.

It is only a matter of time before Maria lets Vesna know that she expects more: 'I've been for four sessions now, and you hardly say anything. I'd expected you to be more helpful, to do more – and you don't seem to be helping. I feel worse now than when we started'. Vesna feels a little defensive – what is it that Maria expects? Did she make explicit her role in the first place – and if so did she stick to it?

In supervision, Vesna is so concerned with her own feelings of incompetence that she feels she has lost the plot with Maria, and doubts whether she can help. Indeed, she is not now sure *how* to help. Vesna is, in fact, feeling very clientish! In this scenario, the counsellor's personal fears and anxieties have sabotaged movement within the counselling process, and the counsellor is left feeling slightly bruised. She is not sure what intervention it is now appropriate to make.

Challenging generally is one of the trickier areas of counselling, and counsellors and clients are notorious for playing 'here we go round the mulberry bush'. This can feel productive; they dance a little dance of intimacy – moving closer, drawing away, twirling around, touching, backing off; they dance their way onwards and through time, learning new movements, dancing into the sunset. Sometimes, however, their dance goes round and round the mulberry bush – a lovely movement, very enlivening and getting nowhere fast.

Dancing round the mulberry bush is easy to do because people *can* enjoy talking about themselves immensely. Have you ever had that experience where someone is actually listening carefully to what you have to say? You may feel that your issues are important, your emotions valid, and your perspective worthwhile. For many people, this is an uncommon occurrence in their everyday life, and is extremely enriching. Thus it can be tempting, when in the client seat, to repeatedly add on to the story in 'and another thing' vein. And if the counsellor is curious, sympathetic, unassertive, or into diagnosis, they will become stuck for a strategy to 'move the client on'. When they try and move towards the future, the client will tell them more of what they don't want, more of what they've always had. While a sense of plateau to integrate change is no bad thing, the clue to the mulberry bush is the never-ending repetition, the endless new aspects to the story. A sure sign to introduce a change of pace and direction. Chapter 4 offers pragmatic instruments to help to make this happen.

## When words are not enough!

In Chapter 5 we outline some perspectives on working creatively with clients who do not respond well to 'traditional' communication methods. Counsellors are taught, by and large, how crucial it is for people to verbally express their emotions, at least in the first instance. The counsellor, traditionally, responds with verbal empathy. This can, however, be too narrow or even inappropriate a response, for different reasons.

The group of people for whom verbal expression and empathic response is not helpful is wide and varied. We have worked with people with off-the-scale IQs and people with learning difficulties who are very cognitive; it was just not their style to talk the language of emotions. Sometimes counsellors can struggle too long in the quest for verbal, accurate, empathy above all else.

In these situations, using other media such as art, music, photography, and even basic cognitive empathy – an agreement to honour the cognitive as being as important as emotions – is useful, and we will briefly explore these options, noting that there is a great deal of literature now which addresses creative methods of helping.

## Off the beaten track

In our experience, both practically and in literature reviews, counsellors are seldom taught about the implication of issues of mental health and illness in their work. It is not, for example, a good idea to open up in one fell swoop all the hitherto repressed emotions of a person with a tendency to psychosis. Unpopular as such terminology as mental illness and psychosis might be at times, we feel strongly that it is ethically and practically desirable for counsellors to have a sound working knowledge of issues common to mental health and of the possible side effects and limitations of certain medications.

Hence, drawing particularly on Graham's broad experiences in psychiatry, we have added a new chapter, Chapter 6, to begin to explore some of these issues.

## I haven't got a clue how you feel!

In Chapter 7 we explore the theme of values from different perspectives. From time to time, counsellors encounter the polar opposite to identification, and find it very difficult to recognise any aspects of the client's story, feelings or context. This may occur when the type of behaviour or situation is alien, the values different. One client of ours had very strong religious beliefs, so that his extreme unhappiness within his marriage was held in tension alongside his love for his god whom he sought to obey. He felt that he had no option but to stay true to the marriage vows despite his unhappiness. It was difficult to understand such commitment to a set of values which were so restricting of this man's potential, and not to be tempted to see the religious belief as an 'excuse' rather than a 'valid' reason for keeping the situation the same.

Such non-recognition may occur within the ordinary and predictable aspects of life when the counsellor has never dealt with a specific situation before. This may be a situation where someone is revealing abusive behaviour, substance abuse, dishonest dealings: indeed, it may be any situation, and these examples are made only to illustrate, not to stereotype – counsellors will have had a range of personal experiences just like anyone else. The point is that we all find 'new' situations, and it is easy to confuse a new 'theme' with unnecessary difficulties. Equally, we all do live by our own moral codes, whether overt or covert. It is useful to remember that clients are whole people, for whom the named problem is only one aspect of their experience. If we believe in some aspect of commonality between human beings, then we all understand what it is to have an emotion or a thought; we do not have to have had the same experiences to work well. On the other hand, we need to respect values.

When we trained counsellors in Kuwait in 1993, in the aftermath of the Iraqi invasion, we were faced with a number of quite new situations. We were advised to read various books in order to orientate ourselves and understand the culture, but chose instead to go 'cold' into the situation. Perhaps going cold should be reframed as 'warm' – we went with open hearts and humility, and learned our way through confidence in our ethos and a willingness to negotiate issues and situations. Our overriding belief system was that the commonalities in our humanity were greater than the differences, and so the

11

'new situations', the 'new culture', were a forum for learning and sharing, rather than an inhibitor.

When we introduced the idea of personal development and self-determination to our group of trainees, we encountered a degree of perplexity – why should professionals need to explore their own personal issues in order to offer a skilled and specific service? A great question, reflecting not only the values of the Kuwaiti culture, but also pertinent to the development of the profession. We were privileged to participate in an exciting and educational process from which we learned a great deal. The chapter explores the different types of issues raised by questions of values.

## A funny thing happened to me on the way through life – anybody know a good counsellor?

In Chapter 8, we look at how and where counselling originated and contextualise the function it serves. We also invite the reader to explore the limitations of counselling, and its downsides. We recognise that counselling is prolific: it seems to be recommended almost willy-nilly, for every ailment, every ennui, of everyday life. In locating counselling as a social practice we make overt some of its foundations and alert the reader to a full range of potential consequences.

## What is counselling?

Chapter 9 explores differences and similarities between counselling terms, how we know that counselling works, how we differentiate between activities, and how we reconcile thorny theoretical debates. Since the last edition of this book, the term coaching has been extensively coined to join the ranks of other psychologically-based humanistic activities, and we look at how this might fit into the range of 'helping' activities which draw upon similar skills and ethical parameters to counselling.

## My genuine response to you is 'you are a male chauvinist pig'

In Chapter 10, we explore some of the paradoxes within counselling, such as the impossibility of accurate empathy, the limitations of unconditional positive regard and the blurred edges of genuineness, and try to make some sense of the demands of such lofty concepts in reality. This chapter remains in its original form.

Feedback has suggested that this theoretical discussion has been useful in understanding practical situations. For example, as a novice counsellor, Janice worked with a heterosexual couple in couples counselling. One day, the husband arrived alone. When asked where his wife was, he laughed and said that he'd given her a good slap, and she was too bruised to come out. Janice went completely blank in terms of sense of purpose, and issued him with several challenges which reflected her *genuine* responses: the emotion of anger, an inability to offer positive regard, responses which were sadly lacking in any skill. She suggested that it would be pointless for the client to come back on his own, at which point he left. Janice felt proud of 'not putting up with any nonsense', and of being true to herself – for about two minutes.

Emerging from the complete blank regarding the client needs and outcomes, realisation dawned that she had acted in such a way that the man's wife was more at risk than ever. The contract had been blown, and neither party returned. Janice had hit her own sticky moment, for reasons which she only understood sometime later, and had confused this with a sense of being genuine. A salutory lesson, and in Chapter 10 we try to demystify these core conditions that we can't always live up to.

## Chapter 11: trained, suited and booted – what does professionalisation mean?

This chapter is new to the second edition, and explores the professionalisation process and some of the nuances within it. What exactly does it mean to be a professional? What does it take to become one? What is the profession anyway, and how is it developing?

In our first edition, we noted the example of a lighter sticky moment for Janice, who used to use a rocking-chair when counselling. She had no idea just how engaged she was with the client, until she rocked so enthusiastically that she rocked all the way over and landed inelegantly. Fortunately, both parties found this to be hilarious, and at least she can say that she remained 'genuine' throughout the ungainly exercise of putting skirts down, dusting herself off, and resuming counselling! Being professional, to us, suggests working within clear principles while shying away from being precious.

Becoming a professional counsellor is an interesting journey: we look at a model of development which may be useful when acknowledging ups and downs of embarking on this journey, and which may be useful for supervision. You will notice that in some of the examples we use in the book, we refer to 'new' counsellors, 'novice' counsellors, 'experienced' counsellors. We do not mean to patronise at any point by this use of language, merely to acknowledge that there may be slight differences in the kind of issues that counsellors have at different times, and that there is such a process as 'counsellor development'. Enthusiastic novice counsellors can be just as, even more, effective than more experienced counsellors: the point is that experience suggests that we might hit different types of issues at different points in professional development.

In wider terms, the process of professionalisation has progressed considerably since the first edition. Virtual counselling is new and brings some interesting challenges – and can you ultimately be counselled by a computer? The status of the profession has risen, alongside the price of counselling courses and books, and the establishment of awards for 'outstanding' professionals – does this make for more exclusivity? We will also be noting the issues around accreditation and registration of the profession, and some of the paradoxes which have ensued.

## The map is not the territory – but without it we'll get lost

Finally, Chapter 12 will reiterate the principles of counselling practice in the form of a four-stage model. We hope that by this time your interest will have been captured and your soul liberated to further your own practice and your own arguments.

Whatever else, we hope that this is an enjoyable and informative book for you, that it will tap into questions that you already have, suggest new ones, and provide some ideas and guidelines that help you to practise in a way that is ethical, engaging and healthy for both you and your client.

## Notes

1   Two comments are noteworthy here. One is that many counsellors, including ourselves, do make careful counselling contracts with friends from time to time. Secondly, we are aware that the term 'friend' represents a whole load of understandings. Some people regard as friends those with whom they share humour and experience of some situations, while others go through a lifetime regarding themselves as having a very small number of friends, those with whom they offer a unique intimacy.
2   See, for example, Ingram (1991) for a clear exposition on roles.

# 2

the inside story: or trapped and alone
with the couch ...

**Abstract:** This chapter is about what can happen to a counsellor – simply because of the job. We explore some of the simple pitfalls which happen for no other reason than because counsellors are human. We highlight some of these 'normal' problems and offer perspectives to help avoid some of the feelings of inadequacy and helplessness that we all feel sometimes in this job. We explore some of the difficulties facing the fledgling counsellor while reminding the more experienced that these can happen to you too! We cover identification and its potential results, such as contamination, control of content, and advice giving and explore such sticky moments as voyeurism, anxiety and distraction. Finally, we acknowledge that there are even dangers in training to be a counsellor!

The life of a counsellor can be pretty tough and pretty lonely. The tendency to isolation can be seriously underestimated by bright and sparkly-eyed candidates on an introduction to counselling course. After all, counselling is about working with people, learning with people, so that at first sight it might seem like a very interactive job. However, those of you who have spent some time in the profession will recognise various experiences which belie the simplicity of this belief. Counselling is interactive, yet in a very specific way which is different from the usual rules of personal encounters. It does have a certain status, it does initially provoke appreciation from successful clients, and it can result in a certain glow of self-esteem when we appreciate ourselves. However, such rewards may not be continuous nor great enough to preclude some 'bad days', and the more surprising experiences of isolation which can occur.

The nature of counselling entails high levels of confidentiality. This in itself may lead to a sense of isolation if counsellors 'box off' their work into 'no-go' areas. For example, in 'normal life' and relationships the cliché 'had a good day at the office', or some version thereof, gives an opportunity for people to share some of their experiences of the day within their close relationships. If this question is met with 'I'm sorry I can't talk to you about that', then there is an increasing possibility that the other in the relationship feels excluded from an important area of their loved one's life. For the counsellor, it can become a burden when their day's work has had effects on them personally, whether to do with graphic accounts of powerful experiences, or to do with some aspect of self-reflection into which we are so relentlessly encouraged. When such effects are screened off within normally intimate relationships, then, distancing may occur for one party in the relationship, and isolation for the other.

The potential for isolation is exacerbated when the counsellor is also working without agency support, for example, when she/he works as an independent or as a single worker without a team. Any sense of frustration, helplessness, or that 'locked-in' feeling can be overpowering and debilitating. This is acknowledged in that one of the necessary benefits of supervision is the great relief felt when one is able to 'tell someone'. The burden of confidentiality can weigh heavy, not always because of the impact of the content of the disclosure one holds inside, but simply *because* it has to remain inside. The 'trapped and alone' syndrome can be made worse on occasions when you may feel that you are not helping 'enough', that perhaps someone else could be 'helping more', that there seems to be no way forward, or simply that you are 'upset' by what you are hearing.

Moreover, counsellors are asked to do something as part of their job which is reasonably unique, i.e. to 'self-develop' towards self-knowledge and authenticity. We might challenge this imperative; can counselling be done by an actor who knows how to operate certain communication styles at any one time? Do we really have to be 'ahead' of our clients? Are we in danger of positioning the counsellor as some sort of idealised self, some role model for the rest of humanity to aspire to?[1] Such arguments aside, the reality is that, currently, counselling imposes an imperative to counsellors to try to 'work themselves out', or at the very least to monitor themselves for 'what's going on', and how it affects the client. The effect of this can be a strong self-preoccupation which can be rather absorbing and extremely demanding, so that the counsellor begins to see the world only in relation to themselves. How exhausting!

All of these types of feelings have been experienced by us or disclosed to us in supervision. We hope that by simply noting them, we may be helping you to realise that you are not alone. Such feelings are seldom aired in public amongst counsellors, sometimes in supervision, and indeed rarely to friends or loved ones (who might notice the phenomenon before we do). It would appear that there are no books that deal adequately with the internal mental life of the counsellor, or indeed, on how the work may affect the counsellors' interpersonal relationships[2]. The best one can hope for is that counselling training or supervision raises awareness of this phenomenon. Through such media, you may be advised to undertake personal counselling when or if the nature of the work distresses you.

This is only one strategy however, and one which continues to focus on your internal life. Useful at times, but we can't emphasise enough that it's equally useful to go on holiday, cut down hours, talk to a friend, have a passionate weekend away, get engrossed in music, film, books, sailing, dancing – whatever you find relaxing, and whatever has a different focus. Often, the degree of isolation felt can be paradoxically connected to how involved you are in the 'counselling world', and in intense self-exploration.

So, our point is that counsellors sometimes will feel trapped and alone. This may be within the counselling relationship, it may be within the general work context, or it may be to do with effects or demands of the work on self. We would suggest, then, that counsellors review some of the principles which they adhere to in the light of the following questions:  ·

- Are my contracts of confidentiality with my clients honest and realistic? Part of one of our contracts now is that the counsellor will discuss aspects of their work with their supervisor, with an occasional consultant, but also with a trusted friend/lover, albeit with anonymity.
- Am I as in touch with other people as I want to be?
- Do I have a network of people who I can turn to simply to have a chat about the nature of the work?
- Do I see the number of clients who I really want to, or are they disproportionate to the rest of my life?
- Have I got a life, or is it all wrapped up in striving to personally develop, in my therapy sessions, in my reflective meditation, in my quest for self-knowledge?
- Do I step back and see counselling as only one part of a much wider existence? Is there life without counselling?

In the rest of this chapter, we will try to elucidate some of the more common responses to and effects of the counselling work. In addition to examining the effects that the counsellors' intrapersonal issue can have on the process of counselling, we hope to present a realistic picture of what is and isn't humanly possible in counselling. Our experience is that counsellors can set such incredible expectations that they are bound to struggle. We also include some thoughts on coping with the more unpleasant aspects of the work.

Firstly, we look at identification, and how it may lead to contamination of understanding, to advice giving, and controlling of the clients' material. Secondly, the issue of voyeurism, or how 'curiosity killed the counselling' occurs. Thirdly, the chapter focuses on anxiety, what causes it, maintains it, and how it can be controlled or dissipated. This section also looks at what we call 'the saviour syndrome'[3] and the issues of stress and overwork which have become known as 'burnout'.[4] We consider a list of possible distractions and categorise these into physiological, emotional/psychological and physical. Some possible antidotes or strategies worth pursuing are considered. We would emphasise at this point that all of the suggestions we make in regard to intrapersonal issues are included to stimulate thought rather than direct you to our particular prescription of what should be done. We do, however, use statements of principle as a means of differentiating counselling from other activities. Where these occur, they may be seen as a guiding light, resound as a motto to be remembered, or simply be an additional thought which stands alone. It is our wish to enable practitioners to address the principles of practice.

Finally, and new to this edition of the book, we offer some thoughts on counselling training, reviewing what we learned in training, and the effect it might have had on us. We sometimes wonder if what is offered in training is a pretty good indoctrination: are we the person we were before we 'trained' and, if not, are we better for it? Although this self-reflective torture can probably do little good after the event, it is interesting to look at the paradoxes and see whether we are still locked in to everything we were taught, or whether we have evolved, loosened up, got sloppier, become more open minded or ... ? Blank minds and the occasional sticky moment might actually be better than having become the counselling automaton.

## Identification

*I know just how you feel and I want you to get better ...*

It is important to try to remember who has the problem. Clients' issues can be disabling and distressing if you identify with them, or indeed the source of a vicarious pleasure when they 'do well'. Many counsellors disclose issues of identification which they are finding troublesome. It is almost as if they have brought the issue to supervision for permission to refer clients on. Clients disclose their responses to life events: bereavements, separations, abuse, betrayal, anger and confusion. If you too are in a comparable circumstance or situation, it is not surprising that difficulties can arise. Counsellors are human beings with the same repertoire of emotions and potential for distress as their clients.

Although counselling training is helpful in order to resist potential 'infections' of emotions, it is unlikely that you become immune. When you consider that counselling training is mostly engineered to enable the trainee to become more sensitive to emotion, it could be anticipated that it will not prepare students to avoid contamination from the clients' distressed world, especially when similarities emerge. As a student nurse, Graham became extremely distressed when working in an operating theatre. As the 'scrub' nurse he had just received an anaesthetised 22-year-old male patient with testicular cancer. The surgeon remarked that the patient was riddled with secondaries in the lungs and would not be seeing another Christmas. The statement of such certainty of death for the young patient of the same age and gender was enough to create an extremely powerful identification. The subsequent emotions were both personally overwhelming and debilitating to professional practice. Although this state was temporary it was enough to render Graham ineffective in his role (who wants a sobbing scrub nurse to assist the surgeon).

---

*Principle:* remember who has the problem

---

## Potential effects of identification

Identification may arise with issues or feelings which are live for the counsellor, or which are rooted in their past. The chances are that the strength of feeling associated with the identification will in some way change the response from useful to less so. It may mean, for example, that more emphasis is placed on one issue than another, or that an issue is avoided, or simply that the counsellor identifies to such an extent that complete misunderstanding takes place.

Before proceeding, we also acknowledge that understanding in general terms of a specific experience can also generate a level of insight which can facilitate rapport and a sense of safety, and we will say more about this in Chapter 4. For now, we are focusing on specific live emotions which can be unwittingly contaminative.

There are some simple antidotes and support where identification occurs. Often acknowledging identification is enough: sometimes more active strategies are needed. Occasionally the identification is so strong it is desirable to terminate the counselling relationship. This is so where the identification results in contamination.

## Contamination

If identification gives rise to the inability to separate the emotions of the counsellor from those of the client, the quality of listening may be damaged. For example, responses to a bereaved client talking about the death of their mother, may be contaminated by feelings that the counsellor had about their mother's death. One counsellor we know made the classic error of 'sympathising' with his client about the death of her mother, stating that 'it must be a lonely and empty life for you now'. This reflected the counsellor's experience of his mother's death, not necessarily the client's. Weeks later the client was able to reveal that the real truth of the matter was that she felt guilty at being so happy that her tyrannical mother was dead. Clearly the counsellor not only could not differentiate between his own feelings and that of the client's, but he also projected his feelings onto the client. This had the effect of making it more difficult for the client to disclose her real feelings to him. It could also be argued that he placed an opinion or judgement onto the situation – i.e. you *should* feel lonely and empty after your mother's death.

Interestingly, discussion of contamination is often limited to the identification with the 'negative' emotions or feelings of clients, those which might consciously distress or disturb the counsellor in some way. Equally, the counsellor might encourage or become enthusiastic about a particular 'positive' statement or desire of the client, as they share it or have previously shared it. We have often seen this phenomenon when the theme is a planned separation from a relationship which seems unsatisfactory or disabling. Counsellors might be secretly cheering for their client's exit from such a relationship, particularly when they have once done that themselves. Or, even more insidious perhaps, would love to but haven't quite managed it! This sort of subtle identification is more likely to be communicated through implicit or explicit 'well dones', under the guise of validation and empowerment.

---

*Principle:* a problem contaminated is a problem complicated

---

Contamination through identification is not a one-way process. A counsellor who is listening to distressful stories which echo for them will be exacerbating their own pain. This is not conducive to good health and good spirit, and when it occurs, there is a message to be listened to. If counselling is complicating the counsellor's life, then perhaps it is time for a review.

## Advice giving

Identifying with the client's situation or experience may in some cases lead to an irresistible impulse to give guidance and advice, as you may believe that you know what is the best course of action for the client. Although suggestions are invariably made with the best intentions, the result is commonly that some client self-determination is lost. The client's freedom and self-reliance is interfered with by the sharing of the counsellor's ideas, and, conversely, the accurate exploration of the clients' resources and strategies has been neglected.

Giving advice or guidance short-changes the client in terms of empowerment and independence. When counsellors give advice they increase the potential for dependency and decrease the potential learning from any client experiment. A really good antidote to falling into this practice of advice giving is to remember that there are usually only two possible reactions from the client:

• The advice is useful, thus the client is grateful and more dependent.
• The advice is unhelpful, so the client blames and resents the counsellor.

In either case the client has been robbed of the opportunity to develop insight into his/her own resources and problem solving, and the counsellor must assume much greater responsibility for the client's outcomes.

While this rather tight way of construing advice is currently the common wisdom of counselling, preservation of self-determination and strict avoidance of advice has been questioned by some.[5] Some pragmatic counsellors see that it is possible to 'blur' the role of counsellor and include a little therapy, guidance, direction, befriending and advice. It is our view that any of these may be appropriate in different contexts.

However, we would argue that if counselling has been purposefully chosen as a particular approach, there must have been a reason. Why did the client want counselling? Why did the counsellor agree that this was appropriate and desirable? There must then be a shared rationale if you are going to change to some other approach. In other words, if there is some reason for 'doing counselling' rather than 'eclectic helping', then the differentiations have to be made clear to the client, and if that decision changes, the change should be overtly negotiated.

> *Principle:* trust your client to find their own advice

## Controlling the content and emotions of the client

Strong feelings of identification may also lead to the suppression of the client's emotions. The unconscious avoidance of strong unpleasant feelings that the counsellor has identified with may result in the counsellor being unable to 'hear' certain parts of the client's story and certain emotions within it. It is easily possible, for example, for counsellors who have a personal history of being sexually abused to 'unconsciously' miss parts of a client's story which share or allude to a similar past history. Strong emotions of guilt or sadness in a client's story of their bereavement may not be overtly reflected if they resemble the counsellors' own currently repressed emotions. Counsellors may not realise that they are doing this until they debrief in supervision.

Conversely, identification may lead the counsellor to want to emphasise or focus on certain emotions and content. For example, if the counsellor has experienced a similar situation to their client, they might want to dwell on what they think is most important, rather than let the client lead. For example, one supervisee disclosed that his greatest distress in the death of his mother was his guilt at 'never telling her that he loved her'. He realised that in subsequent interactions with clients disclosing difficulty in their relationships with their parents, he was insisting upon returning to points in the story that would allow him to probe into the precise nature of undisclosed emotions between them. This type of control over the content of the story is disrespecting the client's right to self-determination.

---

*Principle:* control the process, never the content

---

This is not to deny the possibility of purposeful self-disclosure as a tentative challenging skill. Testing out a hunch as to what the client feels, or what seems to be important, is perfectly legitimate if offered genuinely (see Chapter 4), and when it is used purposefully and prudently, rather than as an excuse to direct the process towards specific content.

Such direction is not always 'wrong', but it is more appropriately associated with purposeful therapy rather than client-centred or nondirective counselling. Once counsellors begin to employ helping strategies which exert greater influence and limit self-determination, they have moved towards the therapy end of the helping continuum. When this occurs, as stated previously, the therapist must assume greater responsibility for the clients' outcomes.[6]

Most of us will recognise some aspect of these examples. We need to be realistic about counselling, and acknowledge that while it is possible to keep largely within the purpose and principles of non-directiveness most of us will slip from time to time. To avoid this slippage, honesty, self-awareness and critical judgement are needed in abundance. We might also argue that there is no possibility of total non-directiveness. Some authors suggest that even the most non-directive-centred counselling is strongly influenced by the values and attitudes of the counsellor.[7]

Counselling is best seen as a helpful approach for some clients, not the panacea for all ills. Our point is that if you know what counselling is and isn't, you become more conscious of what you are doing. As a rule of thumb, remember that whenever your own point of view, experience or preference is indicated to the client consciously or unconsciously, then in counselling protocol, undue influence has been exerted. You are guilty of nothing more than moving along the helping continuum further towards therapy. This may be unproblematic, but it does need client consent, and you do also need to be aware of your greater responsibility for the clients' outcomes.

In summary, it can be seen that in order to remain professional, it is important to pay attention to feelings of identification. Subsequent action will be determined by the intensity and the lasting nature of the identification. To temporarily touch on an emotion is one thing, while to be incapacitated for the whole and subsequent sessions is quite another. Various possibilities then exist:

- Note the identification experienced and move on.
- Discuss how strongly you are identifying in supervision, and make sense of it for you.
- Suspend the counselling if you continue to struggle, and seek whatever help or support you need to minimise your tendency to identify.
- Make a re-referral. It serves little purpose for counsellors to become embarrassed or feel it necessary to seek permission to refer the client to someone else. It is not a matter of letting the client down by referring on, but a requirement to enable the client to receive the appropriate help. The bottom line is that the counsellor should not be working with a client if identification is creating contamination of roles, decreasing effectiveness or reducing the counsellor's ability to be optimally helpful.

In order to remain ethical, counsellors are required to identify their own personal problems and issues and to be aware if they have clients that are presenting with similar problems. This, of course, may not always be as easy as it sounds, as clients can present with one initial problem and later focus on something quite different. Equally, counsellors' issues may be unconscious until stimulated to awareness. Therefore, anticipating the full potential for identification may be extremely difficult! Consequently it is necessary to be alert and sensitive to one's vulnerability and take the appropriate action when necessary.

We take the view that effective[8] client-centred supervision is essential for healthy counselling practice and of course is a requirement of our professional bodies[9] (BACP, 2002; BPS, 2005). Supervision offers opportunities for counsellors to listen carefully to themselves in regard to what they think, feel and do in their practice, and the space to get off the treadmill. Without such space, counsellors may be less aware of how their own processes are affecting their work.

## Voyeurism: pass me those binoculars, they go with my mac ...

So have you ever found yourself just really interested, intrigued, captivated by the story of the client in front of you? Such interest just might trigger the capacity for voyeurism, or perhaps curiosity, which we all have. The tendency for individuals to be curious about their clients is quite normal. An interest in people is, after all, a facet of the attraction to counselling.

Unfortunately, however, clients are not really there to fulfil our curiosity! Counsellors, then, need to keep a spirit of inquiry into what the client is doing and how they want to change, while resisting their natural curiosity regarding the 'content' of the story. Unfortunately, especially to the unskilled eye, a healthy interest in the client and an interrogation may look similar. Have you ever witnessed a session where the questions flow: how often did you do that, what was the position, when did you say your grandma entered the room, where did you say you bought the book?

One of the difficulties in discerning the difference between healthy interest and crippling curiosity is that clients will co-operate equally with both processes. Often the client is delighted to supply endless amounts of information requested by the counsellor, and is forthcoming regarding how many children they have, the precise relationship that exists between themselves and their great aunt Cecily, or the rough approximation of their monthly sexual activities. Why? Simple – the client believes that supplying this information will be helpful to the counsellor. The client believes that with this knowledge the counsellor will be able to tell them what to do!

Such interrogation not only fulfils a need in the counsellor, it also paves another road to advice giving. Curiosity and questioning is used to aid analysis of the client's problem and work out *your* solution to it. The client is accustomed to this; it is what most other professionals, neighbours and friends have done for years. They just hope that this time your advice will be better than the others!

Cynical? Not really: having spent many hours listening to tapes of real counselling interviews, we can assert unequivocally that many counsellors fall into this trap: the trap may be subtly laid, an occasional digressive 'curiosity question' sprinkled amongst orthodox high-level counselling skills. While purposeful open questions can legitimately control the process of counselling, questions that direct the content of the session follow the counsellor's agenda and reduce self-determination. We rest our case – curiosity kills the counselling!

So how do we counter this potential? The antidotes are simple, but require considerable self-discipline:

• Beware of asking two questions concurrently, unless for clarification. This would mean you are interrogating. It suggests that you have neglected to reflect back the content of the answer to your first question, or the second question had to be asked because your first one was poorly constructed.

• Consider asking no questions at all! Or at least for periods of time, perhaps up to 15 minutes. This will help you to concentrate on thorough listening to the client's agenda and to switch off yours, invariably strengthening your empathic skills. We often employ this tactic in counselling training programmes to demonstrate how questions can destroy effective, non-directive listening. It is amazing how quickly even the best of counsellors become dependent on questions to 'bale them out of trouble' in sticky moments or when their minds have gone blank.

• Consider taping your sessions and spending some time counting the amount of questions you asked.

• You could decide to examine each question asked and test it for motive. Why did I ask that? Be honest, why did you ask how many children she has? Does it help you to have the full picture so you can diagnose and prescribe some action from your expertise? Or is it really your honest attempt to challenge the client to bring to consciousness something she is not aware of? Questions should help the client to determine for themselves areas of thought which may be helpful in developing insight. One can't help but wonder what sort of clients would forget how many children they have!

• It may be helpful to check that your questions are open and do not carry a hidden agenda. For example, the question 'What would you like your future to be like?' has only the agenda of directing the process not the content. But consider whose agenda is addressed by a question like 'Have you talked to your children about this?'

Voyeurism sometimes takes another form. The content of the client's story may intrigue the counsellor. In this event the counsellor can be hooked into the perspective of 'I must know what comes next', waiting with bated breath for the next instalment. Some clients become expert at story telling to the extent that they capture the interest of the counsellor almost permanently. This ensures that the next appointment is likely to be sooner rather than later, and that the motivation to move on past the problem to constructive change is largely negated.

Occasionally counsellors are brave enough to admit that the material that the client is disclosing is arousing. It is important to understand that to be aroused by the nature of the client's material is not uncommon. Counsellors are human, and the nature of being human is that we react to stimuli from time to time. We may accept more easily congruent reactions such as rage when told of exploitation of vulnerable people than unexpected arousal at the disclosure of some sexual encounter. What if the counsellor becomes aroused by disclosures of violence, exploitation or perversion? Such reactions are not usually considered consistent with sensitivity and caring, and are often seen as inappropriate. The temptation is therefore to conclude that if we are aroused by such descriptions then we must be abnormal, perverted and definitely unfit to be a counsellor. This, of course, is a classic example of the counsellor being able to be non-judgemental to others but experiencing great difficulty addressing the concept to themselves.

> *Principle:* apply a non-judgemental approach – that means to you too!

Once having discovered that you, the counsellor, are human and therefore vulnerable to experiencing arousal, the next step may be to try to suppress the arousal or deny that it occurred. This seems rather a shame to us; we would suggest that the important aspect of this discussion in regard to the loneliness of the counsellor, is that hidden aspects of the self which can affect effectiveness need to be debriefed. The moral rights and wrongs of becoming aroused are to some extent irrelevant; the fact that the counsellor is distracted from the purpose of counselling is the central point. Preventing voyeurism or distraction, and marshalling self-discipline to get on with the task of effective counselling is a much more valuable goal than self-deprecation.

We recounted in our first edition the illustration recounted to us several years ago. A social worker who had summoned the courage to disclose in supervision the feelings of arousal that he experienced when interviewing a client in a sexual abuse inquiry was immediately suspended and subsequently dismissed. This seemed a poor response to a courageous professional who was prepared to recount real emotions which he had identified as potentially problematic. It is interesting to note that some people have great difficulty in differentiating between what is fantasy and what is a conscious intent to act out. It would seem to us that it is far safer to have counsellors relating their real and potentially problematic arousal states to their supervisors than suppress their emotions and be distracted by their secret fantasies.

The antidote to the voyeuristic nature of humankind is not easy to suggest. The nature of our species, and particularly those of us who are drawn towards the 'caring professions', is sensory, and we are interested in other human beings. The following possibilities seem constructive:

- Learn to listen to yourself; become more aware of your emotions during sessions and ask the question–is this an appropriate reaction? This question deserves to be asked at a human level not just as 'a trained counsellor'.
- Determine what is a realistic level of interest for you to have in your client and at what level it ceases to be non-directive.
- Assess the level of distraction that occurs due to your intrigue or arousal, and ask whether it detracts from the service that you profess to offer the client.
- If you believe there is any possibility of acting upon your arousal, then seriously consider the most appropriate way to discontinue working with the client.
- Review such emotional arousal with your supervisor.

## Anxiety

Whether novice or experienced counsellor, we would hazard a guess that you will have suffered low-level anxiety or something approaching panic from time to time in regard to certain clients. No matter how long you have been counselling there will be times in your life when your confidence deserts you and when those creeping 'self-doubts' allow the demon anxiety to get you. The most extreme of these anxieties are often prefaced by those thoughts in one's head saying 'Do I know what to do?', 'What if?', 'I know I'll get it all wrong', 'I can't concentrate, I'll forget what they've said, I'm sure I'll blow it'. Or there may be anxiety connected to the status of the client – can I really counsel this eminent managing director, this important playwright, this famous musician?

For novice counsellors, these messages may emanate from fear of not being 'ready', being 'a fraud', making it 'worse' for the client in some way. This type of anxiety is often associated with feeling a little trapped and alone. Your supervisor or trainer can't be with you, and because you have a contract with the client and you care about them, you can't let them down. The overwhelming feeling of wanting to be beamed up, go back to bed and pull the covers over you or feign illness are tempting alternatives to 'going through with it'. Well, we all get these feelings from time to time, and we hope that by graphically describing the process that, you won't feel quite so alone again. Moreover, anxieties that we should be helpful to the client can keep us on our toes – no bad thing.

Sometimes, counsellors become anxious when they don't remember the details of the client's story. Some counsellors take copious notes after a session to remind them of the ins and outs of each part of the scenario. They may become anxious about not knowing all relevant names, ages or places. And at times, whilst in the counselling session, they might forget a detail or even get it wrong.

Fear of forgetting, or even actually forgetting factual information, creates a wonderful vicious circle. Anxiety creates conscious attempts to remember–but who for? For the counsellor, in order to reduce their anxiety. As soon as this becomes a primary motivator, if only temporarily, then it interferes with the ability to listen wholeheartedly to the meaning of what the client is telling themselves and you. Counsellors can become brilliant at eliciting flawless case histories–which of course the client already knows.

**So, did I ever tell you that I was married and had three children?**

Forgetting factual information is not a hanging offence. Indeed, often it illustrates that the counsellor is more concerned with the client's process than the content of their stories. There is of course a neat little paradox which then begins to operate. The person who is not anxious about forgetting factual details, who is not embarrassed to check something which they have not remembered, is often likely to be the person who, through paying careful attention to the client, rather than themselves, does in fact remember!

A particular type of anxiety syndrome is created by the 'saviour syndrome'. This is the sense of impending doom that approaches when you feel that a client is not being helped enough. It sometimes occurs when a client asks for an urgent appointment and you find yourself saying yes even as you are thinking that you should say no! The 'no' may have very good reasons attached to it, like the client is becoming dependent, or you are so overworked that your concentration is lapsing; nonetheless the temptation to say yes is too strong to resist.

When this occurs you are in grave danger of acquiring the 'saviour syndrome' and its accompanying stress. This is a particularly nasty syndrome as it has its roots in both the noblest and basest of motives. The noblest of motives are those which arise from the earnest wish to be helpful to another human being, with no selfish purpose or hope for reward; the basest arise from the arrogance and self-serving nature within most of us – the part that wants to be recognised and exalted as indispensable. In either case, the impact of the 'saviour syndrome' is somewhat deleterious for both parties. The syndrome invariably results in the client receiving so much support that they become dependent. This can create a climate where the principle of self-determination and independence is no longer fostered, and is occasionally destroyed – hence counselling has ceased. In this case the counsellor loses humility, cannot see alternatives to being always available, and experiences stress syndromes, damage to personal relationships and the awesome burden of responsibility for other people's lives.

Instant attention to the client can also result in a form of manipulation by the client which is negative to both parties. We are sometimes amazed at how available counsellors make themselves, and the excesses of manipulative behaviour which they will put up with. Not so amazed, however, that we cannot remember our own sorry learning points; for Janice it was only on the third occasion that a client put a suicide note through the door of her home on a Saturday afternoon that she finally realised that being a 'rapid response agent' was not conducive to client or counsellor! At this stage, a blinding flash of realisation that the responses were not helping overrode the initial anxiety of 'What if she kills herself?' Graham's equivalent moment occurred as he found himself clearing the pavement of people in order to get his agoraphobic client to the bank (again).

We may be embarrassed by such moments – surely I'm not daft enough to have let this happen? Once the light has flashed on, however, overcoming the embarrassment and anxiety of disclosing becomes easier, and is clearly necessary. The relief of sharing is well worth it! Renegotiating with the client can be challenging but is a crucial next step.

Antidotes and strategies to anxiety and their associated problems are many. Some suggestions are:

• The absolute antidote to anxiety is relaxation. It is impossible to remain anxious and relaxed. It is surprising how many ways there are which enable you to be more relaxed. Try to remember what they are and employ the suitable strategies when appropriate.
• 'Debriefing' is immensely supportive. Your debrief partner may not even need to respond other than by listening. Clearly the contract with your debrief partner is best if it includes 'non-judgementalness' and unconditional support; however, a shared laugh and a supportive rebuke sometimes work as well. Both of us have friends who can be contactable at any time on a reciprocal arrangement, and they will listen carefully without judgement, and support us through our anxiety, fears, frustrations and humiliations – they are worth their weight in gold.
• Regular supervision with a person who is enabling, who can assist you to focus on your professional goals and challenge any unrealistic demands you or your client places upon you, is invaluable.
• In regard to the 'saviour syndrome', we recommend that you take a daily dose of humble pills. This entails saying regularly to yourself – I'm not the only one that can help – and learn to believe it!

It's good to remember that 'nobody does it right', because in truth there is no absolute right way of helping. As there is always a minimum of 13 possible choices of response, you won't always choose the most beneficial one. What is more, it's almost impossible to evaluate which of the 13 would have been best anyway![10] Once any of the responses has been selected then the opportunity to evaluate the others has passed.

Finally, try to remember and genuinely subscribe to the perception that you are only responsible for your part of the counselling contract with your client, not for the rest of their lives. Counselling is only one part of the client's life; by all means maximise its impact, but don't be deluded into overestimating your importance.

## Distractions

Another seemingly obvious sticky moment is the potential for the counsellor to be distracted. Everyone gets distracted. We know of no one who has on every single occasion given 100 per cent attention to their client in every session. Some common distractions are categorised into three main divisions and are listed below.

There would appear to be little chance that a mere human being would be able to avoid all of these possible distractions all of the time. To go further, we would say that confession of lapses is appropriate and a natural part of the relationship. Most of the clients that we have counselled have had a need to see that we, the helpers, are real and human. So it could be argued that to apologise for momentary lapses of concentration, to admit to the occasional distraction, may add value to the process and relationship formation. This is part of the negotiation which exists in the counselling interaction.

The respectful knack to distraction is genuine management. Although this sounds obvious, it is surprising how, especially within the early phases of counselling, practitioners can be really reluctant to manage distractions, for fear of being thought *dis*respectful. To excuse oneself to the bathroom, to turn a fire on or off, takes on

| Physiological | Psychological/Emotional | Physical |
|---|---|---|
| Tummy rumbling | Anxious | Too hot |
| Nauseous | Depressed | Too cold |
| Headache | Sad | Tired |
| Indigestion | Excited | Uncomfortable |
| Hung over | Affected by client's | Noise |
| Ill–flu, colds | story | Quiet–fear of |
| Hard of hearing | Curiosity | being overheard |
| Visually impaired | Concerned about | Incidents/activity |
| Memory difficulties | someone | outside |
| Need to | | |
| urinate/defecate | | |

an unrealistic magnitude. Yet again we need to remember our ordinariness, with human needs to be fulfilled. Some of these are really very basic, and if we are comfortable, then our clients are likely to be comfortable too. So take time to eat, to relax between sessions, to service your body in whatever way it needs, to negotiate temperature, acknowledge the pneumatic drill which has started up outside, or the window cleaner who is smiling cheerily at you as you determinedly try to empathise!

## Counselling training

Finally, one other aspect of counselling work which will have impact on your inner self is counselling training itself.[11] Despite the espoused ethos of counselling as embracing 'self-determination, and a non-prescriptive approach', counselling training is paradoxical to these values to some extent. In training, participants are prescribed a set of skills, values and attitudes and thus are to some degree denied self-determination. True they have volunteered to do so, but again it could be argued that it is impossible to give informed consent for an outcome yet to be identified.

We are not arguing here that this approach is wrong: in 'training' as opposed to education, demonstrating the right way to do things is a necessary part of developing precise skills. We are simply pointing the reader to the paradox. It is interesting that BACP acknowledge in their ethical framework that the prescription of personal values may be inappropriate, and should only be freely adopted.[12]

One common aspect of counselling training courses is the implicit acknowledgement that 'self-awareness' is a good thing, and there is encouragement for trainees to enhance this aspect of themselves. Indeed we have already recommended this as necessary to understand what effect the counselling is having on the counsellor – necessary for the successful outcomes of both parties! However, we would argue that self-awareness is not *per se* a good thing and perhaps some exploration of the pros and cons of it should precede the activity in training before complete commitment is signed in blood. Our argument rests largely on the point that 'informed' consent cannot be given for such an activity which has such unclear outcomes. It is perhaps enough to say that the counselling student embarks upon a process of significant personal change when initially believing that they are simply enrolling on a counselling course. It is our view that at this time some of the potential problematics as well as the enhancements should be explained to the applicant.

We might also note that the requirement for self-awareness and the adoption (if not already in place) of certain values, beliefs and attitudes are necessary criteria for successful completion of the course ... and these may have significant effects on the conduct of the rest of your life! The quality or nature of significant relationships may alter: you may make explicit goals which had previously merely lurked; tolerance of people close to you may reduce; and you might, quite simply, change the direction of your life (Dexter, 1999).

## Summary

The thrust of this chapter has been very much to underline that practising counselling may affect you intrapersonally. This may be because of the way the job works and the ethics attached to it; because of the content of the client's work; its effect upon the counsellor with their own personality and history; and because of the demands, right or wrong, towards self-exploration and awareness. The overall message is to look after yourself and to make careful decisions as to what work you want to be doing, and what work you are capable of doing appropriately. We believe that such a maxim is in the interests of both counsellor and client.

## Notes

1   Alex Howard (1996) disputes the impossible ideals foisted upon counsellors in *Challenges to Counselling and Psychotherapy*, while Alasdair MacIntyre (1981) draws attention to the role of Therapist as a kind of 'ideal type' in Western society, along with the Ascetic and the Manager, in his work *After Virtue*. Judi Irving and Dave Williams (Irving and Williams, 2001) dispute that it is even a 'good thing' to be 'personally developed', let alone whether it is possible. Gerard Egan (1994) regularly supplies a list of the qualities of the ideal helper in each new edition of *The Skilled Helper*, which we would guess is over and above the attributes of most of us more modest earthlings. The BACP ethical framework (2002) now includes a list of the kind of qualities that we might expect of a counsellor, which are remarkably similar to Egan's. See Chapter 10 for more discussion.
2   Dexter (1997) reports that one effect of training in counselling is considerable unfavourable reconstruing of family and friends.
3   For a more detailed debate on this syndrome see Berry (1991).
4   Burnout is considered in greater detail by some authors in regard to the personality types drawn to the helping profession. It is not our intention to explore theses issues here, but interested readers may find the following texts useful: Grosch and Olsen (1994); Maslach (1982).

5 Carroll (1996), who has written much on the use of counselling in the workplace, focuses on the effectiveness of counselling, and the pragmatics of approaches without great concern for the preciousness of some of the underpinning philosophy or principles.

6 See Chapter 8 for more discussion of this issue.

7 Strong (1968) suggests that the social influence process operates in all human interactions and there are no exceptions. B.F. Skinner (in Kirschenbaum and Henderson 1989) in his analysis of Rogers' practice, identified many behaviourally reinforcing expressions, gestures and verbal statements which could be seen as directive.

8 The word *effective* is used advisedly here. In practice, we believe that people's supervision needs are greatly varied, and that legislating for some norm of supervision is somewhat questionable. However, it is a useful guideline to have the capacity for supervision, by self or others, and to learn to use it when and if necessary.

9 The British Association of Counselling and Psychotherapy, and the British Psychological Society (BPS) require all counsellors to have supervision. BPS (2005) states:

There is an ethical requirement for every practitioner to have regular supervision support from a chartered counselling psychologist, or where more appropriate, from another suitably accredited or experienced supervisor. The supervisory contract will be clearly defined, confidential and proportional to the volume of work and the experience of the supervisee. The basic requirement for individual supervision is 1.5 hours per month for a minimal caseload, increasing proportionally with the case load.

The BACP (2002) ethical framework states:

It is considered important that research and systematic reflection inform practice. There is an obligation to use regular and on-going supervision to enhance the quality of the services provided and to commit to updating practice by continuing professional development.

10 These are the traditional or classic skills usually associated with counselling skills. (An empathic response; a clarification response; a simple paraphrase; a simple reflection; a summary; some self-disclosure; an immediacy response; an information-giving response; advanced accurate empathy; a challenge to a discrepancy, smokescreen or game; a paradoxical challenge; a summary as a challenge; or a question.) In addition to these there are all the non-verbal skills and all the specific skills which accompany the various particular counselling approaches. All in all, if these are taken as potential variables which could be used in combinations with each other, then the potential responses available to the counsellor could be seen as almost limitless.

11 See Dexter, 1999.

12 The BACP ethical framework states in their section on personal moral qualities:

It is inappropriate to prescribe that all practitioners possess these qualities, since it is fundamental that these personal qualities are deeply rooted in the person concerned and developed out of personal commitment rather than the requirement of an external authority. (http://www.bacp.co.uk/ethical framework/index.html)

# 3

# me and you, you and me: interpersonal issues

**Abstract:** We overview the issues and principles inherent in the interpersonal dynamic between counsellor and client. We look at issues of intimacy, sexuality, friendship and culture. We suggest that although interpersonal relationships might defy absolute definition and regulation, within the therapeutic professions, it is encumbent on the practitioner to work with intentionality and awareness of the issues which might affect their work on an interpersonal level.

## Introduction

The concern of this chapter is to explore some of the issues and thinking around interpersonal relationships in counselling. We know that it is difficult to define or code exactly what goes on between people, or what exactly constitutes an 'interpersonal relationship'. Within counselling, it seems that there is a real pull between two distinct philosophies regarding the counsellor/client dynamic. One suggests that interpersonal exploration should have no boundaries, as the very exploration is therapeutic; the other suggests that the interpersonal aspect to counselling be monitored, boundaried and directed to purposeful ends.

It is our view that the interpersonal side of counselling demands an awareness and a direction to a purposeful end over and above the relationship. As far as is humanly possible, it is the responsibility of the counsellor to use their knowledge and awareness to minimise the chances of psychological harm from the interpersonal relationship, and to maximise the benefits. This view accords with the ethical framework for good practice which informs the body of the BACP: the counsellor must make a commitment to avoiding harm to the client (BACP, 2002). This is achieved through a constant process of negotiation of meaning and intent. Even as we write this, we feel the lid being taken off a particular can of worms which provokes uncertainties and dissents.

The nature of the therapeutic relationship has attracted much discussion.[1] This chapter will explore some of the pertinent issues from a wide perspective. Our interest is to try to locate the nature of the interpersonal relationship into a discursive frame: in other words, we are interested in how it is built up and perpetuated through beliefs and practices. We will then elicit some principles which help the practitioner to ensure, as far as possible, ethical and effective practice. In particular, we will address issues of intimacy, self-disclosure, sexuality, friendship and culture.

## Keeping our distance: boundaried intimacy

We begin by spending a little time noting some of the assumptions regarding counselling as a relationship of intimacy. As stated above, there is a curious paradox which seems to operate in relation to intimacy within counselling. On the one hand, intimacy is seen as desirable, even unavoidable within the counselling relationship (Feasey, 2005), while on the other, it is made clear that there are certain rules to be obeyed regarding its nature. The whole area, then, is very uncertain.

Research has elicited several key points which are salient to issues of interpersonal relationships within counselling (Russell, 1997):

- Intimacy is commonly assumed by counsellors to be a desirable part of the counselling relationship, offering fulfilment of the highest value.[2]
- There is no consensual concept of intimacy within counselling discourse.
- No specific reason can be given as to why intimacy is desirable, other than reasons of faith that it is a 'good thing'.
- Many counsellors believe that the counselling relationship may be the first time that the client is experiencing intimacy, and therefore take upon themselves an obligation to 'model' an intimate relationship.
- Within counselling culture generally, intimacy is generally viewed as a positive concept in terms of making for successful counselling.[3]

We believe, however, that the insistence on intimacy, and the value attributed to its achievement within relationships, is questionable. In practice, there is no evidence that intimacy enhances the chances of a 'good' relationship. Within marital therapy, for example, it has even been suggested that marital therapists might be better to dispute the notion of intimacy as being crucial to the good relationship. A recent article in a popular women's magazine suggests that sex within intimate-couple relationships is adversely affected by the high degree of intimacy because the partners become so close that they feel almost familial; one study suggests that 60 per cent of American marriages are affected by a lack of lust associated with overfamiliarity, and an inability to see partners as other and different from self.[4]

Intimacy can of course lead to experiences which are evaluated as destructive, or intrusive. Interestingly, the research cited above showed that where clients described 'negative' intimate relationships, counsellors concluded that this was not then 'proper' intimacy. Their implicit definitions revolved around the notion of intimacy as both beneficial and constructive. This kind of well-intentioned arrogance denies thousands of years of philosophical inquiry and human experience, to fit in with a modernist notion of the self wherein 'open' equals 'healthy'. Our own brand of well-intentioned arrogance causes us to caution strongly against such naïveté!

Further, there is no evidence that the counselling relationship *must* be intimate in order to succeed. Indeed, such generalisation inhibits

**Don't be getting intimate, darling. I want this marriage to last.**

us from being able to make a useful definition of counselling. We believe that it is crucial that counselling be differentiated from other relationships by its purpose and its principles. Currently, the 'unique, interpersonal nature' of each counselling relationship is sometimes cited as evidence that we cannot define what we do. We would say that this is not the case. Psychiatrists, teachers, social workers, all need an effective working relationship with each individual in order to succeed, yet this does not stop us from defining the activity. A major principle underlying the relationship aspect of counselling is that:

---

**Principle:** the nature of the relationship in counselling must be instrumental to the purpose: it is not itself the purpose

---

To forget this fundamental principle is to do something other than counselling, and may have repercussions for the client or the counsellor which are unexpected and unhelpful. The counsellor might become obsessed with the client's life, rather than concerned to offer the best possible service in the time available. The client might feel exposed, or have expectations of a 'specialness' between them and the counsellor which are unrealistic. We do well to be somewhat challenging to the claims made for intimacy *per se*. The counselling profession owes it to clients and to the profession alike to carefully examine its fundamental philosophies before building on shallow foundations. We cannot 'prescribe' the level of intimacy necessary to effective counselling, but we can make some useful observations.

## Production of intimacy

We might observe that the counselling relationship is one which is actively and deliberately produced. In other words, it is not accidental. We do not begin work with clients and leave it to chance as to whether we 'get on with them' or not. We endeavour to offer some qualities and mechanisms of relating which will be useful. Where these are not useful, or even dangerous, or where the purpose of 'relating' is not therapeutic, the client will not be best served. Some accounts of intimacy within the counselling relationship are experienced as inappropriate.[5] There are three key points to be made pertaining to the deliberate nature of the counselling relationship.

- When intimacy occurs within counselling, it has a situational aspect to it. Thus the intimacy which might be found within the counselling room, or session, may not be replicated outside the contracted time/space: it is appropriate to the situation.
- The notion of appropriateness, or 'propriety', is engaging. It seems that practitioners must establish with their clients a sort of optimum condition, whereby anything can be said or done, providing it is 'appropriate' to the context. In this sense, counselling may be seen as being a defined role. The view that counselling may be seen as a form of 'role' relationship is compatible with notions of authenticity: I can be 'real' with you, and acknowledge that you are originally attracted to me because of my role as counsellor, my perceived expertise and authority.
- Where intimacy in counselling occurs, it is different from when it occurs in relationships of attraction: there need be no mutual attraction between counsellor and client. The client is initially attracted to the role, the promise of help, rather than the person, and the counsellor need feel no attraction to the client in any way in order to pursue activities which are geared towards generating intimacy. This renders it available to analysis in the paradigm of the production of intimacy as an active social process, rather than within the tradition of relationship as chemistry, as in courtship or marriage.

The conditions for intimacy to occur, then, are deliberately produced or engineered through the qualities and skills which the counsellor offers. This leads us to our second principle regarding interpersonal relationships in counselling, namely:

> *Principle:* interpersonal intimacy within counselling is functional only to the extent that it helps the client with self-knowledge

This is not always a popular perspective, and many counsellors believe that the intimacy within the counselling relationship is a two-way process – both must be intimate for useful change to occur. To this end, counselling is conceived of as using enough elements of self to constitute a mutually intimate experience. We would like to dispute this in the next section.

## The myth of mutual self-disclosure: I really feel this with you

What implications do our arguments have for practice? One common debate within counselling has been around the wisdom and acceptability of the counsellor demonstrating their emotion. Such demonstration

**You think your sore head is bad: I'm raging!**

may be seen as a form of self-disclosure which is powerful in effect, and the key question must be, as ever, what effect will it have on the client?

The answer, of course, is that we do not necessarily know. Several years ago, one of us counselled a woman who had been raped. She disclosed that one of the responses which she had found most difficult to handle had come from a previous counsellor who had demonstrated her own distress at the client's story. 'I felt', this client said, 'like this was much worse than any other client's experience, and that my telling her was too upsetting for her to handle'. This was not conducive to further disclosure or to the formation of a useful therapeutic alliance. In contrast, a colleague recounted her experience of a client who had undergone severe physical and emotional trauma which they were now disclosing for the first time in many years. The counsellor quite deliberately allowed their own tears as a device to facilitate the client, and indeed this was effective in catharting the client to usefully express pent-up emotion. The level of emotion was empathic and yet contained, and was used in the interests of the client's work.

The difference between the two events is not about whether self-disclosure of emotion is wrong or right. Rather, we are back again to the issue of intent. In the first of these two examples, the counsellor became caught up in her own responses within an interpersonal situation, and neglected to observe the effect of her revelation on her client. For her, self-disclosure of itself had value. In the second instance, although the emotion of the counsellor was genuine, the decision to reveal it was considered, and the focus of the counsellor was ultimately with the client. The counsellor was ready to 'catch' empathically the client's response, and would not have continued her self-revelation if it did not seem helpful. This is an important principle within interpersonal dynamics within counselling:

---

*Principle:* the client's well-being must be the central focus of the counsellor

---

This is quite different from having free licence to reveal aspects of the counsellor's feeling because it seems an intimate thing to do, or indeed because it is just necessary for the counsellor to do so.

## You see as much of me as I do of you

When intimacy is spuriously valued *per se*, it is possible to make some universal and some misleading claims about the nature of self-disclosure. Some counsellors claim that being 'present with self', or being 'genuine', or sharing the detail of their domestic surroundings, displaying personal taste through choice of furniture or clothes, constitutes a mutuality to self-disclosure in the therapeutic relationship.[6] We would advocate caution to this view. It is not that there is anything wrong with wanting to offer an openness, a window into our own beings, or a glimpse of our preferences and histories. It is just that we can, if not careful, construct a false view of mutuality which can miss the integrity of the one-way self-disclosure which necessarily occurs in counselling.

We can identify two distinct areas of self-disclosure. One is the content of what is disclosed: do counsellors actually reveal of themselves and their emotions as the client does? This would depend on the definition of self-disclosure as being the traditionally accepted version, i.e. 'a communication process in which one person verbally provides personal information about his or her thoughts, needs, or feelings to another person'.[7]

However, this definition may be seen as narrow. Talk may be the medium which most obviously defines relationships, yet we know that a high percentage of communication revolves around the non-verbal and the paralinguistic, which construct more subtle and indirect signs of disclosure, intimacy or distance.[8] A second perspective to self-disclosure, then, is that which delineates it as the revelation of self through manner and surroundings.

We can easily distinguish differences between the counsellor and the client's levels of self-disclosure. A counsellor who works from home will know that whatever picture she/he puts on the wall is open to public gaze, that his/her choice of clothes and hairstyle will present some aspect of self to others for their evaluation. Their manner will reflect their motivation, their personality, and their training in communication and social skills, all of which will be deliberately presented in a learned sequence. The counsellor will be disclosing in a way which is both appropriate and purposeful to their role, and will not be seeking a particular response in terms of their own self-esteem. This is quite unlike the rules of other developing relationships where reciprocity is part of the normal sequence of events.[9] The counsellor in a professional role and surroundings is making a controlled disclosure which does not entail high degrees of emotion, risk or trust, which have been identified as constituents of intimacy. Any client may come and see the pictures on the walls, all will be offered warmth and genuineness as these are part of the ethos, principles and skills of counselling, requiring no negotiation dependent on patterns of response usually required for developing relationships. The uniqueness necessary to an intimate disclosure is missing from the counsellor's perspective, whilst when a client discloses, this may be a unique experience. It is common for clients to disclose events or aspects of self which they have never previously voiced: it is crucial that this is respected for the activity which it is, and that we do not pretend a mutuality which does not exist. The risk involved in the unique revelation, the trust, is not to be underestimated or camouflaged.

This is not to say that self-presentation cannot change to become more intimate self-disclosure, or that there might be some facets of the therapeutic relationship which are challenging to the self of the counsellor. This is certainly suggested within some schools of therapy.[10] However, there are two apparently obvious principles attached to the use of counsellor self-disclosure:

If these principles are adhered to, then it can be seen that counsellor and client self-disclosure cannot be equated; they are of different natures and they demand different levels of intentionality and response.

> *Principle:* counsellor self-disclosure demands no therapeutic response from the client; therefore it entails a certain degree of 'having dealt with'

> *Principle:* counsellor self-disclosure is offered tentatively, and specifically to aid therapeutic movement

Gill Frost (2006) introduces an honest and provocative angle to the debate in her frank and entertaining exposé of menopausal manifestations within the therapeutic relationship. Her preferred stance is to keep self-disclosure to a minimum so that any transferred feelings of the clients may best be used to the client's advantage. However, hot flushes introduced a new challenge, and Frost's exposition of her responses to this involuntary tendency cause her to question whether or not she should bring her own self-consciousness to bear within the therapeutic relationship.

Deurzen-Smith (1994) suggests a rather elegant and principled slant to the conceptualisation of self-disclosure which enriches the understanding of shared or witnessed emotion within the counselling relationship. She suggests that the deliberate creation of intimacy within the therapeutic relationship is not about exposing the inner self of either party, but rather the creation of a mood, context or 'space' within which both parties can explore and create new understandings, insights and possibilities. The intimacy for her is then not in any counsellor revelation, which might indeed 'burden' the clients with her own internal emotions, be they joy, sorrow, fears or desires. Rather, the counsellor may openly be touched or moved by what occurs in this 'therapeutic space'. This seems to encapsulate more realistic understanding of client–counsellor intimacy without making claims of reciprocity which are simplistic and inaccurate.

## Sexuality: a powerful part of the human condition

What about the interpersonal issues pertaining to sexuality within counselling? There are many ways in which the development of psychology and sexuality are intrinsically linked in terms of theoretical development, from Freudian theories onwards. The construction of sexuality is complex, and deserves brief mention before proceeding.

Our position here is that sexuality is itself a social construct which is a part of how we construct our identity.[11] It is clearly too simplistic to reduce sexuality to the physiological or essentialist view of sex: in other words, it is about much more than just a physiological urge to union, inherently given and acted upon. It is about a more complex set of social and intrapersonal relations, both physiologically driven and entangled with issues of identity. Thus we describe ourselves as

**Where we come from, we all cross-dress. So what?**

gay, straight, bisexual, monogamous, polygamous. Our understanding of sexuality is culture bound, and differs between individuals, depending on their experience and view of the world.

Through various means of social discourse, e.g. family, school, religious institutions, the legal system, peer groups and mass media, we receive strong messages about the shape our sexuality should take, indeed even what shape our bodies should be to be sexy. We are provided with 'legitimate' or 'illegitimate' representations of sexuality. Thus while media can present images of women in any state of sexual

exposure or arousal, the erect penis is still effectively outlawed in the UK – in image form, that is – relax, you guys! This makes for a social construction of sexuality which is under constant review and challenge, as to what is 'normal', what is permissible. Such construc-  ·
tions vary from society to society and across time. In Mesopotamia, all married women were expected to have sex with a stranger in return for money on at least one occasion: traditionally, Polynesians saw love as the 'life force', with no words in their language for sexually obscene, indecent or impure, illegitimate, adultery, bigamy or divorce.

Examples are ubiquitous, and it is clear that sexuality is a complex construct, which intrinsically has no norms to adhere to. Concepts of gender may also be suggested as discursively constructed, and an issue for counsellors to address, as Angie Fee (2006) has eloquently and convincingly argued.

Equally, we must recognise that the development of counselling is located within a specific culture; so that it would be reasonable and ethically desirable to acknowledge the norms of that culture when it comes to specific behaviours within the counselling process, regardless of gender. We say this with caution, given the appalling narrowness and bigotry that has been associated with various schools of psychology.[12] By norms, then, we mean norms of conduct on an interpersonal level. Thus we might accept that behaviours which involve either primary or secondary sexual characteristics are likely to be experienced as sexual. All behaviour which is motivated by the sexual urge or gratification of either party in an interpersonal relationship may be deemed sexual: and any behaviour which stimulates the client into any kind of eroticised response must be acknowledged as sexual.

What then are the interpersonal issues of sexuality which affect the counsellor and their client? Broadly speaking, we have found that blank minds and sticky moments may be banded into four categories, as follows:

## Wow – my client is a sex god/goddess

Counsellors, being humble human beings, are physiologically attracted to others. Therefore it is reasonable to expect that at some point in our counselling careers, we might encounter a client who we find very sexually attractive, whether in their looks, their manner, their dress, or some other source of stimulation which appeals to our taste.

There is nothing wrong with such attraction – how can we possibly say that attraction can be graded as 'right or wrong'? What is inappropriate, however, is for the counsellor then to act on that attraction, or to become preoccupied with it in such a way that it contaminates the counselling.

For example, one counsellor we know, a heterosexual male, had a female client who was classically beautiful, in his terms. He felt low-level sexual arousal almost instantly. He had several choices to make:

- Leap across the room and embrace her with declarations of lust.
- Pretend nothing was happening.
- Disclose the attraction in the first five minutes, with reassurances that he would not act on it.
- Disclose the attraction with no reassurances.
- Suggest continuing the counselling over dinner.
- Acknowledge the attraction to himself, and take this issue to supervision.

There are many more possibilities of course, some more appropriate than others. In the event, the counsellor acknowledged the attraction to himself in the first instant, and then disciplined himself to focus his attention on the whole client, not merely her sexual persona. He then discussed his responses in supervision. He felt less threatened about the sexual element, and was then able to manage it appropriately. At some stage in the process, when a strong working partnership was established, he was immediate about how attractive he found her, at a point when she was talking about her self-image and effect on others. Thus it was relevant and purposeful information for her to incorporate into her reflections. He was also able to refer to his initial contracting where he had discussed the parameters of the counselling relationship in some depth, including the stipulation that this was not a social relationship, a move which had helped to set the context for both parties. Thus the client was able to experience her sexuality as a positive attribute which was not an overpowering force to other people, rather just one part of her whole being. Such a perspective can be crucial where clients have experienced abuse and exploitation, in which, falsely, they consider themselves at fault.

We are aware that this is a contentious area, and that sexual attraction can be a very subtle process – it is not always a case of 'Phwoar, isn't he gorgeous!' Nevertheless, we believe that self-monitoring is crucial to safe practice. Just as it is difficult to legislate for sexual licence or rules in life generally, so it is within counselling. The extreme arguments are that sex with a client is fine – after all, everybody's adult aren't they, through to sex must never ever be allowed between two people who have had a counselling relationship. This begs questions of equality and autonomy.

We do know that manipulation of a counselling relationship to satisfy the sexual gratification of the counsellor is detrimental to the client.[13] Therefore, it is safe to say that the counselling relationship should not be a sexual one.[14] It is incumbent on the counsellor to self-challenge and seek support and supervision if they find themselves attracted to the thought of ending the counselling in order to free the boundaries of the relationship. We do not believe that sexual attraction is an uncontrollable desire – flames must be fanned to make fire. However compelling a sexual urge may be, we will not explode if it is not instantly gratified!

## My counsellor turns me on

Sexual attraction to the counsellor has been well documented in all the therapeutic traditions, particularly those of Freudian origin. Whatever paradigms we operate in, we do well to remember that we are in a very particular and specific role in relation to the client, which carries with it some expected norms and some responsibilities. While it may be flattering or frightening, then, to be the object of someone's sexual attraction, it is imperative that we understand that all our activities and responses remain intentional to the client's welfare.

Where we are tempted to respond to a flattering invitation to sex from a client, we need to evaluate our own lives, in terms of our relationships and levels of fulfilment. This is not to say that sexual misconduct is always the product of sexual dissatisfaction: this could be a dangerous view, claiming 'mitigating circumstances' for unacceptable conduct. However, if the counsellor is playing games with the client, if his/her counselling practice is so much the whole of life that it has to provide his/her titillation and erotic gratification, then we would suggest that something might be out of balance – time to get a life!

We need also to carefully consider the role aspect of being a counsellor. Clients who invite their counsellors to a sexual relationship may be simply repeating entrenched patterns of behaviour which have little to do with the counsellor's individuality. In other words, they might be attracted to people who are in positions of perceived authority. They may confuse the pleasure of being carefully listened to with love. They may have never had a close relationship which did not include sex. In such a circumstance, to accept the invitation is to deny the client the opportunity to develop insight into his/her behaviours, and to preclude the possibility of change. It is highly unethical and ill-advised to collude with such behaviour.

**He's so caring. So non-judgmental. And has obviously got the hots for me. If only he wasn't so professional – just can't stop wanting him to want me ...**

*Tell me more about where she touched you ...*

We may become aroused by the content of the client's disclosure. One of us once had the experience of hearing a client recount in some detail an episode which she had experienced as abusive. On listening to the taped session, the counsellor found themselves feeling sexually aroused. The real event which the client had described matched a private sexual fantasy which the counsellor had created. An instant response of self-aberration was helped enormously by acknowledging what was happening, and the counsellor was supported by being able to discuss the occurrence without fear of judgement or recrimination.

As ever, there are no hard and fast rules about what should be done in such a situation. Each person needs to use their own resources and strategies to separate out their own responses and feelings so that they

**She'll be coming soon. Is it my imagination or does she want to fuck my brains out? Mmmmm.**

can focus on the client's world. What must *not* happen is that the counsellor direct the client to reveal more about this event for their own gratification: this constitutes abuse. We need also to understand that feelings of sexual arousal may be just another form of identification. After all, we don't hang someone because they have felt sad at an account of bereavement: we simply recognise that such feelings need to be managed and channelled so that they are not contaminating the counselling. Sexual fantasy is no different in principle from this.

## He did what? Urgh, how revolting

Conversely, we may feel disgusted by what the client is telling us. We might feel angry or uncomfortable with accounts of abuse, or with some of the practices between consenting adults which clients describe and which are not to our personal taste.

Either of these possibilities may present a danger: the counsellor might unwittingly direct the content away from disclosure. People are not stupid; when we divulge *risqué* material, we can tell from physiological indicators demonstrated by our confidante whether our revelations have caused disgust or alarm. So in a counselling relationship, the counsellor who is repelled but who tries not to be may well have the effect of suppressing any more disclosure. Equally, the counsellor who tries to steer or direct the client towards some ethic of 'normal' behaviour will be acting oppressively.

These can be tricky areas. Three approaches strike us as having realistic and helpful outcomes. One is to be self-educative in the arena of human sexuality. If we conceive of sex as a heterosexual procreative activity which takes place in bed with the light off, man on top and not too much noise, commonly offered as the best 40 seconds of a woman's life, then our shock threshold is likely to be low. If, however, we have an awareness that sex can constitute a whole range of pleasure-focused activities, then shock is not so likely. Secondly, we need to distinguish honestly between where we are ignorant and where we are prejudiced, and to challenge both. And thirdly, we would say to have confidence in the use of immediacy if we do feel taken aback. An honest admission of shock, if accompanied by a genuine desire to understand, is rarely offensive, and is a constructive way forwards – much more respectful than pretending we know everything, or pretending that we have no response at all.

In summary, then, it is possible to elicit some principles as to what is appropriate sexual behaviour in the therapeutic situation. Counsellors need to be able to:

- Facilitate the client's exploration of sexuality when this is intentional to the client's goal.
- Take responsibility for setting and maintaining clear boundaries.
- See the client's psychological needs as being paramount in the relationship.
- Communicate intentionality of their own actions.

We believe that if these principles are adhered to, in sexual matters as in others, then counselling will remain productive.

A final noteworthy issue is that of physical touch in professional helping relationships. In Portugal, it is a norm to shake hands or kiss on meeting and greeting. We are sometimes likely to continue that habit in the UK when training – which can be disconcerting and perceived as inappropriate, leading to apprehensions that 'Oh lordy, the trainers are predatory/perverse/provocative'. The key, as ever, is to be aware of our intentionality and the responses we elicit.

Touch in the therapy room is a thorny issue: do we really want to be in a position where we never show warmth, compassion or just 'humanity' through the use of touch? (See Swade et al., 2006.) Again, we revert to our well-worn but sturdy exhortation to examine intentionality: offering a nice cup of tea or a hug to comfort someone may actually prohibit the expression of emotion whilst refusing ever to shake hands, pat a shoulder, or hug may be demonstrating an unnatural inhibition.

# Friendship

It is easy to feel friendly with a client, and to imagine that we could indeed be good friends. However, we need to be careful. One person in this dyad (the client) has revealed her story, her emotions, her hopes and her fears. Something has occurred which has resulted in a close rapport. You feel so strongly for this client, that you really would like to help them, and you know they have such potential, and you understand their feelings so well. Hmm. As yet, she does not know your feelings, your potential, or your hopes and fears. She sees someone who always listens, who understands, and who is positive in all respects. She does not know your 'weaknesses', your failings, your values. Hey – she would like you to be her friend too.

Of course it is possible that of all the clients who we meet, some of them might be our 'type' in terms of friendship. It is equally possible, however, that we don't always identify those who would be most likely, for often the bits we hear in counselling are the bits that clients *don't* tell their friends. We offer a contract which guarantees to try to make the conditions for intimacy to occur. Would we really like our friendships to be the same?

Feeling friendly with the client may also be a smokescreen for feeling flattered. The trap is that you can be lulled into an inability to be challenging – after all, how can you challenge if you're seen as really nice? At its worst, this may even be, intentionally or unintentionally, a part of a manipulative behaviour pattern by the client.

Does this mean we can't counsel where the friendship predates a counselling contract? Some counsellors acknowledge that they do counselling with their friends from time to time.[15] This is of great interest, for it is *contra* the received wisdom of counselling culture. We have both on occasion either given or received counselling from both colleagues and friends. For demonstration purposes in groups, we have also counselled each other, and on occasion, have given each other some 'time' in which we have clearly designated roles in line with counselling ethos. We would both practically and ethically defend such practice.

We also know that, sometimes, students on counselling courses become so enthusiastic about their skills and newly found direction that they practise them on friends and loved ones, only to provoke hostile responses, along the line of 'If you check out what I'm feeling just once more, I shall have to slap you'. People get sick of 'being counselled' when all they want from their mates is a sympathetic ear, or a little guidance or advice, or some dependency.

How do we decide what is okay? What are the rationales, arguments, beliefs and myths around the practice of counselling friends?

**Sorry Margery, I just can't! I know you're suicidal but I can't help you – you're one of my closest friends!**

And why could it be different to counsel friends than to make friends through counselling? Let us first look at the myths which surround counselling friends, and then look at the principles which can make such activity feasible.

## Putting you before me: trick or treat?

One of the common (mis)understandings of counselling is that the anonymity of the counsellor and, indeed initially, the client, is of paramount importance because it can provide a certain form of 'objectivity', and allow the counsellor to be an uncontaminated mirror for the client, in which they suspend their own agendas and interests. There are two relevant arguments to consider here. Firstly, the nature of objectivity. Objectivity implies that the counsellor has no prejudices, no invested interests in the client's welfare, no preference as to the client's choice of action, no concerns and no identification. It is highly doubtful that such a state is possible. Many counsellors, when asked what they bring to counselling, will answer a part of such a question with 'myself'. The uniqueness of each counsellor is unquestionable; the desire to be 'for' the client is often paramount; the objectivity is already questionable.

In order to minimise contamination, therefore, counsellors are in a constant state of monitoring themselves to check whether they are following the client. At best, then, they are able to work in a manner which suspends their subjectivity, or produces a critical subjectivity – i.e. they reflect on how their presence in the relationship affects that relationship, and use this informed stance to best advantage. The second key argument then to debunking the myth that anonymity is necessary to 'objectivity', or rather to this state of 'critical subjectivity', is that if a counsellor can perform such activity with strangers, who may provoke all kinds of feelings within them, then they can produce it with friends. The suspension of personal agenda is a technique, a deliberate enterprise, which can be managed if motivation, self-awareness and skill level is present. This is why counsellors go on courses, and, indeed, why they read books. Being 'client-centred' and suspending self-interest are not some tricks which occur because 'we don't know each other'; it is a deliberate strategy which can produce a helpful intercourse which focuses on the 'content' of one person, and as such may be seen as something of a treat available to all.

The strategy might be easier or harder to apply depending on circumstances and relationships. Few of us would want to counsel a loved one who was suicidal, say, or who needed to express deep anger towards ourselves, or to address issues which are private from us. And clients themselves may prefer anonymity: we realise this. Where both parties are willing, however, we suggest that the carefully contracted counselling of friends is possible.

## No safety in knowing you ...

A myth surrounding the anonymity of the counsellor is that it is essential to providing safety for clients. For some clients, it is important to know that they might choose not to return to the counsellor at any stage, and to know that they do not have to face in social circumstances someone who knows certain intimate areas of their life. Anonymity is certainly one way of achieving such safety. It is not, however, the only way. It is perfectly possible to achieve safety, control over 'material', and trust within counselling, with someone who you know.

How can this be? Because states of relationship are actively worked at within counselling, deliberately pursued and produced. It is possible, through contracting and self-discipline, to create safety without anonymity. We mentioned earlier that during counselling training, we model sessions using each other as client. In the interest of authenticity, we always use 'real' material. This could be dicey, or at the very least uncomfortable. However, it isn't, because we contract very clearly to leave the modelled material in the classroom. It is only ever opened up again when both of us agree and we recontract to do so in the appropriate place. Indeed, our prior knowledge of each other challenges us to demonstrate a very clear negotiated understanding without contamination.

Trust is key to this endeavour. We have to know that it works, that statements made in a counselling contract are not 'used against us'. Once such trust is established, however, then the real safety, the intrinsic worth of an honoured confidentiality, can be experienced. It is even possible to argue that making anonymity essential is rather devaluing, going for the 'quick and dirty' rather than the more robust route. Rather than invoke this polarity, however, our key point is that anonymity is a choice, it is not essential to the counselling relationship; confidentiality, however, is.

## *Only strangers leave their black caps at home ...*

A third myth which leads people to rail against the thought of friends counselling friends is that knowing someone automatically means that you will have some judgement about their course of action, their perspective, their feelings. Again, we would argue that should this occur, then the counsellor has the same task as when they experience judgement with any other client – this is a conscious activity.

We might also take a perspective wherein part of the essence of friendships is that we are accepting of each other, that we do suspend judgement. Friendship is commonly held to embody expectations of honesty, openness, and the sharing and keeping of confidences. Respect is another common feature of friendship. Sound familiar? There is, then, no reason for counselling not to be feasible with friends, where it is acceptable to both parties. Such feasiblity hinges on four basic principles:

- Counselling and communication skills are the property of the human race. They have developed from human interaction and can be applied to any human interaction.
- The contract is the key issue to being able to counsel friends; informed consent by both parties enables counselling with friends to work.
- Sharing the art of counselling with friends is different from procuring friendships via counselling.
- Counselling is a strategic activity: it embraces an ethos and a repertoire of skilled approaches which can be applied to anybody.

## Culture

We always operate within a cultural framework.[16] We use this term broadly, to encompass myriad forms of differentiation: societal culture, race, class, gender, levels of education, political leanings, mental state, physical state, religious beliefs and background, organisational cultures.

Our cultural perspective influences all our interactions through their value systems and behavioural manifestations of communication.

There is always debate on whether or not counselling can ever be totally value free. There is also debate regarding the significance of how cultural difference or similarity affects the effectiveness of counselling. Such debates are huge, and deserve to be the subject of great consideration. Within the scope of this work, it strikes us that there are at least four ways in which values enter the counselling relationship with specific regard to culture:

- moral values;
- helping paradigms – the intrinsic value of counselling;
- clinical judgement – evaluation;
- communication patterns.

In this section, then, we will take all in turn and discuss briefly some key salient points.

## You don't want to be doing it like that, you want to be doing it like this ...

Moral values underpin behavioural norms, and can challenge the counsellor. In pure theoretical terms, it is seen as antithetical to counselling to adopt a moral position on the culture or the behaviour of other people. We are taught to suspend judgement, to be acceptant and to offer unconditional positive regard. It is not considered acceptable to perceive one race of people as of higher value than another, or to behave in a prejudiced way against groups who exhort one sexual preference over another. In terms of culture, moral values may lead to prejudice and oppressive practice: if we believe that people from certain countries/areas are 'thick', or shifty, or all white middle-class people are arrogant sods, for example, we will prejudice the counselling. We are urged to self-challenge such values in pursuit of unconditional positive regard; such pursuit may be complex, an issue which is discussed in some detail in Chapter 10.

Ultimately, we never achieve unconditional positive regard, because we give ourselves let-out clauses in the guise of limits of confidentiality. We may argue that such caveats are desirable, if we are not to perceive the individual in a societal vacuum. Thus if you are a client and tell us that you want to become a more effective rapist, then not only would we not counsel you, but we might break confidentiality in the name of precluding exploitation. This stance is justifiable under the heading of moral values, because as members of a society we have a moral duty to pursue shared values such as equality or fairness. Thus to condone racism, or sexual harassment, is as unacceptable as to practise it oneself.

In practice, then, we are not bound by the promise of unconditional positive regard no matter what. However, we can aspire to suspending judgement for the greatest part of our counselling negotiations, and to offering respect to the client, and again we discuss this further in Chapter 10. In regard to culture, however, it is clearly not acceptable to take a moral stance on someone's behaviour on cultural grounds, or through ignorance of cultural norms. At its worst, such ignorance and prejudice has resulted in people being confined to psychiatric units on the basis of cultural and racial difference.[17] We would suggest, then, that while we need to acknowledge the reality that counselling as a social practice is not devoid of moral values, it is incumbent on the profession not to offer valuation on the basis of culture or race.

## Counselling ten, witchcraft nil points ...

In addition, counselling as a social practice is inherently value laden. It presupposes a particular model of the self in society, a self which is open, honest, self-determining and authentic – in dominant Western terms. While this point is expanded and contextualised in Chapters 8 and 9, one or two points deserve mention here in direct relation to culture.

Firstly, it is well to remember that the development of counselling in Britain has been closely linked to the Christian church. There are of course also strong links between the philosophies and practices of counselling to Judaism. The notion of selfhood propagated through counselling, which embeds a concept of free will, is compatible with these religions.

This is not the case with all other religions. Counselling is being increasingly experimented with in Muslim cultures, and our own involvement in the initiatives taken by the World Islamic Council, in Kuwait, and with Bosnian Muslims, was educational.[18] Implications of the mix of the very different philosophical tenets of Islam with those which advocate self-determination are as yet unclear. It has been argued that Western and Islamic paradigms are irreconcilable, and that Muslim human development theorists should heed this stance as they develop their conceptual frameworks.[19] The main point is that for counselling to be adopted with all of the tenets so far advocated, cultural norms would have to be severely challenged.

Further, there is a real cultural value given to the 'internal' life in counselling, with not much room for the unknown, or for magic which we do not understand. The counselling venture is very much a part of humankind's attempt to be able to understand, predict and influence human behaviour, a part of the 'rationality' of the twentieth century. There are attempts to reconcile counselling with cultures where internal misery is conceptualised as 'being bewitched', the argument being that the structures of therapy are less important than the discovery and reinterpretation of shared meaning.[20]

There is undoubtedly a process of negotiation and change to be encountered between the cultural norms of counselling discourse and those of whole societies or sections of societies. Our guess is that such a process could be enormously enriching and very exciting if some sort of real integration and shared learning takes place. However, there is also scope for the imposition of one version of self, written through the symbols and icons of Western psychology, onto others. It is important to remember, then, the value-laden nature of the counselling movement.

## Tell me what you want, what you really really want

The third kind of values which we might operate are to do with clinical judgement, an evaluative process. In a first interview, the counsellor will be, hopefully with the client's involvement, assessing whether they can offer help which is appropriate to the needs of the client. A number of factors will influence this process; expressed wants of the client, level of articulation, orientation of the counsellor, the nature of the issue or problem, whether the client is on medication and if so what effects that might have, expectations of responsibilities, whether ethical codes are acceptable, and so on.

Later in the process the counsellor will constantly be making 'judgement calls'. Acting on the data they receive from the client, they will be choosing an intentional response. This may be on the micro level: I will empathise here, whereas here I will offer a challenge to perspective, and so on. There may also come times when the counsellor wants to challenge the motivation of the client, or indeed may want to break confidentiality for ethical reasons. These are all forms of evaluation of what is going on and what will be useful next.

Culture may be one of the variables which influences clinical judgement. The client might want a counsellor who is the same race, the same religion, the same gender, experiencing a similar physical impairment, and so on. This must be a matter of choice for the client. Counsellors, meanwhile, need to be careful to work in a way which is open to a cultural awareness – in other words, they must accept different norms of expressive behaviour, without letting this cloud clinical judgement. So the impassioned revelations of a person from one culture might contrast with the apparent passivity and lack of eye contact from a person from a different culture. On their own, however, such different behaviours should not influence clinical judgement. This leads on to patterns of communication, which are key to transcultural work.

## *It could be like being like me, to be like you, or it could be very different – what shall we go for?*

Values always underpin how we communicate, as all communication is produced and modified through cultural filters. In mainstream counselling culture, making 'good eye contact', is regarded as valuable, as a sign of respect, even of authenticity. It is regarded within Western counselling culture as jolly good form to vent the emotions. It is not considered particularly nice to say fuck or shit. Our language is a powerful trigger, and measure, of cultural prejudice.

What can we say about this subject in a general work, so great is its potential. We can only share views here. We have worked within multicultural settings and on a transcultural basis. Many of the books on the subject urge us to find out as much as possible about the other culture before working. Our attitude, however, has been to see the challenge of how we communicate in the here and now as the most fruitful way forward. So we have gone into situations 'culture blind', and learned from them. We follow a belief that effective communication relies on sharp observation, and the production of negotiated meaning, with a lot of checking out. We are not embarrassed to ask, or to get things wrong.

On the other hand, we want to be respectful, so for example in Kuwait we observed certain dress codes, in order to facilitate intercultural communication. We challenged some of our own interpretations of behaviour, particularly in gender relations, and kept an open mind. Working cross-culturally hinges on a belief that 'goodwill' is available and recognised in all cultures, and can be conveyed in a thousand ways. Ultimately, we need both cultural and individual sensitivity.

This is not to say that taking active steps to educate ourselves, to be proactively anti-discriminatory, is not valuable, indeed essential. We would also like to see far less control of the production of counselling discourse in the hands of society's dominant group, i.e. the middle-class white man. By this, we mean the 'owners' of developmental notions of self and models of counselling, key editorial figures, and so on – this claim is discussed further in Chapter 11.

But perhaps our worst fear is that 'reading' about it, and trying to do all the right things, can produce a rather stereotyped version of culture. Some people brought up in Catholicism practise birth control, some Muslims drink alcohol; every culture will have people within it who are more or less orthodox in their beliefs and practices. Cultural groups are not homogenous. We would advocate against becoming Dolly the counsellor, learning how to bleat self-consciously towards the appeasement of cultural difference.[21]

## Concluding remarks

In sum, then, it has been suggested that although interpersonal relationships cannot be defined and legislated for, their nature can be clarified, and they can be conceptualised as purposeful. The difficulties which lack of pure definition invokes do not make counselling impossible to define. Other professions whose success hinges on the formation of rapport and the offering of personal qualities still manage to define themselves, and so can counselling.

We have acknowledged that there are some themes regarding interpersonal relationships which cause speculation and difficulties. We have questioned whether intimacy is a necessary part of counselling, and challenged some understandings of this concept, particularly in relation to the myth of mutual self-disclosure. We suggest that issues of sexuality, boundaries of friendship and issues of culture are all negotiable in a spirit of good heart and integrity.

It is not possible to be value-free within counselling, and neither is it necessarily desirable. While moral judgement is not useful to counselling, we suggest that clinical judgement is necessary to safe and effective practice. In terms of intercultural work, negotiation is the best we can do. Finally, we have suggested that the practice of counselling itself is a value-laden venture; the challenge is in retaining flexibility and negotiating its values among different cultures.

## Notes

1   For Carl Rogers (1951, 1961), the nature of the relationship within counselling is of paramount importance, and is the substance of much of his writing. Elements of relationship were also of course paramount throughout Freudian theory and its derivatives. Extreme lassitude in boundaries within Freudian theory can be found in the practices of Sandor Ferenczi, who was

very much of the 'let's take the client on holiday with us' school, the rationale being that the unboundaried relationship was the therapy.

2 See, for example, Berne (1964); Dryden (1989); Ehrenberg (1992); Lerner (1989); Rogers (1951); and Rowe (1991). Dorothy Rowe, for example, states that 'intimacy with other people [is] the greatest pleasure we can know' (1991: 244), while Eric Berne suggests it is the 'most perfect form of human living' (1964: 55). High praise indeed!

3 One piece of research into counsellors' 'successes' offers the observation that:

> [A] common feature of these descriptions was the degree of *intimacy* between client and counsellor. Indeed some of the descriptions seemed to equate success and intimacy; as one counsellor reflected: 'Such caring, such willingness simply to be fully in each other's presence, always led to creative movement in the end'. (Mearns, in Mearns and Dryden, 1991: 195)

We would see this as a representation of what *might* happen, rather than what *must* happen for counselling to be fruitful.

4 Paul Nicholson, in *She* magazine, November 1995.

5 See Russell (1993, 1996) and Rutter (1990) for discussion regarding inappropriate sexual intimacy. Little work is yet available on inappropriate intimacy in wider contexts, although this is becoming an increasingly important theme.

6 See, for example, Argyle (1987: 44) and Goffman (1959: 33-40) for discussion on presentation of self. Ingram (1991: 408) discusses the intentional nature of the therapeutic relationship, and therefore the improbability of self-disclosure as being mutual.

7 See Falk and Wagner (1985: 558) for further discussion on this point.

8 Duck and Pond (1989: 26-7).

9 See Duck (1988: 44).

10 See, for example, Ehrenberg (1992) and Ingram (1991) who both elucidate on the uniqueness of each relationship while focusing on the particulars of situational and role-oriented disclosures.

11 For excellent discussions of sexuality as discourse and as construct, see Foucault's (1981, 1987) work on *The History of Sexuality*, or Weeks' (1986) *Sexuality*.

12 Psychology has been instrumental in providing theories of human development which have actively outlawed homosexuality and masturbation as unnatural practices. Of course, as trends change, so do the psychological norms; nowadays it might be seen as 'abnormal' not to masturbate!

13 See Russell (1993) for a client-centred discussion of these issues.

14 This perspective is compatible with the BACP ethical framework which suggests that sexual relations with clients are prohibited. 'Sexual relations' include intercourse, any other type of sexual activity or sexualised behaviour (BACP, 2002: Point 18).

15 See Feltham (1995).

16 We will be looking more closely at the impact and relevance of issues to do with specific cultural differences in Chapter 6.

17 The pioneering work of Littlewood and Lipsedge (1997) on this issue makes classic reading, and illustrates perfectly the dangers of moralising from an oppressive position.

18 Note that the BACP conference in 2007 explored the issues of counselling going 'global'.

19 See, for example, Rashid (1992), who argues for such articulation in the language of the Qur'an.

20 See, for example, Ross and Lwanga (1991) for a detailed account of such transcultural experiments.

21 This point is made eloquently by the main character in the book *Primary Colors*:

> Most white people do this patronizing number: they never disagree with you, even when you're talking the worst sort of garbage. It is near impossible to have a decent, human conversation with them. They are all so busy trying *not* to say anything offensive – so busy trying to prove they aren't prejudiced – that they freeze up, get all constricted, formal. They never just talk. (Anonymous, 1996: 27)

# 4

## challenging: do i really have to sit here and listen to anything, even when i think it's drivel?

**Abstract:** The art of challenging can be one of the most difficult areas for counsellors to grasp. They can become good at empathising, clarifying, finding out more and more story: thus counselling can become a hand-holding support exercise rather than a dynamic process of negotiation with opportunities for change. The word 'challenge' provokes images of throwing down the gauntlet, somehow challenging the validity of what the client is saying.[1] We use the word 'challenge' advisedly, to refer to interventions which invite the client to find a new perspective on their situation, feelings, thoughts, behaviours or wants. Counsellors need assertiveness to challenge, as well as skill. In this chapter we describe ethical principles of moving clients on. We explore what to challenge, and what not to challenge; when to challenge, and when not to; how to challenge in ways which encourage the client to make self-determined change.

Some counsellor trainers will tell you that the answer to the title question is 'Yes'; the more adventurous trainer might say 'Maybe'; and we say 'Probably not'! This does not imply that we disrespect the client, nor that we do not try to follow the principles of self-determination and non-judgementalness. It simply acknowledges that a lot of time can be wasted listening to comparatively trivial substance trotted out by the client because both parties believe that this is what is expected! The client thinks it necessary to describe every bit of his/her life minute by minute, and the counsellor has been trained that it is disrespectful to stop them 'in full flow'.

Clients often come for counselling because they have got as far as they can using their own resources at that particular time; they keep on reaching the same old stumbling block, maybe have a fixed solution in mind which they dread; they know the kind of changes they

**It might be fun, but I'm getting dizzy and confused.**

want but have become frozen in fear; they have hit some sticky moment in their lives from which they cannot move on their own – yet.

And counselling can be frustrating as well as rewarding. We would like to think that the better counsellors become, the more rewarding the work. By 'better' we mean having acquired greater skill, increased their range of techniques, being more confident and assertive, and being generally more at ease and at home with the process of challenging. When a client is unclear, reluctant to disclose to themselves, or going round and round in circles, the feeling of connecting to this client, helping them clarify their thoughts and reach a point where they can make changes for the better in their life is satisfying. Alternatively, if the counsellor is not able to help the client do anything other than go 'round and round the mulberry bush', they too may become frustrated.

While it's easy to theorise that the client is 'resistant', challenge is essentially about the counsellor challenging themselves. Resistance is one of those nice theoretical terms that we can nominalise and then attribute to the client. Counsellors talk about 'the resistance', working with 'it'. What on earth are they really referring to?

The term 'resistance' is used to cover a number of dynamic situations. What the counsellor really means is that the client is not willing at this point to confront some area of counselling work. Now this can have a number of possible explanations. It may be that they are afraid: maybe they are ambivalent about whether or not they really want any exposure or change at this stage; maybe counselling just isn't the right activity for this client; or maybe the counsellor is so naff, that the client would rather tell their cat about their troubles and the intimate details of their life.

What we can be sure of is that resistance is not some concrete entity. Its only use as a concept is to describe the fact that at this particular moment, or period, the client is choosing to resist the counselling process as conceptualised by the counsellor. Although this may seem obvious, when we demystify resistance in this way, we open up possibilities and limitations of the work. In other words, this is something that the client is doing responsively. The challenge for the counsellor is to examine what they are doing, or not doing, that may be part of this dynamic, and whether counselling is really the activity that is appropriate here for this client.

Consider the following. A counsellor asks for help with a resistant client, a young man of 15 who had been sexually abused. She could not help him through the trauma, she said, as he had tremendous resistance. She wondered if one of us would see him, which we duly did. In the subsequent session, the client disclosed how distressing he found it to talk about the abuse. He had been to court, and publicly testified against the abuser. He now wanted two things: one was to go to college, and the second was to stand up to his rather strong-minded father. No resistance at all. It was simply that the counsellor had not accurately negotiated the direction of the work, and once this was clarified, was able to help her client move on.

Recently, we undertook some couples counselling, wherein one party had dubbed the other as resistant to working through the problems. In fact, these clients wanted different things. More subtle variations on 'resistance' occur which may only be noticed in hindsight. For example, have you ever noticed that when you do some work on a theme, such as bereavement, sexuality, relationships, your clients tell you more about such issues just as you become more open to hearing about them? Often this is because clients will discern how open a counsellor is to being able to understand: if the counsellor has resisted listening carefully, then the client will say no more.

- If a client is 'resisting', what is it then that I, the counsellor, am imposing?
- Or what am I missing that would enable more work to be done?

It is far more useful to ask these questions than to attribute some 'thing' called resistance to the client. Those activities in which we are engaged, can be changed. Those mysterious occurrences which we dub resistance will ... resist!

Ultimately, of course, some clients have genuine difficulty in doing work that they want to do, but which causes apprehension or ambivalence. Challenging such ambivalence is perfectly legitimate and helpful, within a crucible of rapport and empathy. And certainly, some clients do not yet (or ever) want to make changes. Such situations need to be respected.

How we challenge, in the end, is a matter of judgement, knowledge and creativity. The rest of this chapter is concerned to look closely at the principles of challenging so that the practitioner remains ethical while challenging themselves into helping the client move purposefully towards change.

## What to challenge

### Ownership

Many clients will bring problems and goals that are not owned, that are 'other' stated. It is easy to portray oneself as a victim of other people's circumstances, to present with unowned problems such as:

- My wife's an alcoholic.
- I'd like to be more assertive, but they won't let me.

We can accept that the client is encountering problems because of his wife's drinking habits, or feeling unable to change behaviour at work. It is simply that, currently, the problem is not stated in terms of 'me'; it is therefore insoluble.

Similarly, people are brilliant at stating unowned goals:

- I want my children to be happy.
- I want my lover to be free of pain.
- I want my mother to realise what she did wrong.
- I want my partner to love me more, to bring me surprises like she/he used to.

We may want these things as much as we like, and could spend a lifetime ruing the fact that we cannot/did not attain them. Out of respect for the client, such goals need to be challenged in order to enable the client to see how they themselves are involved.

Without the problems and goals being owned it is impossible to help the client to see strategies or develop insights that will work for them. We know (however frustrating at times!) that we cannot control other people. Sometimes clients are not clear on this, and counsellors might collude with passivity. The key question, then, is 'How can the counsellor convey the importance of owning the problem to the client without just "telling"?'

We might manipulate clients with 'pseudo-counselling' manoeuvres such as the following:

> 'Everything you try leaves you feeling frustrated, and you know, this is because you can only control yourself.'

Or:

> 'So when you say you want your children to be happy, you know that's not completely under your control, so I'd guess you really want to feel you're doing your best for them – that way you'd find some peace of mind.'

Either of these gets the client headed towards an owned state, but through trickery: the responses involve some counsellor expertise and short circuit the more insightful path where the clients realise for *themselves* what they can and can't control.

The easiest, crudest and most neglected challenge to an unowned problem is simply:

> 'And what about you?'

This is a direct invitation to the client to take some ownership of what is going on, and of what they might want: 'So your wife's an alcoholic – where does that leave you then?' The client may well respond with a vague answer and return to the fact that his wife *is* an alcoholic. The counsellor, then, needs to be able to gently persist in the intervention; you may pick up empathically how the client has responded – 'So you sound as if you feel quite helpless.' Already this begins to identify what the problem is for the client, not for their wife.

The information giving challenge is slightly more sophisticated:

> 'I could just let you tell me more and more about your wife's behaviour, but it's my experience that you can only change the things which are under your control.'

For the unowned goal, the simplest challenge is:

> 'And what will you get out of that?' or 'What would that achieve for you?'

So, for the client who wants their children to be happy, the response could be something like:

'You also said that you want your children to be happy – what would this achieve for you?'

Although this does have a 'teachy'-type component to it, it remains acceptable because it makes clear what is the counsellor's view/ knowledge and then uses the client's material to return immediately to the client's chosen disclosure. It is of course directive, yet follows the next principle.

---

*Principle:* control the process not the content

---

The challenge to ownership is a very strong one. We are at pains to say here that it is not a challenge which ignores the situation the client is in; all problems occur in a context. However, if a problem is suitable for counselling, then it must be stated in terms which the client has some hope of changing. This means that some situations do not justify counselling, such as acute/immediate stages of bereavement, or social situations such as homelessness. Individuals facing such situations may benefit from support, which will often entail the use of counselling skills. Problem ownership is essential for effective counselling; to personalise social problems to this end is unrealistic and ethically questionable.

## Strengths

One of our first clients told a tale of woe. This 50-year-old woman had two children in a loveless marriage. She had promised herself that when they were both independent she would have her life back. Being a person who believed in her marriage vows before God, an important value for her, imagine her feelings of suffocation when her husband became seriously disabled shortly after her second child left home. She felt trapped, desperate, alone and futureless; Graham reflected this back to her in true Rogerian fashion. At the end of this first session it was clear that the client had been given every opportunity to ventilate her terrible situation, explore every negative emotion, and inspect every facet of her problem scenario.

Perhaps it should not then have been such a surprise to hear her response to the question 'Has that been helpful?' She simply and sadly said, 'Yes. When I came I realised it was bad, now I understand just how hopeless it really is!'

Further experience has shown us that typically the less experienced counsellor does not always remember to feed back strengths. We are trained to empathise with emotions and to listen carefully to the client's story, and this was done impeccably with the client in the vignette above. However, what was sadly missing was reflection of the *full* story and empathy with all the emotions. It is so easy to listen only to the problem, and then only to empathise with the misery and negative emotions.

You may at this point be thinking, 'Thank goodness I don't make mistakes like that!' Perhaps it's worth taking a moment to consider:

- What were the strengths in the client's story?
- What would you have reflected back to her if you'd been her counsellor?
- What were the positive emotions revealed in her story?
- What could the counsellor do in these circumstances to enable the client to have some hope, without compromising the fundamental principles of coun-selling (i.e. without reassuring, comforting, guiding or advising)?

We now see that there are many strengths and qualities that need reflecting back to our client:

- She is seeking help, she has insight into her dilemma.
- She has a clear commitment to her faith, despite this presenting a problem to her currently.
- She is a person who has integrity.

The counsellor had opportunities to reflect back to her the strength that she demonstrated in waiting so many years, how steadfast she had been to her promise and how much integrity she had demonstrated in her resolve to ensure the children could grow to independence.

The positive *emotions* revealed but not reflected were numerous: the *love* for her children; the *concern* for their independence and for herself in her promise to have her own life; the joy of anticipating a different life; the patience she has had in waiting.

Finally, the client could have been challenged to look more closely at what she wanted for her future that could still be possible. The clas-sic challenge of 'what would it look like if it was just "a little bit better"' might have been immensely liberating.

The potential challenge for clients to look at the positives in them-selves is lost in the intensity of negative reflection and in going with the superficial 'mood' of the client. Our view is that the client is served better when all aspects of themselves are reflected back to them, not only the selected negatives.

## Discrepancies

Opportunities sometimes arise for counsellors to challenge discrepancies, games and smoke-screens that are presented in client disclosures. These fall largely into the following categories:

(i)     What clients say they do/what they actually do.
(ii)    What they say they want/what they actually want.
(iii)   What others think about them/what they imagine others think of them.
(iv)    What they believe happened/what actually happened.
(v)     The relationship between cause and effect, i.e. he started to cry – I made him cry.
(vi)    What was observed/what was interpreted.
(vii)   Overestimating their impact/underestimating their impact.
(viii)  What is said/how it is said.

Each of these possibilities creates opportunities for the counsellor to challenge. One of the most powerful of all challenges is accurate empathy; another is simply to paraphrase discrepant statements together and invite reflection. The following examples illustrate the point. Using the categories from the list above, we give firstly an illustration of how accurate empathy (AE) could be used as a challenge and then illustrate how paraphrasing discrepant statements (PDS) together would create a challenge:

(i)     You feel really proud when you support your partner, and irritated by her when she's moaning (AE). You say you always support your partner, and yet you tell me that on occasions you refuse to listen to them 'moaning on'. (PDS).
(ii)    You feel insecure when they manage without you, but really pressured when you're left to do everything (AE). You have said you want more relaxation yet you say you need to feel indispensable (PDS).
(iii)   You feel inferior to the other workers and surprised that anyone seeks your advice (AE). You imagine that people think you a fool, and yet you tell me that your advice is often sought by your managers (PDS).
(iv)    You feel responsible, in some way to blame, and yet you are certain that you were clear about saying 'no' (AE). You say you must have led him on, seduced him, but when you said 'no' he ignored you (PDS).
(v)     You seem absolutely certain that when he cried you were the cause (AE). After you told him you were leaving, he became tearful (PDS).
(vi)    You worry about his drinking and have no doubt that it's connected to the loss of his parents (AE). You notice that he drinks heavily at Christmas, and assume this is because his parents died around that time of year (PDS).
(vii)   A lot of the time you feel ignored (AE). No- one listens to you, but they all seem to know how troubled you are. You are fearful of being deserted so you don't criticise them (AE). The merest hint of criticism from you and

they'd leave home, but they've stayed on despite the row you had with them last week (PDS).

(viii) You tell me that you feel afraid, and yet you look very excited (AE). You are fearful of making these changes, yet have already begun by saying no to your boss (PDS).

The discerning reader will be able to spot that some of the so-called accurate empathy may have a paradoxical effect. Clients receiving their intense emotions accurately reflected and attributed so tightly can quickly sense any implied message from the reflections absoluteness, i.e. 'Should this be so, is it really that simple, or am I right to be so sure'. The experienced and confident practitioner will also know that to inflect some sarcastic tone to an accurate empathic response, or to issue it with a questioning tone, automatically changes it to a challenge.

## Thoughts

Thoughts, as expressed in language, offer some potential areas for simple and yet effective challenge. The technique here is calculated to throw down an invitation for the client to reflect upon what precisely they mean. Most of the groundwork and thus credit for this approach must be given to the cognitive therapists.[2]

Often clients use words such as 'must', 'should', 'ought', which the counsellor can simply echo in a questioning tone. For the less speedy client this challenge can be elaborated to 'When you say "must" does that indicate some sort of pressure to do that, as opposed to simply wanting to?' The more confident counsellor may try something like 'You say you must, I wonder if you could tell me what it is you would do if you were free to choose?' This approach has the effect of gently challenging and also inviting the client to briefly visit their goals.

Other powerful words are those which indicate the client's thoughts are somewhat concrete or absolute. Words such as 'always' and 'never' are in this vein; they are almost always challengeable and should (!) never be missed! Once again the same parroted word in a questioning tone is usually enough to invite the client to reflect. Challenging conceptual thinking is one of the most powerful interventions that can be made, and such challenges need to be considered before hurling them at the client impulsively!

Challenge can also be made using both laddering and pyramiding which are based on Kelly's Personal Construct Theory (1955a). Taking time with this approach is important because in the process of asking about preferences some underpinning values are often disclosed.

**Everybody always wants to do everything. They're ruining my life.**

In the illustration below, the client's concepts such as loyalty, trust and warmth were very important to him; asking him to explore possible disadvantages to them cannot only be uncomfortable but alarming. Care should be taken in this regard, as the client's value orientation is exposed and potentially vulnerable. The following comparatively light illustration exemplifies:

A student on a cognitive approaches course was the subject of a demonstration. His problem elaborated out to his neighbour's rude and aggressive behaviour in regard to this student's dog. No empathic reflecting nor gentle invitation to consider the neighbour's view was successful in challenging the student's position. The student was asked to say what he preferred about dogs as opposed to any other animal. His list of preferences included such concepts as loyalty, friendliness, trust, warmth, acceptance and peacefulness. When subsequently asked to say what the opposite of these concepts were his list included betrayal, unreliability, uncaring, cold and standoffishness. Without much need for probing, but by simply asking if any of this related to his stated problem, it was revealed that his list of opposites almost directly applied to his neighbour. To challenge the student's thinking it was simply a matter of asking him to examine what the disadvantage of his preferred list were and the advantages of his list of opposites. Although at first this was difficult for him, it eventually led to some rather different conclusions about what he had recently quite firmly believed to be obviously correct. Eventually the student disclosed that he could see that barking in the night, the occasional smell of faeces, the trampling of plants and being jumped on with dirty paws might be unpleasant for other people.

## *Behaviours and proposed behaviour*

Perhaps one of the most obvious opportunities for challenge presents through the client's behaviour. At first, this may seem paradoxical – counsellors are trained to be 'non-judgemental', so how can they challenge behaviour? Yet all behaviour is linked to a goal: behaviour is the result of a person trying to achieve something. The challenge then is not directed towards whether the client should or should not act that way; it is just to check out whether that behaviour is getting them where they want to be.

One acquaintance of ours spent some time in prison several years ago, and was incensed at being kept in cells at the police station in poor conditions. He steamed himself up and threatened the police that, if they didn't treat him better, he would urinate in his cell. They didn't, and he did: who got to stay in a urine-soaked cell? Thirty seconds of satisfaction generated several hours of discomfort: not really what he wanted to achieve.

It is our experience that people often act without thinking about where they want to get to – give a person a problem, and 95 per cent of the time they will move immediately into what they're going to do about it. Thus all behaviours presented to the counsellor can be challenged by asking, 'When you do that, what exactly do you expect to achieve by it?' This rather crude challenge holds good in a whole variety of situations. For example:

- A self-harming client – 'So when you cut your arms, what do you achieve?'
- A sulking child – 'What do you get out of refusing to talk, going to your room?'
- Or – 'What would you prefer instead, and what would you have to do to get that?'

This approach to challenging behaviour need not be reserved for challenging present behaviour; when clients make impulsive decisions about what they are going to do, the same challenging approach is useful:

- The suicidal client – 'So if you were successful in killing yourself, what would you have achieved?' Once the goal is identified, you can follow up with – 'Can you think of any other ways of achieving that without killing yourself?'

- The desperate client – 'If you walk out right now, with nowhere to go, what exactly will you realise for yourself?'
- The violent client – 'If you do attack/kill him, what do you really gain, what are the likely consequences for you?'

Essentially this simple technique halts the impulsive client in their tracks and enables them to reflect carefully upon their behaviour and what it intentionally and unintentionally achieves for them. This does not require the counsellor to be judgemental, simply alert and questioning to previous or future behaviours which are as yet unconnected to goals. Otherwise the counsellor colludes with unhelpful behaviour for the client.

For example, one of us had occasion to counsel a young woman who had recovered memories of sexual abuse and had immediately confronted both her parents. She wanted them to feel punished, and her to feel better. She subsequently regretted this action, as it had totally unforeseen consequences. Had she been helped at the time to consider her goals more clearly, she might have realised that they were unclear and unrealistic, and could have avoided a lot of pain and wasted energy.

## Prejudice and stereotyping

We are taught to be non-judgemental. However, this can leave us vulnerable to allowing our client's prejudices to pass unchallenged. Doubtless, we all to some extent hold some prejudice, whether this arises from a form of preference – i.e. I prefer to chat to someone who is extroverted rather than introverted – or whether it is oppressive and offensive – I would never give a job to someone black. Both hold some prejudice and discriminate behaviourally against the disliked person. However, one issue that separates the two examples is the oppressive nature of the prejudice, and the power base for its exercise. It is not sufficient to argue that *I don't have prejudice, I simply exert a preference*, when this translates into an oppressive practice. Hence, by degree, it could be seen that to ignore all extroverts would be oppressive practice, while to avoid excessive social contact with a particular extrovert might be eminently sensible!

In considering whether to challenge prejudice in client disclosure, the counsellor has to contemplate whether the prejudice constitutes a serious threat to a greater social justice. They have to also consider whether it is useful for the client to be challenged, in relation to the contract. Further, they might simply be compelled by their own response to use immediacy in terms of how offended they might feel.

The issue is complex, but the reality which each counsellor has to face is that they will feel the periodic need to challenge client prejudice. There may be tension between this need and the drive to a non-judgemental, warm and genuine relationship. However, to be genuine means treating both yourself and the client equally, and therefore being able to challenge prejudice from within your own value system. We offer some ideas here in an honest attempt to be realistic and practical, rather than give some half-arsed theoretical answer that leaves the reader no clearer as to what to do. We will use the example of a client we had who was derisory to his gay single-parent neighbour, who has not kept her part of the garden tidy. This seemed to be a trigger for the client to run down all women, to want to outlaw lesbianism, and to slate single parents. Some options we considered are:

(A)  Challenging the client's qualities, strengths and values to expose discrepancies between the client's potential positives and their disclosed negative attitudes:
   • You give the impression of being a very caring person, and yet you seem to think so badly of your neighbour who you don't yet know very well?

(B)  Using self-disclosure of emotion and challenging the prejudice from our frame of reference:
   • I suppose I am a bit surprised (disappointed, frustrated, irritated) to hear you say that, especially when you yourself have been a target of prejudice for being unemployed.

(C)  A straightforward empathic response with a questioning tone accented on the paraphrased prejudicial thinking:
   • You sound absolutely certain that your neighbour is lazy, and you seem to think that that is because(?) she is female, gay and a single parent.

(D)  A combination of empathy, self-disclosure and challenge of the prejudice:
   • You seem resentful towards your neighbour because you think she is lazy: but I'm a bit confused: are you also saying that *all* gay women that are single parents are lazy too?

(E)  Immediacy:
   • I feel really uncomfortable with you asserting that all gay single parents are lazy wastes of space. Is that an effect that you hope to achieve with people?

We don't propose these as ideal, and proposing such ideas without stereotyping examples is quite difficult. Our main point, however, is that while suspending judgement of the person, we cannot help but have some responses to prejudices.

It seems to us that there is a complex relationship between disclosure of prejudice and goals of counselling. If we work with an extremely sexist man, for example, who wants to better his relationship with women, then the declaration of prejudice is an integral part of the work, and can be challenged easily in relation to goals, in order to develop insight and change. If, however, our client tells us that he really cannot stand anyone in a wheelchair, and wants to gather strength to form a campaign to have all known spinally defective foetuses aborted, then the counsellor might not only challenge such prejudice, but refuse to be involved in the work. There is a sense, then, in which we are never fully non-judgemental – we make constant clinical judgements as to what we can work with, and constant value-laden interactive and personal judgements about what we want to be involved with. Ultimately, some of our challenges around prejudice are from a position of our integrity rather than necessarily in the interests of the client as defined by them.

## Unrealistic expectations of self, others and life

We believe it is one of the counsellor's responsibilities to enable the client to see themselves as clearly as possible. This requires the counsellor to challenge the client's objectivity in regard to the social, cultural and behavioural norms in which they are confined.

Take Raymond for example. Raymond complains that his partner doesn't love him enough. He states that life is dull for him, and his job is boring. He feels that it is wrong to gossip about others, but he finds it too great a temptation to resist; he says that if his partner found out he was gossiping the scene would be awful, he would not be able to cope. He describes his worst fear as his partner admitting that they don't love him any more, and that this would be disastrous.

Losing the will to live? This is the sort of client that, just sometimes, you want to take hold of and shake, or to offer some *slap* therapy to. However, this is not fair or useful; no client means to be irritating, and everyone's problems are important to them. Sometimes, this is challenging to fully accept. This may especially be the case if your other clients are comprised of victims of identifiable and extreme trauma, such as sexual abuse, bereavement, war, homelessness, terminal illnesses. In comparison, Raymond's issues are in danger of paling into insignificance, even though to him they may be awesome. Some useful challenges for Raymond at this

76

point are suggested from the rational emotive school of therapeutics; for example:

'Raymond, can you tell me exactly what would happen if your partner discovered you'd been guilty of gossiping?, 'It would be awful!'
'What feelings would be associated with this awful situation?' 'I'd be embarrassed, and uncomfortable, I'd feel really silly.'
'So what you really mean is you wouldn't like it to happen, but if it did you'd survive it?' 'Yes, I suppose so – now I've said exactly what I'd feel, it's uncomfortable but not so awful.'
'Raymond, you say that if your partner admitted he didn't love you any more it would be disastrous; when you say disastrous can you be more specific, I mean what exactly would be the result for you?' 'Well, I'd have to leave, wouldn't I? It would mean I was no good, useless, and everything would be over forever.'
'Well, I can see the prospect distresses you, but let's just see how accurate all of that really is ... you'd have to leave, it would be a **certain** indication that you were **no good, useless** and **everything** would be over **forever?'** (Questioning accented hesitation on all words in bold).
'Raymond, you seem resentful about your dull life and boring job, and **helpless** because you have no influence over those emotions?' (Helpless accented with irony.)
'You feel unhappy because your partner doesn't love you enough; I wonder if perhaps you could take some time to think about the exact amount of love he should offer you?'

The point about such challenges is that they reality test. We are a culture who tend to verbally dramatise. Much critical and popular theory of the last 30 years talks about life in terms of 'surviving' divorce, 'surviving' redundancy, 'surviving' cellulite. People talk about being 'devastated' by their boss's attitude, by the failure to reach an expected promotion. If we use such language frequently enough, then we exaggerate our feelings and reduce our coping mechanisms.[3] Survival and devastation used in the context of the former Yugoslavia, Rwanda, Iraq and Sri Lanka have a very different meaning. It can be helpful to check out exactly what we mean, not to deny problems, but to exercise some responsibility and choice about the reality of our emotional and cognitive world.

## *Unrealistic goals*

I want to train to be a ballet dancer, says the 83-year-old woman with arthritis. I want my dead husband back, says the bereft young widow.

I want to win the lottery, says just about everyone! Unrealistic goals are nearly always phrased as strategies rather than true goals. What the person asks for is usually an action, experience or something to happen, rather than an emotion or state (true or absolute goal). Thus the automatic challenge, which is almost always effective, is the one which helps the client discover what it is that they will achieve through the action, experience or happening. For example:

'So if you could actually become a ballet dancer what does that feel like?' 'A sense of freedom, feeling the audience appreciate me, feeling proud, a sense of achievement.'

'How many other things can you think of, perhaps easier to achieve, that might result in those feelings of freedom, pride, being appreciated and that sense of achievement?'

'I know that you realise that to have your husband back is impossible, but perhaps you could tell me what you miss about him most?' 'Him just being there, to hold me, to be able to share things with him, to be part of someone. To feel loved.' 'So if he was here with you now holding you, what would you feel?' 'Secure, loved, connected.' 'So you might hope that at some time in the future, when the sadness and loneliness you feel now is less acute, you may be able to find ways of feeling loved, secure and connected – again?'

'I guess lots of people want to win the lottery, but if you did what exactly would you want?' 'Lots of things: new car, house, boat, to live in the country, give up work, have a holiday, oh all sorts of things.' 'Okay, so say you've got all those things, what do they all achieve for you – what do you get from a holiday, giving up work, living in the country?' 'Freedom, space, to be able to choose what I want to do for a change.' 'So the lottery is just one way of getting those things – I'll bet you could get some of those things without having to win the lottery though?'

It is important that the challenge is issued to the client for *them* to determine what is realistic and unrealistic, even when it is tempting for the counsellor to assert their own view of what they believe is a realistic goal.

*Goal hierarchy or ladder*

It seems to us that there is a lot of confusion about what constitutes a goal, and how it differs from a strategy. We meet many people who are not clued in to their own personal or professional goals. For example, notice what you say to yourself when in a crisis or stuck: often, it's

'What shall/can/should/ought I do?' Effective facilitators help people ask the more appropriate question, 'What do I want instead?'

Helpful prompts which help people get in touch with their futures are the WILLI-wobblers:

* What Would It Look Like If It Were A Little Bit Better?
* What Would It Look Like If It Were A Lot Better?
* What Would It Look Like If It Were Perfect?

All these are ways of asking *What do I want*? The question may be qualified by the use of suffixes such as 'professionally' 'personally' or 'organisationally', but it is always specified as a future wish, desire or want, *not* in terms of an action. Knowing what you want and examining the ethical, moral or consequential issues surrounding it must logically come before action. Goals can be seen as being on a ladder, or hierarchy.

Goals are closely associated or synonymous with values, and ultimate goals are *always* consonant with a person's value orientation. Ultimate or pure goals are always specified in terms of emotions or states of being, e.g. at peace, stimulation, challenge, freedom, free to choose, independent, relaxed, fulfilled, satisfied. It is important to notice that it would be highly unlikely for an individual to have only one ultimate goal, as goals often need to 'cohabit' for fulfilment to be achieved. For example, one may want peace, but to have nothing but peace might produce a state of boredom. Therefore, the goal of peace would be tempered by other goals such as excitement and challenge. This leads to the insight that a way of helping people to practically express their ultimate goals is to insert the word 'more' in front of them. Thus, once someone's goal to achieve 'peace of mind' is uncovered, it can be converted to 'more peace of mind', immediately making it more feasible. Through this process, we can convert ultimate goals to first level goals.

Second-level abstract-type goals are the next level of the hierarchy. These are often expressed with some behavioural component attached, but are not yet behavioural goals. For example, people may say that they would like to be able to be successful, have greater self-esteem, to be more socially skilled, assertive, and so on. These are **not** the highest level of pure goals or even first level goals, because the question 'What will that achieve for you?' will take the client further up the ladder.

The next level can be termed behavioural goals, as they are specified in terms of what will be happening if the ultimate goal was achieved. Note that this is still expressed in the future tense: i.e. I will be able to, say ... do ... go ... see ... think ... feel ... . It is vital to note that this is different to expressing what has to be done in order to achieve the goal! Although this is subtle it is extremely important to differentiate a goal from a strategy. Behavioural goals are generally useful to clients because they can be tested for criteria that ensure they are realistic. You can ask of them:

- Is that under your control? (Ownership)
- Is it within your resources? (Ownership)
- Is it worthwhile? (Substantive)
- Does it seem right? (Appropriate)
- Will it really be so different? (Substantive)
- Will you know that you've achieved it? (Measurable)
- Will you feel okay with that if you achieved it? (Values)
- What will be the consequences of achieving that goal? (Commitment)
- What would be the consequence of not achieving that goal? (Commitment)

Remember at this point to help clients develop positive goals. For example, saying 'I won't be anxious any more', 'there'll be less hassle', 'people won't belittle me', re-specifies the problem, not the goal. When meeting these negative goals simply say: 'So what would you feel instead of anxiety?', 'So what would you like to replace hassle with?', 'So what would people be doing instead of belittling you?'

Any subsequent work on goals after this level will probably be approaching strategies. Bear in mind that some grand strategies look very much like goals. For example, to win the lottery looks like a goal; it is of course simply a means to the goal, or something that has to be done (or appears to) first before the goal can be reached.

To explore up and down the ladder between goals and strategies, two very simple questions can be used:

- *To go up*: In response to any client utterance which involves an action ask, 'And what would that achieve for you?'
- *To go down*: In response to any abstract or vague description ask, 'And what exactly would that look like in practice?' Variations on this may be any of the following specific questions: What would you be saying, thinking, doing? What would other people be saying, thinking or doing? In this better future vision what would an average day look like?

An example of a 'goal to strategy' ladder might look like this:

**'Goal to strategy' ladder**

Ultimate/pure goal: Security.

First-level goal: More secure.

Second-level goal: Able to cope with stress, be successful, more assertive.

> Behavioural goal: I will be saying what I mean. My heart rate will stay down. I will be able to make decisions. I will communicate openly with my partner. I will work more efficiently.
>
> Grand strategies: Get demoted. Win the lottery and retire. Find another job.
>
> General strategies: Work on my assertiveness. Take up a relaxing hobby. Do a course on decision-making.
>
> Possible strategies: Talk to my children. Say 'no' more often. Learn to prioritise.
>
> Micro strategy: Buy a cinema season ticket. Take the earlier bus to work. Do feel-good session when I come in.

For us, this detailed work with possible futures is **key** to change work. So often people make a change with no real consideration of what they would like instead, rather than what they want to be doing.

## example

A recent client of ours, Fernanda, has a son who is a crack cocaine addict. The addiction has resulted in him becoming homeless, disoriented, violent on occasion, and, latterly, suicidal. She is understandably distressed and fearful. She has already given him a huge amount of money to try to help him, much of which has gone on drugs. Her husband Miguel is angry and fed up with the whole situation.

Initially, Fernanda states her goal as saving her son's life. While this is fully understandable, we challenged this goal as it is not under Fernanda's control – it is, in fact, more of a passionate desire, a never ending hope.

Working through the scenario, Fernanda discovers that while it is her prerogative to keep on hoping and desiring, her realistic goals are:

- To know that she is doing all that she can for her son, doing her best.
- To find a degree of peace of mind within a traumatic situation.
- To feel that she is acting within her own values of compassion and forgiveness.
- To be able to relate to her husband in an honest way without compromising either him or her.
- To have more control over her life.
- To feel more fulfilled.

As Fernanda realises that she has several abstract goals, she is able to measure her plans against them and to make her decisions in a more informed way. She devises a policy of when and where she will see her son; she begins to accept that she may not be able to either save her son's life, or indeed to influence him to a different way. She decides that what she wants is to enjoy whatever times she does have with him, and to help him within her own limitations. She also resolves that she will only discuss her son with her husband when her husband is not being angry. She also accepts that she and her husband have different attitudes, and that it is important for her to be true to herself while considerate to him. This carries some possible costs and consequences if her husband cannot accept this point. Fernanda also begins to look for what else might give her fulfilment in her own life, outside of the relationship with her son – she has another three children, and she is also an accomplished seamstress, with considerable business acumen.

Over time, Fernanda feels a greater degree of control and fulfilment within her life. She continues to have strong emotions regarding her son and his habits, and allows herself the permission to feel these and to seek support for herself. She spends time with other members of her family who are precious to her. She develops her business to the point of employing two other people within it. When she sees her son, she treats him to what she would like to, and says no to other things. She sees that he is less suicidal and has sought medical help. Although this has happened before, and she knows that it might not signify lasting change, she continues to have hope without feeling responsible for righting the situation.

This example shows that clear goals are key to helping people move through the helplessness of being unable to address their own wellbeing within difficult situations. They carry risks, which need to be explored thoroughly before people commit to them. Most people have more than one goal which need to sit beside each other – Fernanda has two key relationships which may be seen to conflict, yet nevertheless she is working to her best with them both, while having identified an empowering goal of being true to herself. Life is complex, and it is a counsellor's role to help their clients to know what they want within it *before* moving to action.

Finally in this section, a lighter story that illustrates how strategies and goals are connected, and how, ultimately, fate often has a hand. Have you ever heard of Lupe Velez? Lupe Velez was a movie star in the 1930s, who went downhill and hit skid row. Lupe's ambition, her goal in life, was to achieve immortality and notoriety. Since she hadn't been able to do this through her acting, she decided to make one final act to achieve her ambition – to be remembered – by becoming notorious for the way that she died. She planned a lavish suicide.

Picture the scene: a beautiful hotel bedroom decked with flowers and candles, favourite music playing; sheets made of satin; and Lupe's gown made of silk. Lupe takes her tablets and lies down, imagining how beautiful she will look on the front pages of tomorrow's newspapers.

What Lupe hasn't reckoned with, however, is the chemical reaction between the tablets she has taken and her last chosen meal, lobster thermidor and fresh strawberries. Feeling distressed and nauseous, Lupe stumbles to the bathroom, trips on the marble steps and falls head-long into the toilet. There she stays until she is found the next morning. Her unusual death hits the headlines.

The moral of the tale? Things might not happen the way we planned – but if we know where we want to get to, they have a habit of working out anyway.

## Summary

This has been quite a lengthy exposition of what sort of things we might challenge within counselling. These have been suggested as the following:

- Ownership – of problems and of goals.
- Strengths, qualities and 'positive' emotions.
- Discrepancies in behaviour, wants, others' evaluations, perceptions, cause and effect, fact and interpretation.
- Thinking patterns: absolutes, behaviours and proposed behaviours, prejudice and stereotyping.
- Unrealistic expectations of self, others and life.
- Unrealistic goals.

It is perhaps equally important to have some idea of what not to challenge, and the next section addresses this question.

## What not to challenge

### Values and beliefs

Generally speaking, it is not appropriate for a counsellor who believes in the fundamental principle of self-determination to attempt to challenge a client's values or beliefs. This is perhaps quite easy to appreciate when the belief is, say, religious, for it then seems obvious that we would not challenge a commitment to Judaism, Islam or Buddhism – doesn't it? In 'good' counselling practice, no one would challenge such self-defining issues. However, it can be easily seen how this might get complicated.

What if the religious fundamentalist wanted to join an abort 'imperfect' foetus group, that in fact their value system generates prejudice which is detrimental to others? What if the client had some obvious delusion (a false belief that cannot be shaken by reason or argument and is not in keeping with the person's cultural context) such as a belief that they are God? What if their religion is a Satanic cult which makes live sacrifices? Here the counsellor would have to make decisions on the basis of their contract with the client, their personal and professional ethics, and their experience and judgement, as previously discussed.

Generally, however, it is not the place of the counsellor to challenge values which are simply different from ours. For example, we might not agree in the sanctity of the heterosexual Church-blessed marriage, but some clients will consider this as an important value even if they are unhappy in their marriage. Such intrusions into the spiritual areas of a client's values and beliefs should be avoided – unless they are detrimental to others. A veritable minefield!

Of course, values and beliefs will be affected during the counselling process. It could be argued that this is a part of the efficacy of counselling, and we believe that it would be impossible to interact in some deep and meaningful way without *engaging* with the client's (and in a certain sense, the counsellor's) values and beliefs. However, it is not generally our job to challenge them from our perspective, but simply to invite exploration of those that exist in the client's selfhood, for them to consider if change is required.

Both of us have come across clients that have antithetical value systems to our own. Working with sexual abusers, for example, has required courage to invite them to explore their values and beliefs; without such exploration, no change is possible for them. Where we consider that there is motivation towards change, it has been both reasonable and possible to suspend judgement in order to facilitate exploration. On the other hand, it has been mostly quite obvious, with careful attention, when the client has no intention of exploring their values, with a view to changing their behaviour towards a more social end. For these individuals, the most charitable interpretation is that they are not ready for challenge, and the most forsaking conclusion is that they are beyond the pale. Whichever of the latter conclusions is drawn, the counsellor is faced with a client who is currently choosing to stay as they are; it is not within the remit of the counsellor to continue working with this person. Sometimes society says that this person requires treatment in order to *compulsorily* effect change. We do not believe that this is possible with a counselling approach.

Values and beliefs are a complex area, inviting many paradoxes to operate within counselling:

- Respect values and beliefs, acknowledge they might need to be explored.
- Don't challenge your client's beliefs – unless they're prejudicial or oppressive (and guess who gets to evaluate?).
- Suspend your values, unless you make an ethical or clinical judgement not to work with this client.

Ultimately, we do the best we can with an awareness of these paradoxes. The best check we can think of for ourselves in unclear situations is what challenge will achieve for the client, for us personally, for us professionally, and for the agency – what purpose will it serve? We can only make our best judgement based on skill and experience.

## Past behaviour

Challenging past behaviour is largely a waste of time. The past has gone, the present and the future are of paramount concern to the counselling practitioner. This does not mean it's not sometimes useful to reflect upon past behaviour in order to explore the rationale for its manifestation, or that lessons can't be learned from it. On occasions it may be helpful to cite examples of past behaviour in an attempt to enable the client to see what it achieved; the purpose is to challenge the present behaviour or proposed behaviour; it is not in itself a challenge to the behaviour of the past.

# When to challenge

## When confusion exists

Confusion is a sure sign that some sort of challenge is required. Mostly this simply means that the client needs to be challenged to slow down, to sort out exactly what is going on, and to carefully attribute the emotions experienced to the events that they derived from. Sometimes confusion indicates that the client's thinking about something has been shaken, or that values that previously served them well are now under review. The counsellor's task in these situations is to enable a thorough exploration of the confused ideas.

## When the relationship is solid

Strong challenges are like strong medicine; they are powerful and therefore need to be used in small doses. One thing that we are both sure about is that strong challenges will not be heard unless the relationship between the client and counsellor is sound. Any lack of trust, or insecurity within the relationship precludes a strong challenge. The relationship needs to be one that leaves the client in *no doubt* that the counsellor is on their side, and definitely not critical of them; counsellors need to be very honest with themselves about this. Without this certainty, challenge may be perceived as an attack.

Gentle challenge is sometimes appropriate when there seems to be difficulty in the relationship. If there is a perceived lack of trust, or reluctance from the client, then the counsellor might want to be immediate about this: 'I notice that you look uncomfortable with me today, and wonder whether you have difficulty with trusting me with this material'. This can be part of the formation of the relationship, as the negotiation of slight risk might increase trust levels.

## When the purpose is clear

The counsellor should know *why* they are challenging. Challenging skills require a significant amount of confidence from the counsellor, and effective challenges can be difficult to teach. The basic skills of counselling can be simulated into practice groups using real material, and students gain confidence in using them. Unfortunately simulating situations where challenge is appropriate is more difficult, and so fewer opportunities arise. Given this lack of opportunity to practise, it is not surprising that it can be difficult to know exactly when and how to challenge in real sessions with clients. This may mean that our preference to have a clear purpose before you challenge might be a little obscure. However, there are some guidelines in regard to purpose which we can offer. Challenge is purposeful to the following ends:

- To help the client avoid making assumptions about themselves, their world, and their relationships.
- To enable the client to look at their story from all angles, to consider a wider view and to see their story more objectively.
- To see the positives of their account, not just the negatives.
- To be able to see themselves and their behaviour as others do.
- To help clients take care about decisions; to consider cost and consequences of actions; and to weigh carefully all of their options and choices.
- When you know what you're doing.

It is necessary to practise challenging, and useful for more inexperienced counsellors to plan appropriate challenges and discuss these with their tutors and supervisors rather than to plunge in impulsively.

## When the data is accurately perceived

Be aware that challenging should be based around accurate data acquired from the client. Wild guesses or stabs in the dark are not an appropriate starting point for a challenge. Imagine a client discloses his story which is about his divorce. Although the story is related calmly the counsellor responds with:

> 'You felt upset when your marriage broke up and although you sound very calm, you must be angry.' 'What on earth makes you say that? I didn't feel at all angry until you said that.'

The counsellor who is guessing or making wild stabs in the dark can do nothing but apologise in such situations. However, the counsellor who based the hunch on accurately perceived data can recover:

> 'Well, I can see that you're upset by my remark, but it was simply that I noticed when you talked about your wife leaving, your hands were clenched and your knuckles looked white; however, I'm sorry if I got that wrong.' 'No, you didn't really get it wrong … it's just that I am angry and I suppose it irritates me to be so transparent.'

There is no substitute for accurate observation, and it is these observations that are the precursor to good data-based challenges.

# When not to challenge

## Too early, impulsively or constantly

- The relationship must be one of negotiated understanding before challenges can be made effectively. There is no fixed time on how long this might take – five minutes, 40 minutes – but the counsellor must have understood the issue and concomitant emotions/thoughts before challenging.
- Impulse might arise for different reasons. Something might seem strange or foreign to you – try understanding. Likewise, you might feel emotionally affected by the material. If you are unsure of your motivation, best not to challenge.
- Constant challenge will place a strain on the relationship between you and the client and may be experienced as judgemental. Be sure to demonstrate empathic understanding throughout the process.

## How to challenge

*Invitationally*

Challenge is best achieved by invitation. That is, the client feels invited to reflect upon an issue, goal, discrepancy or behaviour, freely contemplating the alternative possibilities and ways of addressing issues, not being dragged kicking and screaming into the counsellor's cold reality. It is easy to distinguish an effective challenge from an ineffective one by watching the client's reaction. If the posture changes to one manifesting offence, hostility or defence, then you've probably wasted your breath. On the other hand, if the client becomes pensive, then the challenge has probably been successful, inviting careful thought.

As well as stating the obvious, that effective challenges are delivered in a timely, tactful and sensitive way, there are some useful technical skills which have been most helpful to us in our endeavours in counselling. We offer next our version of some of the 'classic' challenging skills.

## To do or to dare: the classic challenging skills

*Empathy sandwich*

The 'empathy sandwich', or data-based hunch, is our version of advanced accurate empathy. At some point the counsellor may have a very strong feeling, based on some information gathered, that the client is feeling something other than what has been overtly disclosed. At this point the counsellor may start with an empathic statement, then offer the hunch or strongly suspected emotion that the counsellor is fairly sure of, and then follow up with a 'here and now' empathic response. This final part prevents the counsellor losing the client if the hunch is inaccurate. It prevents the client feeling 'second-guessed' or that the counsellor is in some way making assumptions. Thus the final empathic response is a safety net, to keep the counsellor with the client.

*example*

A client has described an incident where they were attacked by someone they considered a friend; as well being surprised, they are angry. The empathy sandwich might go as follows:

- *Empathic response:* You say that when you were beaten up, you were both surprised and angry, and you still seem angry.
- *Playing the data-based hunch:* I'm not absolutely sure, but the way you told me makes me wonder if perhaps you feel … a little bewildered by the whole incident. (Client looks relieved, yet startled.)
- *Follow up empathic response:* You seem a bit surprised, and yet relieved.

The important thing to note here is that even if the hunch had been wrong the follow-up empathy would have ensured that the development of the relationship and the growing understanding would not be entirely lost. Consider what might happen if the hunch was wrong:

- *Empathic response:* You say that when you were beaten up, you were both surprised and angry, and you still seem angry.
- *Playing the data-based hunch:* You still feel some hatred towards your friend even though it was a long time ago. (Client looks startled and irritated.)
- *Follow-up empathic response:* You look startled and a bit irritated … I guess I got that quite wrong.

When hunches are data driven, they are not likely to be too far wrong; however, when they are, it is helpful to know that the situation can be retrieved.

## Immediacy

Immediacy is a skill that a counsellor may need to use from time to time to get things moving. Sometimes clients and counsellors can get stuck because of the relationship between them, or the feelings of the counsellor.

It may be, for instance, that the counsellor believes that the client is avoiding the issue, and because of this she or he is getting irritated and frustrated. It may be that previously the counsellor got something wrong and the client has lost trust with them, or even that some emotional issue is arising such as love, sexual arousal or revulsion that requires resolution before effective counselling can continue. It may also be that the counsellor is fantasising about what she/he *thinks* the client is thinking, when actually they themselves have some uncertainty or embarrassment. These sorts of barriers need to be skilfully negotiated with the client in order to move on. Immediacy is therefore one of the most powerful tools to prevent circular discussion: it addresses what is going on here/between us.

For example, a client of ours who had experienced considerable homophobia amongst his peers talked at length about his suspicions that straight people always had some prejudice against gay men. He had disclosed much about his sexual preferences, history and disappointments, and had developed considerable insights into what he wanted in a relationship. He had then moved into bemoaning how difficult it was to find this and what hostility he was up against. The counsellor had questioned their own responses to the client, and was now imagining that the client was feeling hostile towards them. Immediacy was appropriate:

> 'I am aware that recently the tone of the sessions has changed. Forgive me if I'm wrong, but I'm wondering if you feel a bit uncertain of me, or a bit hostile towards me just now? I know I've just felt a bit uncomfortable, and I was wondering what it was about.'

This disclosure from the counsellor makes it clear that any issue between them both can be addressed directly and that there is no need for game playing. Such immediacy enabled the client to declare apprehensions and also his own ambiguity in terms of totally trusting the counsellor, suspecting at times that 'really' he was just like everybody else. The work could then continue. To be this direct on quite sensitive issues can take considerable courage, but is essential to maintain an effective professional relationship.

> *Principle:* get the shadows into the light – don't let hidden agendas prevent good practice

## Confrontation

Confrontation is not adversarial: confrontation really means to confront the client's strengths, to confront the client's resources, talents and skills, and place these into the framework that the client has brought. This can sometimes be used in combination with immediacy to invite the client to look at blocks or unacknowledged barriers to good interpersonal client/counsellor relationships. It may also involve confronting discrepancies in what is said, or how it is said, from data-based observations.

Challenging strengths such as courage to proceed, trust in the counsellor and commitment to be honest, are extremely valuable. Clients may feel hopeless, or helpless, and yet the counsellor may be able to help them to marshal all their resources. As previously mentioned, sometimes clients make smoke-screens, and sometimes clients will play games. Confrontation is a way of enabling them to use their resources, skills and talents to prevent these disabling strategies: it can help the clients see their skills, talents and resources in a more objective and focused way.

## Information giving

Information giving is the skill of neutrally offering information which may help the client see their problem from a different point of view. This is **not** by offering advice **not even** in disguise. It is often possible to present facts and information that challenge the fixed perception of the client and then to look at the problem from a different perspective. For example, bereaved clients may believe that they are going mad because they keep seeing or sensing the deceased's presence. To be able to inform them that this is in fact a common phenomenon experienced by many bereaved people, is not reassurance for the sake of it, but information which invites the client to reframe the way they have construed themselves. A client diagnosed as being HIV+ may think that this means impending death, whereas accurate information challenges this perspective, while empathically acknowledging fears.

## Self-disclosure

Self-disclosure is most appropriately used when the counsellor briefly shares an emotion or experience that was similar to the client's. This is usually done only when it appears that the client is having difficulty disclosing. The invitation to share the counsellor's world is issued in the hope that it will serve to reinforce the client's courage to discover more about their own world and disclose it more freely. For example, if the counsellor has personally been through a similar experience, some of the more deeply held feelings and issues may be shared if there is a hunch that these deeper hidden feelings are also being experienced by the client.

For example, having been deeply affected by sexual abuse in childhood, we are open to the complexity and depth of feelings it arouses. Counselling someone in a similar situation, Janice thought she was detecting some issues around a sense of failure for the client, while being aware that this might also have been contamination through identification. Any self-disclosure was very tentative:

> Counsellor: When you talk about your past, I can see that you are both angry and shocked by what has happened ... One of the things that really got to me in this situation was a deep sense that in some way I'd failed ... I sometimes get the sense that this might be true of you too; would that be right, or am I miles off beam??

The task then is to observe the client's response to be certain that they agree or disagree honestly, not simply to please, and thus ensure that words have not been placed in the client's mouth.

## Summarising

Summarising as a challenging skill is slightly different to summarising as a basic skill. It is often possible to summarise a whole range of issues and resources back to the client for them to review within a more systematised and structured approach. The counsellor using summarising as a challenge would pull together any themes running through the individual's life, which in isolation may mean little, but together may well be enlightening. As previously stated, care must be taken to ensure that negatives are seen in context to the individual's strengths and resources; a good summary is a full summary, not a selective trip into the mire and the mud.

## Paradoxical challenge

Both of us have developed skilled and sensitively timed sarcasm in our counselling practice: paradoxical challenge is, we understand, the technical name for such challenge! On occasions we have found it almost irresistible to sensitively provoke the client to respond when they seem to have lost all sense of proportion. The sort of style we are advocating does need to be carefully executed, and counsellors need to understand the potential of this approach to backfire. However, it is invaluable.

You may remember one of Graham's early clients, the one who reminded him of his mother, and whose planned exit from her marriage (once the children had grown up) was thwarted by her husband becoming ill. Well, she did come back despite Graham's initial doomy reflections, and struggled as she now felt that she couldn't possibly take any time or quality of life for herself. Having empathised for Europe, Graham moved to paradoxical challenge:

> *Counsellor*: So, for 29 years, you have cooked, cleaned and supported your husband and sons through all of their difficulties. You have put their needs first, taken a back seat in all situations, and now, when you had hoped for a future of your own, once again someone else is more important than you. And you feel disappointed. Well, how selfish can you be? That's all you think of, isn't it? You, you, you! Quite right, you don't deserve anything better at all.

The counsellor's hope that this would provoke the client to restore the balance of reality paid off, as the client 'retaliated' with how she was not selfish, and deserved better.

We have found this approach invaluable in terms of reality testing when clients feel really stuck. In work with the abused or violated, it is a very useful challenge when the client insists on feeling responsible for the abuse because of an ingrained feeling of guilt. It helps to put together the data you have heard with the irrational feeling of the client:

> 'So you tell me that you were five-years-old, about three foot six in height, and weighed four stone; you were frightened for your life as you really believed that if you told anyone, you would be killed: and your abuser was about six foot tall, maybe 16 stone, and in his 40s. Yes, I can really see how his systematic assaults on you were all your fault, and how easy it would have been for you to stop them.'

Of course such a challenge needs to be well timed and in a context of other challenging and supportive behaviours, but it can help the client to see how unfounded her (his) perspective is, and this can begin to challenge the strength of feeling which accompanies it.

## Challenging from time frames

While skills fuel the process of effective challenge, there are also frames of challenge, which work through a variety of means. One of the most effective frames which we use for challenging is that of time. However stuck a client is, a change in time frame can be very liberating. This is why life-threatening illness can be so powerful an energiser – it reminds the individual that they are truly mortal, and that each day will never come again. Sometimes, then, it is an effective challenge to simply ask the client to imagine that they have only six months left to live – what would be truly important? This can help to get in touch with goals and priorities. Similarly, we can take the client on a little time travel, invite them to stand in a position which represents a year hence – where will they be, what will they be doing, and what might they have had to do to get there? Possibilities are endless in how we approach this frame.

Time frame can also be used to help to challenge the client in the here and now. For a client who repeatedly beats about the bush, or who might have a habit of dropping a bombshell at the last minute, a simple invitation to treat the first five minutes of the session as if they were the last, can be helpful. What things really must have been addressed? What feelings/attitudes/behaviours must really be changing? Playing with time brings creative challenge.

## In sum

We have outlined some principles of what to challenge, when to challenge and how to challenge. Clearly, there are many more ways of challenging, and we would particularly direct the interested reader to some of the cognitive-behaviourists cited earlier in the chapter. However, our concern is not too much with exactly how you challenge, and certainly be creative and individual: our concern is that the general principles of challenging are better understood. **Not** to challenge is to do the client a disservice; counselling cannot move forward without it.

We use the paradigm shown in Figure 4.1 to summarise some of the principles of challenging. In counselling, the degree of understanding will enable the degree of challenge, and vice versa. The counsellor and client must take risks in order to increase the level of trust. These qualities have an incremental relationship to each other.

If a climate is engendered of low risk/trust, low understanding/challenge, then little movement will take place. In this quadrant of the diagram (quadrant A), the client will feel somewhat confused and anxious; nothing is happening, and there is no movement. For a short time, this might engender a level of comfort, which will quickly turn to boredom. If there is an increase in trust and understanding, but no challenge or risk, then the client and counsellor will stay in quadrant B and develop a very cosy, very gratifying in-depth understanding of

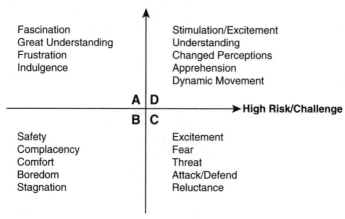

**High Trust/Understanding**

Fascination | Stimulation/Excitement
Great Understanding | Understanding
Frustration | Changed Perceptions
Indulgence | Apprehension
| Dynamic Movement

**A | D** → **High Risk/Challenge**
**B | C**

Safety | Excitement
Complacency | Fear
Comfort | Threat
Boredom | Attack/Defend
Stagnation | Reluctance

**Figure 4.1 Risk/trust paradigm**

the client's life, which will lead to a certain level of indulgence and a high degree of safety. If we move to quadrant C, where challenge and risk are high, but the right to challenge has not yet been earned through understanding, then the client will feel unheard, attacked, unsafe, jolted, and yet there may be something of an adrenalin rush which makes them prepared to risk that quadrant again. If the risk/challenge is incrementally increased in proportion to empathic understanding and trust, however, then we move to quadrant D and get some dynamic movement. Here change is likely to occur. Sometimes this will make for dissonance or discomfort in the process, but this is part of shifting perceptions, habits, ways of thinking and ways of feeling. It is therefore crucial that the counsellor as well as the client can take risks, and this depends on their ability to self-challenge.

- Have I really understood? Have I even listened accurately?
- Am I really assertive enough to interrupt my client?
- What stopped me using immediacy there?
- Am I frightened that my client won't like me if I challenge? Do I want their approval?
- Am I avoiding whole areas here?
- Am I scared that I might fail?
- Am I scared of the emotions I might uncover here?
- How can I change some of this?

These are just some of the many questions which a counsellor might ask themselves in order to be really self-challenging. We are quite sure, however, that the ability and willingness to challenge effectively are crucial to fruitful counselling. The key is to challenge incrementally from a position of understanding and to remain empathic with the client's response to the challenge.

## Notes

1   There is some irony here, as the word 'challenge' has infiltrated common parlance to become almost ubiquitous–horrendous situations or life transitions are described as challenging; difficult or unacceptable behaviour is described as challenging; undertaking a physical pursuit such as a sponsored hike or bike ride is described as a challenge; and levels of disability or physical change are described as challenged, both seriously and humorously–visually challenged, follicly challenged etc. However, we continue to notice that challenge is a tricky and skilled process within the counselling contract, and one which many practitioners still struggle with.
2   Albert Ellis, Aaron Beck and Arnold Lazarus are accredited as the key founders of cognitive therapies, Ellis (1962) with rational emotive therapy, Beck (1976) with his cognitive therapy, and Lazarus (1971) introducing the term 'behaviour therapy'. Initially unpopular with the humanist movement, cognitive behaviours therapy has been keenly researched and developed over the last 20 years. See initially Wilson and Branch's *Cognitive Behavioural Therapy for Dummies* (2005) and Westbrook, et al. (2007) for cohesive introductory texts.
3   Lasch (1989) offers an excellent exposition of this phenomenon.

# 5

# tight lips, heavy hearts: articulating without words

**Abstract:** This chapter looks at how and when we might communicate using alternatives to spoken language, which might be the case at particular stages or in particular situations, or when the client is not practised in talking about themselves or their feelings.

What happens if the client isn't very articulate, as in is not used to voicing their personal world? Counselling should not be a precious activity, only accessible for those who can articulate emotions. Counselling relies on the skills of communication: if the client is not an 'orthodox' communicator, the challenge is for the counsellor to find a way of building rapport and understanding.

This may be at the level of speaking plainly. For example, we can describe a helping framework in terms of 'past issues, current issues, future scenarios and strategic planning', and we can allude to transferences, projections or whatever jargonese we choose. Or we can ask 'What's up? What d'you want instead? What can you do to get it?' And we can just say if it seems that the client is putting us in a particular role, or if we feel particular vibes or energies – we don't have to explain in psychodynamic terms. Language needs to provide a description of human behaviour: it need not be a mystical science.

## Contexts for creativity

Years ago, Janice had occasion to develop a counselling service for young adults who were identified as having learning difficulties. This somewhat catch-all expression described a whole range of people: those for whom the school system hadn't worked, those who had a specific condition such as dyslexia, those who had emotional and behavioural difficulties, and those who had suffered some measure of brain damage. This was a group of people with diverse needs and abilities. What they had in common was a lack of practice in expressing themselves in conventional or mainstream ways. The challenge was to find ways to invite and facilitate articulation in the widest sense.

Interestingly, experience of counselling on a university campus offered similar challenges. Again, the clients were a diverse group of people who at that period of their lives were clumped together under the label of students. A certain cluster of students presented who were at the top end of the academic range, highly competent in articulating academic ideas. In other words, they had tremendously well-developed learning *abilities*. However, they found it surprisingly difficult to identify or articulate their emotional lives, and presented with relationship difficulties and issues around low self-esteem. The same challenge presented – how to find effective channels of communication which had meaning and impact.

Both of us have also worked in the field of mental health. Many of the people we worked with were in states of being where they were mentally dysfunctional in some way. How could we find means of expression where realities were distorted, distractions high and concentration span low? How could we help people express themselves in a way that they could take some charge, and where the expression of emotion was going to relieve distress and dysfunction rather than exacerbate it. We had to develop creative ways of counselling, where counselling was an appropriate option.

Much of conventional counselling revolves around the agreed activity of articulating emotion, or expressing feeling through words – the 'talking cure'. Words are immensely helpful; we negotiate shared meaning and understanding to the same ballpark via the use of words, and we develop useful shorthand. Words are good representational symbols.

Words are also impoverished. Have you ever experienced an occasion or event when you just could not find the words which would describe the portrait you wish to paint, or the sensation you wish to recount, or which would capture the sound which you had in your mind. Have you ever had the experience of thinking that you have described something in a way which others will understand, only to find that their inference from your words is different from their intended meaning?

And have you ever noticed how, sometimes, words just rob the experience of its uniqueness, or else make real that which is only a concept. For example, the experience of a new relationship, whether with lover, close friend, child, parent, mentor, which fills us with glee and incorporates magical moments might change in expression when related to another. It may become more mundane, less special, less unique, less enchanting. We all know the expression 'It loses something in the telling', or we might have the experience of 'Once I'd said it, it sounded wrong: I wished I could take the words back'. Words can be very powerful in their effect, and yet limited in terms of their accuracy.

Further, the expression of emotion is far more complex both in its form and its desirability than we sometimes acknowledge. For example, it can be tempting to think that in order to express anger, the individual must conform to some standard of clenching fists, shouting, becoming red, and so on. Yet this is not necessarily so – some people's version of expressing anger is much less visible to the outsider. It can also be tempting to think that in order for effective counselling to occur, then the emotion of anger (or whatever emotion is appropriate) must be expressed verbally.

Such an idea is specific to Western psychology. Our experience of teaching counselling in Kuwait, Poland and with refugees from Bosnia-Herzegovina led us to question the notion of selfhood with the emphasis on expressing emotion suggests. Colleagues working in Hong Kong relayed that they could not teach empathy in the Western conventional sense: to empathise with an emotion was seen as intrusive upon the self. It is more acceptable to empathise with a less personal state, for example an acknowledgement that the bus journey had been frustrating today, or something similar. There is a fine line in counselling culture between the attempt at careful understanding, and the insistence on openness to the exclusion of privacy.

So we wish to encourage the counsellor to become imaginative in forms and modes of communication, whether focusing on emotion or thoughts. We are sensory creatures, and can use many media. We don't want to devalue or oversimplify the skills and expertise of the trained art therapist, or the drama therapist, yet we wish to use any medium which helps tap into the human senses and urge you to experiment with what seems helpful to the client.

The use of 'alternative' or 'creative' techniques remains client centred. This is not a case of the counsellor thinking, 'Hmm, think I'll get Bashir to do a bit of drawing today, that'll make it more interesting'. The type of medium introduced needs to be either responsive to the verbal cues and clues of the client, or, if these are sparse, to be introduced as an invitation to experiment. Cues and clues to a person's preferred communication system can often be picked up through language patterns. Some people talk in terms of what perspectives they adopt, what vision they have, how they see things. Some people talk of how they feel about things, how they want to grasp the nettle, or feel their way forward. Yet others talk about whether or not they are

**Of course it won't sing: it's a robin, not a canary!**

in tune with people or policies, whether they are on the same wavelength, and whether they can hear clearly what is being said. While language alone is not an infallible 'diagnostic' as to what medium might work, it is often a powerful indicator. Equally, it becomes apparent very quickly what is not useful for clients – some people find imagery very difficult, for example, or drama therapy. So, although it may seem obvious, it is important to try to match the medium to what might work best for each client.

If there is little clue or cue, then the counsellor might take a different tack, that of experimentation. Obviously, participation in any activity is voluntary, and so the client needs to know that this is really an experiment. The counsellor needs to be upfront. For example:

> We've had four sessions so far, and it seems you find it really difficult to speak about what's troubling you. I was wondering whether you'd like to try some other form of work, like drawing, or perhaps playing with clay? There aren't any guarantees that this'll help, but sometimes it does, and they're often fun to do. What do you think?'

The counsellor needs to be sensitive to the client's propensity to limit themselves through constructions regarding their abilities; a common reaction, for example, is 'I can't draw', as if the client is immediately evaluating their capability in terms of technical competence, rather than expressive potential. It is important then to try to negotiate a way through this which remains sensitive to a real 'I don't want to', rather than an externally imposed 'I can't'. Once we are happy that the client will 'play' then we can try different methods of communication.

There are some excellent texts available to look at alternative methods of working creatively,[1] and doubtless you have many more ideas than us. What follows is just a snapshot of some of our practices, to illustrate how we might blend the principles of counselling with more media than talk.

## Painting the picture

As stated earlier, words are only symbols, which can be interpreted visually or aurally. And indeed for those who are hearing impaired, it is possible to understand words through the medium of touch, through their vibrations. It is possible of course to construct other visual symbols which help people to express themselves, to develop insights and, literally, to envision a different future.

The most commonly used approach which taps the visual sense is painting or drawing. This is simple to set up and use, requiring only pens, pencils, crayons or paints, and some type of paper. There are a number of ways of using pictures which are created by the client. You can use free drawing – whatever comes into your head; drawings of how you feel now; self-portraits, past, present or future; events and experiences, past and present. Sometimes it is useful to draw a lifeline, starting at birth and leading up to now, with pictures of all the key things which pop into your head. Pictures are invaluable when helping people to envision what they would like in the future. This can be done by asking a client to draw a picture of how they would really like it to be, or it can be done as a continuation of the lifeline – what events would you like to see on there in a year's time, two years' time, five years' time. This introduces the possibilities of change and control, in a way which is measured and manageable.

However a picture is created, we must use counselling principles to 'debrief' it.

Principle: the picture is owned by the client, to be interpreted through their schema of understanding, not the counsellor's

In other words, stay within the client's frame of reference. Because a picture becomes concrete, this is not an excuse to start offering our own insights over and above those of the client: 'Ooh, isn't that interesting, you've drawn yourself smaller than everybody else. Ooh, there's a lot of red, obviously lots of anger there.'

Pictures are powerful media. We say that a picture paints a thousand words, and, through creating pictures, a client might very quickly develop an insight or perspective that was previously not available, and which is quite stunning. One client drew a picture of herself as having a dark line between shoulders and neck, and a steel cage with a padlock around her heart. The realisation of what this meant for her, that her heart and head were severed from each other, was initially disturbing. The strength of such powerful imagery, of course, is not only in the revelations it can provide about what is happening now, but also in the potential which this then holds for change. The art work allowed this client to see the iron cage as metaphor. She explored it further, the strengths, functions, weaknesses, then drew what she would like instead, and discovered what would have to happen to remake the connection between the heart and the head.

One of our clients once drew a picture of her ideal place to be and, initially, it seemed rather a commonplace fantasy. However, as she talked through the scenario, she made a powerful and significant point.

'I'd be on a deserted island, the sun would be shining, and I'd be lying tanning myself. A hunky slave would bring me my Bacardi and Coke whenever I snapped my fingers. He'd apply sun-tan lotion delicately and sometimes vigorously wherever and whenever I wanted. He would be at my beck and call for *anything* I want from him! The island has got everything I want, things to do that are interesting. What I like best about the island is that, as you can see, on each end of the beach is a machine gun turret.'

The most important thing on this client's island was that it was safe and secure. The machine-gun posts were there 'because no one gets on my island unless I want them to!'

Pictures are effective in creating group dialogue and movement. We worked with a team that was in dispute with their employers. An arbitrator asked each side to produce pictures of their organisation as if it were some sort of sea vessel. The team produced images which depicted slaves in galleys, and shark-infested waters; the employers were drawing versions of a cruiser! The impression that the pictures made cut through a lot of the impasse which had been reached through talking.

**Prepare to repel boarders!**

We also use collage, with individual counselling clients, training groups and management groups. Pictures made from cut-up magazines and brochures can all help to inspire clients. The 'third-person' aspect of collaging can also sometimes make it feel safer to create a depiction of a particular event, or of a state which feels uncomfortable.

Another visual medium is the camera. You might invite clients to bring in photographs from particular periods in their lives, of themselves or significant others, in order to help develop new insights and perspectives. When working with young adults with learning difficulties, we used a Polaroid camera along with a box full of props. Clients were invited to dress up and pose in a variety of ways: how they see themselves, how they imagine other people see them, how they think they were seen at school, at home, among friends: how they would like to see themselves; and how they would like to come across to others. This was generally experienced as fun, and generated a tremendous amount of self-awareness and energy.

It is becoming increasingly easy to find visual resources in the form of cards. The tarot card has long been a consultative resource to people, a focus for personal reflection. There are many types of cards which can provide excellent visual stimulation. Packs of 'inner child' cards are available; whether or not this particular concept is meaningful to you or your client, the cards themselves can be used as invitations to explore. Which card best illustrates how you feel now? How you felt then? How you would like to feel? What happens if you imagine yourself as the character in this card, where do you think it leads you? You do not have to be an 'expert' with cards to use them as visual resources to stimulate thought and exploration.

Visual media can be put away. We have found this immensely useful for two reasons in particular, although we're sure that there are many more! Firstly, the story committed to some form of paper or other material can be metaphorically closed. When emotional material is painful, this can be useful. It can help clients to take some control over when they 'open it up' again, and in containing their emotional world and influencing their mental process. Secondly, pictures can be compared with one another to develop some sense of progress or change, and this can be enlivening. The client who had a padlock around her heart, went on to find a key, to draw an unlocked heart. Her earlier drawings reminded her of her courage and her abilities to change, as well as creating a sense of identity formed through all these self-images.

Finally, a word on using inner pictures to create change. The world of Neuro-Linguistic Programming has drawn attention to how we create our own mood states through making pictures in our heads, running scenes which evoke emotion. When working with war refugees, we encountered one woman who created a daily flashback through evoking a horrendous image, complete with sounds, smells, and so on. While working to understand the function of the flashback and to acknowledge the emotions within it, we also worked rapidly to help her to be able to control and replace her internal images to the point of removing the flashback completely. This is skilled work and can be very powerful, and we would encourage the interested reader to explore it further.[2]

## Feeling our way

There are those people who find it difficult to visualise or to articulate thoughts and emotions, but who find the experiences of touch and movement the easiest medium of expression. Touch may involve using the skin, the hands, the body, in parts or as a whole; movement may be isolated, or carry a sense of the body as a whole, alone or in interaction.

The sense of touch can be stimulated through a number of different materials. One counsellor we know developed expertise with the use of clay, to offer clients the opportunity to literally mould whatever they wanted to. The finished product is of course not the only benefit; it is also the feel of the material, the texture, the consistency, the production process. Plasticine or Play-Doh are easy and flexible, and give instant results.

Stones, coins or any other objects which seem appropriate are useful for making 'mini-sculpts' of current situations and future wants. One client who had a complex family relationship which included a number of children and stepchildren, as well as ageing relatives, found the use of coins a powerful aid. He was invited to use the coins to represent the people who were important to him in his current situation, and surprised himself at how he grouped individuals as far or near, and indeed he speculated what value he had given them. He was able to make instant adjustments to his coin-sculpt to represent where he would like to be in relation to everybody else, and vice versa. We were then able to work around what changes would have to occur to make this happen, and to develop both insights and strategies to facilitate such change.

These media can be conceptualised as crude forms of play therapy, and play is liberating. If the counsellor is prepared to take a few risks, they will help the client enormously. For the 'playful' counsellor, the use of dolls and figures can be helpful; Lego people, rag dolls, teddy bears, all have their part to play if it seems that they might be useful to the client's ability to express themselves.

Movement is a great medium of expression for some clients. Dramatherapy as a 'pure' discipline is well documented and derives from the pioneering work of Moreno, the Viennese psychiatrist. We believe that some of the simpler techniques are useful in different ways within counselling. If the counsellor is confident with their own framework and ability to 'catch' if things don't work out, then we would encourage a little experimentation. Four methods in particular seem especially useful to us.

**I didn't know that self-awareness could be so much fun!**

105

One is that of 'sculpting', which we have mentioned in relation to the use of objects. Sculpting lends itself particularly to group sessions, where an individual can take others as representing members of the family, or of a love relationship, a work situation, or whatever is applicable. They can then position them as if they were marionettes, in relation to each other, and, of course, to the client. This can be helpful to both seeing and feeling how each position is; actors can give feedback on how it is to be standing over/under everybody else, and clients can be helped to take a 'third' position on what is happening in their situation.

Another common technique is the 'empty chair' derived from gestalt work. While gestalt is a whole system which can be studied alone, it is not highly mysterious, and some of the techniques may be used in integrative counselling when offered with integrity, skill and purpose. The empty-chair technique has two distinct uses. One is to imagine someone who you wish to dialogue with as sitting in an empty chair, and to express what you really want to to that imaginary person. You can then change places and respond in the position of that person. The exercise facilitates expression of emotion and thought, encourages a fresh perspective on the other person, and facilitates self-acceptance. A second use of empty chair is when the client is caught in internal conflict, originating from ingrained messages received in years gone by, internalised and kept alive by the client's self-talk.

A client who came for counselling following a long illness featuring depression and anxiety, told us that he had become ill after the death of his mother. Once we had listened and helped him to understand and express his sorrow and guilt, we asked the question 'What would you change that to if you could?' He replied: 'Just to say goodbye and say I'm sorry.'

This answer suggested the technique of empty chair almost immediately. After explaining the technique, its purpose and its risks (sometimes powerful emotions can be overwhelming for a client) he agreed to try it. Graham demonstrated the process first, which helped reduce any feelings of embarrassment. Then the client was invited to speak freely to his mother and see perhaps what she had to say to him. At one point he was prompted to ask her how she viewed his behaviour when she was dying, and if she held him responsible or to blame in any way. The client imagined immediately that his mother not only forgave him, but told him off for being so silly! It needs to be said that *mostly* this is the outcome: occasionally you could have a client whose mother (or whoever is in the chair) is not so charitable. Even a difficult encounter, of course, can have the benefit of raising self-awareness, although it may be more painful to hear a mother say, 'Yes, you did let me down, but then you always were a selfish little so and so, weren't you?' Empathic responding remains the ground skill alongside this technique.

A third liberating method is acting 'as if'. This can be used in two ways. One is in a situation which seems irresolute. For example, one couple who we counselled had a situation where the wife had taken a lover two years previously. The affair had been short-lived, and the couple had derived several benefits from having their rather complacent relationship shaken up. They were highly motivated to stay together, had a great investment in providing security for their children, had many things in common, enjoyed their sex life together, and respected each other. They identified some mutual goals and some disparate goals, and acknowledged that they would like more 'quality' time together. Despite the pain and jealousy which had been experienced, this couple had a lot of pluses on their side.

However, there was a mutual problem of trust. The woman in the relationship had a longstanding distrust of men, which originated with her father. The man distrusted the woman; she had had one affair, who was to say she would not have another? They found that they were caught in a vicious circle: they went for days and sometimes weeks getting on very well, then one of them would start talking about the affair, or how they did not feel trusted. The insecurity question acted as a barrier which inserted a step back for every hard-earned step forwards.

When the couple were asked how life would be different if they were secure, they identified a number of behavioural manifestations. They would not ring each other compulsively when they were apart, nor would they insist on accounting for their every move. They would not worry about what the other was doing; they would not talk about the past hurts. What would they do instead then? Well, they would trust each other, and believe themselves loved. They would ring when apart only if they wanted to express something positive to one another, or to use each other as supportive resources. They would spend free time apart on pursuits which were relaxing: reading, jacuzzi, cinema, sport. They would spend time talking about their future; and they would always know when their next 'quality' time together was coming up.

We contracted with this couple that for the next three months, they would act 'as if' they were secure with each other. The couple found it astonishingly easy. They had to check themselves once or twice, but they found it easier to enjoy the positives which they had. Behavioural changes led to changes in both cognition and emotion, a great example of the 'as if' technique in interpersonal relationships.

The technique has a broad application. We might be taking on a new training contract, and feel a little nervous. While some anxiety may be useful, we also want to acquire confidence. It can be quite simple to approach the situation 'as if' we were our version of the greatest trainers on earth, someone who we really respected. How would they do it? How would they gain rapport? How would *they* introduce themselves? This can be a very simple and effective aid to personal presentation, useful in self-development.

## If music be the food of love ...

The sense of sound is of great importance to human development, although its importance is sometimes understated (and as you read this, just take a second to check out what senses you are using to do so). It is often the internal representation of sound which we allow to reinforce habits, behaviours and feelings which we do not wish to have. In other words, it is the words which we tell ourselves, the tones which we hear, and the frequency of their use which influence us. This means that we can allow our aural sense to be confining. The best thing about knowing this is that we then have the power to make it liberating.

Consider the power of self-talk. Many people talk to themselves over the course of an average day. Such self-talk is relatively unresearched, although some little work has been carried out into the nature of such talk which suggests that it is rooted in our distant but apparently not so dim past. An average trail of self-talk is illustrated by the following story.

Picture the scene: Fred is sitting in his living room one Sunday afternoon in spring. He is in his armchair, pleasantly sated after lunch, feeling warm and full, watching an afternoon movie. His eyes wander to the window, where he notices that the grass is long. A thought passes through his mind – maybe I *should* mow the lawn – yes, I think I'll do that. Somewhere inside, he knows that *it's good to keep the grass tidy*. Fred feels good. Suddenly, however, he realises that he hasn't had his lawnmower fixed. He swears, inwardly – inwardly, because *a gentleman doesn't swear*. Immediately, he wonders how to solve his problem, and it occurs to him that Elena next door has got a lawnmower – *he could ask to borrow hers*.

So far, Fred has gone through a commonplace process. He needs a lawnmower, Elena has one, perhaps he could borrow it. But wait – Fred hasn't finished talking to himself yet. As he rises from his armchair, he stops mid-movement. A voice in his head is whispering insistently – *neither a borrower nor a lender be* – it isn't good to borrow. He realises that he cannot possibly ask Elena for the lawnmower, because she will think *what a damn cheek; haven't you had your own lawnmower fixed yet? You really are hopeless.*

Fred sits down, disappointed. He ponders – no, of course Elena won't think that; after all, *most people are only too pleased to help out.* And after all, mowing the lawn is a socially productive act, as well as being personally gratifying. *Your neighbours will appreciate the place being looked after.* He must have been wrong; he will go and ask Elena for the lawnmower. He rises again, exhaling, feeling more relaxed, and strides across his living-room. He is hit by a moment of doubt – didn't he recently borrow the jump leads when he'd inadvertently run his car battery down? *Stupid fool, you're always so forgetful.* So wouldn't Elena think he really was very rude indeed – *don't go bothering people, son, and don't show your weaknesses.* And so he pauses, sits and thinks some more.

Five minutes later, Elena, who is feeling mellow after doing her yoga, hears a knock on the door. She sees through the glass that it is Fred, and thinks nonchalantly how nice it is to have friendly neighbours. She is shocked, therefore, to open the door to a crazed looking Fred who is red in the face and spluttering:

'Sod your bloomin' lawnmower. I never wanted to borrow the flaming thing anyway!'

We once told this story to a colleague who was agonising over approaching her manager with a difficult issue. She battled with self-talk which consisted of limiting messages and fantasised responses. We talked it through, and then left her with the story of Fred. Some days later, a postcard arrived from this colleague. It said – *Thanks, I borrowed the lawnmower.*

It is immensely useful to introduce clients to the idea that you can influence your own self-talk. This can be easily demonstrated, through inviting them to turn the volume up or down, to slow it down, or speed it up. People can play music in the background, and note the changes to physiology and feeling when they do. They can even change the content, once it has been challenged.

'External' sound is also a source of memory stimulation. We hear a piece of music and it transports us back in time, either to a specific memory or to an emotional state related to such a memory. It's very difficult to stay 100 per cent down when we play our favourite upbeat music.

## In sum

The possibilities are endless. You can develop and create myriad ways of helping your client to understand their world, and to convey to others their wants and needs.

Remember that whatever you do, whatever strategies you use, it should always be at the service of the client – just because you learned hypnosis last week, or new approaches in transcendental guruing, does not mean that you have to try it out on your next client. That said, we would say there's a great deal to be gained from using creative approaches

## Notes

1 McNiff (2004) and Simmons (2006) offer good overviews of creative therapies, while Martinovich (2005) explores their use with young people with Asperger's syndrome. Silverstone (1997) remains a great favourite for her expertise in client-centred art therapy.
2 Bandler and Grinder's classic *Frogs into Princes* (1979) is hard to beat to give a spirit of this approach rather than representing it as a set of techniques.

# 6

# counselling clients with mental health problems

**Abstract:** This chapter on mental health is for those counsellors who require further knowledge about mental health issues which they might encounter, in order to serve this particular client group and ensure effective help. An exposition is made of various mental states with recommendations of when counselling is suitable or contraindicated.

Aldridge and Pollard (2005) recently identified that 41 per cent of psychotherapists, 38 per cent of therapists and 18 per cent of counsellors, stated that they work with clients with psychiatric disorders. Our impression is that issues of mental health and illness can create some problems. It is also our impression, wrongly or rightly, that mental health issues are not addressed in depth on most counselling courses.

There are many definitions of mental health. The United States Department of Health and Human Science defines mental health as:

> How a person thinks, feels, and acts when faced with life's situations. *Mental health* is how people look at themselves, their lives, and the other people in their lives; evaluate their challenges and problems; and explore choices. This includes handling stress, relating to other people, and making decisions. (http://mentalhealth.samhsa.gov/resources/dictionary.asp#m)

The World Health Organization (2001) defines mental health as:

> a state of well-being in which the individual realizes his or her own abilities, can cope with the normal stresses of life, can work productively and fruitfully, and is able to make a contribution to his or her community. (www.who.int/mediacentre/factsheets/fs220/en/)

Our working definition is:

> an ability to interact with the environment, people and oneself in an organised manner, and to communicate and understand the world around one in

a meaningful way which ensures a state of well-being and stability. This stability includes mood, thinking and behaviour that is congruent with the person's situation and cultural context.

Given these definitions we could assume that all clients coming to see a counsellor or therapist are therefore not experiencing complete and robust mental health. However, many clients simply have some personal, situational or life-demanding issue which provokes the desire for assistance from a counsellor/therapist. Sometimes they ask for help only to accelerate a necessary and quite normal process – such as bereavement, separation, career change or simply exploration of future options. Clearly these could be described as issues rather than mental health issues.

It is our view that there is a qualitative difference between someone who comes to see a counsellor with an issue or a mental health issue, and a client who has an identifiable mental disorder which may require expert attention. While labelling people with mental illness can be stigmatising, yet for clarity it is sometimes necessary to acknowledge the difference between those clients who can be helped entirely by psychological means, and those that require the intervention of antipsychotic medication, antidepressants or mood-stabilising medication. Whatever we decide to call these mental health issues, it is clear to us that a reasonably advanced understanding of the complexities, symptoms and jargon used in context to our potential clients is essential.

So what exactly do we mean by mental health problems, and why have we added this particular special term into this book? Basically, because some of the thornier issues where minds go blank and situations get sticky involve clients with symptoms and behaviours which are outside of the range of most counsellors and therapists. It is helpful to know some general rules of thumb, such as that which says that clients suffering from psychotic illnesses should be referred to psychiatric services. Counselling such clients using empathic responses and challenges may induce emotional responses far in excess of the 'normal' range of response, and can produce such an overwhelm of emotion that the client is injured by the therapy – certainly to be avoided if possible! Clients experiencing psychosis may have delusional patterns of thinking, which are not only hard to keep track of, but may produce unpredictable results if challenged unskilfully.

This chapter is designed to help the counsellor to understand more about mental illness in the interests of safe practice. Firstly, let's simplify key terms before examining common 'labels', meaning and implications. Then we will look at some of the common drug therapies.

# Psychoses

Psychosis, more commonly known as 'psychotic illness', is the term commonly used for more serious mental illnesses which are characterised by the following:

- Little or no insight into the disorder.
- Personality changes, often permanent.
- Serious symptoms such as 'delusions' and 'hallucinations'.
- May require continuous treatment, usually tablets or injections, to prevent relapses.
- Often 'triggered' by circumstances involving some degree of stress.

Psychotic disorders are often 'familial'. Prognosis is poor for a complete recovery: however, the later the age of onset, then generally the better the prognosis. Additionally, lifestyle changes which offer a protected and nurturing environment, and stress reduction, reduce the frequency of psychotic episodes.

# Neuroses

Neuroses are commonly viewed as less serious disorders: however, they are not trivial. Some neuroses are extremely serious and even life threatening. Neuroses are contrasted with psychoses as follows:

- Usually complete insight of the problem is retained.
- Most neuroses are completely treatable, often without the use of drugs, or with combination therapy – drugs and counselling/psychotherapy follow-up.
- Usually the personality remains intact.
- Mostly, less serious symptoms (with the exception of suicidal risks), health problems associated with some neurotic behaviours; for example, anorexia.
- Complete recovery for most neuroses can be expected.

# Common mental health problems

## Schizophrenia

The primary symptom in people suffering this condition is 'thought disorder'. Thought disorder is the person's inability to think clearly, almost as if the filter we all use to concentrate on any particular idea is missing. Imagine having to verbalise every thought that enters your head. Without the ability to order, focus and organise your thinking, it would be chaotic and frightening. A high percentage of people with this disorder have auditory hallucinations: all of these are known as 'primary symptoms'. To have disorganised thoughts and with voices superimposed is distressing, and may lead to distorted perceptions and bizarre behaviour. Additionally, other possible symptoms include: emotional disturbances such as incongruent reactions to events; flatness or blunting of emotions; emotional lability; psycho-motor excitability or retardation; incongruous behaviours; significant change in pre-morbid behaviour; hallucinations – commonly visual and/or auditory; and delusional ideas.

Schizophrenia was classically described as having four types – simple, paranoid, hebephrenic and catatonic. Although these sound technical they are quite easy to distinguish.

## Simple

People with simple schizophrenia have the 'primary' symptoms which often lead to further symptoms such as poor motivation and drive. These in turn lead to poor personal hygiene, reluctance to get out of bed, lack of appetite, poor communication and subsequent breakdown of interpersonal relationships. Very few of these people will seek help from a counsellor, as their motivation is reduced, and their insight poor. Most referrals will be from concerned relatives and friends.

## Paranoid

This type of schizophrenia is the most widely speculated upon – reporters seem to like to use this term in relation to any offender that is classified as 'abnormal'. In fact, the term relates to people who have the primary symptoms of schizophrenia plus a 'tendency' to be wary and suspicious of others: indeed, the clinical definition of 'paranoid or paranoia' is that the primary symptom is 'delusional thinking'. People with this distressing form of mental disorder often have a bizarre web of ideas that may include egotistical 'ideas of reference' – everything heard or seen by the person is in some way about themselves. For example, the newsreader is actually talking about them, the television play has in some way been directed uniquely towards them to give coded instructions or information understood only by them, or the new posters being pasted onto the hoarding are actually a special signal that can only be accessed by them.

Unfortunately, anyone debating with someone in this condition is likely to become included in the delusional thinking. It is important for counsellors/therapists to realise this. People suffering this disorder can be dangerous and/or violent. Imagine that you believe that you are being poisoned, plotted against, betrayed by your friends or family, sometimes with strange voices in your ears whispering obscenities, instructions or death threats: it is not surprising that you may be tempted to react against your betrayers.

However, it is also true and important to say that, despite this internal provocation, many sufferers deal with their torment without any thought of striking out, and instead manage their lives, their fear and their panic.

Both *catatonic* and *hebephrenic* schizophrenia are somewhat old-fashioned terms but serve to demonstrate the wide range of symptoms that are clumped together under the umbrella term of Schizophrenia.

### *Hebephrenic*

This form of the disorder causes similar primary symptoms and reduces the sufferer to a childlike or immature state, manifested in giggly, nonsensical or gibberish-type talk. The sufferer behaves like a totally distracted child who is completely absorbed into their own world. Communicating effectively with this person is highly unlikely; the chance of anyone with this rather rare form of schizophrenia being presented as a client is even more unlikely. If it happens, however, immediate referral to psychiatric services will serve the client best.

### *Catatonic*

Those unfortunate enough to suffer this condition, which thankfully is very rare, are prone to all of the other symptoms plus what is termed 'psycho-motor' disturbances. The latter can be seen to range from frantic unco-ordinated, erratic or random behaviour – running, jumping, touching, slapping – to the complete opposite, staring into space with no movement at all. The latter is characterised by what is known as 'waxy flexibility' (*flexibilitus cerea* – why does the medical profession have to have such terms in Latin?). This refers to the strange phenomenon of the sufferer adopting (or being posed) in unusual physiological positions in which they will remain until moved, or they spontaneously change position themselves. This can only be clearly visualised by asking the reader to remember the flexi-dolls of the 1970s which were basically padded wire dolls that could be bent and would remain in the acquired position. It is highly unlikely that anyone with these symptoms would be telephoning for an appointment!

As some of these categories of schizophrenia are now used infrequently, the counsellor is more likely to hear new terms which are clearly designed to adopt more approximate diagnosis. This shift allows more flexibility in treatment programmes and may avoid some of the stigma attached to certain labels. 'Schizoid' is a favoured term to describe symptoms similar to those of schizophrenia, sometimes linked with other diagnoses – e.g. schizoid sociopath, schizoid depression, schizoid anxiety states. Many mental health problems which mimic schizophrenia may simply be referred to as psychotic episodes. These may be quite transient, and are often used to describe a period in someone's life when they portrayed the symptoms of schizophrenia, i.e. behaving bizarrely and out of character, then returning to a quite normal state. The person is not 'labelled' here, but a vulnerability to temporary states is acknowledged.

On this note, the descriptions above, and indeed below, are used to help the reader to better understand some of the manifestations of mental disorder in the context of whether or not counselling will be appropriate, not to buttonhole people into stereotypes. In the words of an artist we know:

> The label schizophrenia is inescapable. Call me schizophrenic by all means, but understand it is not something I 'have' or 'got', it is something I am. I regard my experience as a natural, integral and vital part of my personal evolution, a blessing. I am: because I am. (Shingler, 1999)[1]

## Bipolar disorder (previously known as manic depressive psychosis)

This disorder is characterised by uncontrollable mood swings which lead the sufferer to deep depressions or unrealistic euphoria: it can be dangerous and distressing. There are obvious risks with such extremes: deep depression can become suicidal depression, and manic euphoria can result in the person being so distracted by fantastic ideas that they have no time to eat, drink or sleep. One client revealed that she 'surreptitiously' danced all night instead of sleeping: another client related to us her near-financial doom after a spending spree costing thousands of pounds she simply didn't have. Another client described 'feeling in a deep dark pit and having neither the ability nor the inclination to climb out'. Despite its descriptive title, bipolar disorder does not mean that all sufferers flip from one extreme mood to another: some sufferers are locked into one end of the axis and never experience the other extreme.

Bipolar disorders are categorised as psychotic because in many cases the sufferer has symptoms which include a lack of insight, and some may have delusional thinking. This is especially true in sufferers who have stopped taking medication – 'logically' – because they didn't see why they needed them. Equally some sufferers experience some significant change in personality from their 'pre-morbid' personality. We can only stress that this is the case for *some* sufferers and certainly does not apply to all. Many bipolar sufferers control their state using lithium carbonate or similar medication. This combats the biochemical imbalance in the brain which is thought to be responsible for this disorder.

## Endogenous depression

Depression is said to affect many people, and is a normal reaction to difficult circumstances and situations. 'Endogenous' refers to the type of depression that is inherent in the sufferer's personality, and may have psychotic overtones such as delusional thinking and associated behavioural difficulties. Generally, those with endogenous depression manifest thoughts of 'unworthiness' and failure, and although this is also common in other forms of depression, the unshakeable character of these thoughts make them a considerable threat to the individuals' well-being. Early waking and oppressive thoughts of doom and disaster 'going over and over in my head', make this an upsetting disorder, which usually requires ongoing medication in order for the sufferer to participate in a 'normal' fulfilling life. Counselling/therapy is often helpful, although not normally in the acute stages before medication has been prescribed, although it is not contraindicated. Once the 'delusional' dimension of the disorder has been relieved, reframing thoughts and challenging is useful. Challenging whilst delusional thinking is still in process, will have little effect and may result in the counsellor being incorporated into the client's delusion.

## Multiple personality disorders

The idea of 'multiple personality' intrigues us: there are many books on the subject, and at least one movie.[2] It is a particularly difficult syndrome. Sufferers of this disorder have within themselves independent personalities that 'take over' and live independently of the others within the same mind. Clearly in these cases it is possible the personality of a murderer, and a devout religious person to co-exist.

Generally speaking, we would say that counselling such individuals is inadvisable. This is a generalisation that not everyone would agree with. On a personal note, we know one very skilled counsellor/therapist who had remarkable success with this disorder, with some very careful, taxing and supervised work. We have also encountered counsellors/therapists whose own intrigue/fascination has seemed to be more the agenda than the absolute welfare of their clients or those for whom the client might have responsibility.

Whatever view you choose, we do believe that the inexperienced counsellor should refer on a client with multiple personality disorder as quickly as is ethically possible. Counsellors/therapists should not confuse this psychiatric disorder with the espoused theory of 'sub' personalities, which is a respected way of working with some individuals in order to enable them to see themselves as being different in different settings. Writers such as Goffman (1959) have endeavoured to help us see that we may present our 'selves' differently in changing environments or situations. Many hold the notion that our personality is not static or fixed, and some counsellors/therapists from the school of psychosynthesis help individuals exploit this fragmentation in order to help them cope better with changing and difficult circumstances, or simply to enhance fruitful lives.

## Personality disorders including psychopathy

The term 'personality disorders' is a blanket term which covers a multitude of disorders which may or may not be amenable to treatment. Psychopaths – those individuals who are actively anti-social in the sense of acting against society, and sociopaths who are anti-social in the sense of shunning or feeling that they don't fit into society, are included in this group. People with 'coping difficulties' or people who are often considered to be 'inadequate' are also included in this group. Often other 'abnormal' behavioural patterns such as alcohol and drug dependency and even occasionally eating disorders can be included by this umbrella term. Sometimes these states can be induced in periods of drug (including alcohol) withdrawal, as can psychotic episodes.

A term that we have heard somewhat bandied around is 'borderline personality', which refers to 'borderline personality disorder'. This term is generally used as a pejorative and seems to indicate that the client is on the edge of being a personality disorder and thus unlikely to benefit from counselling. It seems to us that these terms are really not too helpful and only add to an already overcrowded 'labelling' stigma.

So where does that leave the counsellor when presented with an individual diagnosed as having a personality disorder? Well, we may wonder whether the condition is produced by 'nature or nurture'. Clearly, Carl Rogers believed that nurture was the major factor, and that the process of disorder could be reversed by providing the core conditions of unconditional positive regard, warmth and genuineness. As idealists and pragmatists, our heart is with this view. Equally, our practical instincts tell us that the job of re-nurturing is huge, maybe too big for many of us; there may be disappointments along the way; and fantastically rewarding for the counsellor who is in for the long-haul therapeutic journey, with very clear focus and good support and supervision.

## Obsessive compulsive disorder (OCD)

The specific difference between obsessions and compulsions is clarified in the glossary of terms. Mild symptoms of OCD can be seen in some form in even the most 'normal' of people. You have met the fastidious, tidiest and most organised of individuals and have possibly admired them, perhaps even been in awe of them: you might be them! Whilst this trait in a person is often an asset, once it becomes an interference in 'normal' daily living, it becomes a disorder. One public house we know had beer-mats on each table that had to be placed the 'right side up' at all times. If the publican noticed a beer-mat (believe us he never missed one) the 'wrong way up', he would make his way to the table, engage the customer in small talk and obsequiously turn the beer-mat back to its 'proper' position. This could sometimes take up most of his time, requiring his bar staff to do the rest of the normal work routine.

Now although this seemed to his regular customers like a bit of 'silliness', it eventually led to his business failing, as he would become extremely irate when he realised that some of his customers were deliberately turning over the beer-mats to vex him, obviously. He would bar people who played with the beer-mats, and eventually had to seek help to regain some control over his obsessional–compulsive behaviour.

The treatment of choice for this disorder is cognitive behavioural therapy, and is well within the remit of most counsellors/therapists. However, some sufferers have severe, almost psychotic, overtones to their condition, and these may need more specialised help. Repetitive hand-washers who scrub their hands raw with disinfectant in order to 'calm' their thoughts of death and destruction can often not be relieved of a belief that without this ritual, untold misery will befall them or those they love. These sufferers could be described as 'delusional' and their disorder is often beyond the counselling remit.

## Anorexia nervosa and bulimia

Anorexic clients can be helped enormously by counselling; despite having a psychiatric 'label', they may well have many issues whose understanding and resolution becomes instrumental in their recovery. Severe cases associated with extreme weight loss are seriously life threatening: long-term emaciation can produce long-term physiological difficulties and disorders, so no time should be lost in referring clients to psychiatric care centres where appropriate. Treatment can sometimes include complete bed rest with permitted increase in activity correlated strictly to weight gain.

The use of psychotherapeutic programmes including behavioural programmes, occupational therapy and counselling are the main thrust of care. On occasion, some clients may require compulsory treatment under the various legislative acts: thus serious consideration of the tenets of 'client self-determination' as a philosophical stance is crucial. Our own view is that *on occasions* the principle of self-determination of a client may have to be deprioritised as their need for survival becomes paramount. We say this cautiously, as it is complex – age, state of mind, physiological conditions, previously negotiated contracts, what we can live with – these factors vary. Counsellors and therapists have to reach their own conclusions as to when and where they consider the right to self-determination by the client may be superseded.

## Puerperal depression

This type of depression affects women who have recently given birth. Typically, this is a serious 'delusional' disorder, often with heartbreaking symptoms, such as abandonment of the baby, disbelief that the child is really their own, lack of bonding with the child, sometimes child-harming behaviours, and an inability to show or feel affection towards the child and or others usually close to the sufferer. Fortunately, although this is classified as a psychosis because of its severity and delusional overtones, puerperal depression is often a temporary mental disorder. Swift referral to psychiatric services is helpful, as antipsychotic medication can facilitate an early recovery. Counselling/therapy is often welcomed and helpful as follow-up, as there is often an adjustment period which might entail self-recrimination and regret.

## Postnatal depression

This is depression associated with the period following child birth, a neurosis rather than a psychosis. Mothers presenting with this problem may be distressed by the lack of bonding they have with the baby, and the emotional blunting they experience. Although the 'baby blues' are experienced by many mothers shortly after delivery due to hormonal changes (thought to be associated with a drastic reduction of progesterone following childbirth), postnatal depression is quite different. It is not as transient as 'the blues' and may last for several months following the birth of a child.

We can speculate that postnatal depression may be a result of the rapid life-changing events of becoming a parent and the associated feelings of inadequacy, self-doubts and general overwhelm. Counselling/therapy can be most helpful, especially when combined with behavioural programmes aimed at helping the mother to engage in specific time-boundaried 'mothering' exercises. Although it does not have the psychotic overtones of puerperal depression, postnatal depression is a serious disorder with inherent risks. It is therefore important that therapeutic approaches complement and are sculpted into the overall treatment programmes co-ordinated by the psychiatric services where appropriate.

## Reactive depression

Reactive depression is the commonest of mental disorders and affects many of us from time to time. It is not to be confused with being 'fed up', or even 'seriously fed up'. Common symptoms include change in appetite, sleep disturbance, nightmares, disturbing dreams, lack of libido, emotional flatness, deep dark moods, often with a sense of foreboding. These symptoms may be associated with anxiety, feelings of unworthiness, lack of energy, inability to concentrate, and a general lack of motivation. Thinking is also affected, with clients having recurring negative thoughts such as, 'I'm a failure', 'I don't deserve to live', 'I've let everyone down', 'I do everything wrong', 'I'll never be any good at anything'.

Counselling/therapy is almost always useful for those with reactive depression, and of course there are claims for different types of therapy as most effective. Commonly, cognitive behaviour therapy is acknowledged as highly effective, as it challenges 'faulty' and unhelpful thinking. We may also argue that unconditional acceptance is equally effective. The possibilities are endless.

Whichever approach one uses, the counsellor/therapist needs to be aware that suicide or suicidal attempts are not uncommon. This is especially true in the early stages of recovery. At this point, the sufferer has regained some motivation, but low moods have not lifted. It can be effective to contract with client not to self-harm, even if only for the duration of the counselling programme. It always amazes us how often a contract such as this acts as a simple but pervasive strategy to avoid the risk of clients self-harming!

It's also helpful to enable clients to identify their abstract goals and to separate these from their strategies. For example:

*Client*: 'I am going to kill myself.'
*Counsellor/therapist*: 'What do you hope that will achieve for you?'
*Client*: 'Peace.' 'Escape from this hell.'
*Counsellor/therapist*: 'How would your life look if it was a bit more peaceful? How many different ways can you think of to help you have a bit more peace in your life?'

## Anxiety states

All of us experience anxiety: it is our mind's way of helping our bodies to be alert and ready to 'fight or flee' in situations of danger. Anxiety *states* are of a similar nature to normal reaction, only more intense and longer lasting. Although it is physiologically impossible to remain in an intense state of 'panic' for any length of time, some sufferers do maintain low and continuous levels of anxiety.

There are said to be two types of anxiety – 'free floating' and 'phobic'. The former is more commonly associated with reactive depression and anxiety states, the latter specific to phobias. Free floating anxiety is the *state* of anxiety. While many of us become periodically anxious about our finances, relationships or employment, clients with free-floating anxiety are anxious about almost anything. If the counsellor helps the client systematically resolve anxiety in regard to one area of their life, it simply moves to another.

Another form of free-floating anxiety is manifested without the client being able to verbalise exactly why or towards what they are anxious – they just feel anxious! Anxiety states have associated symptoms associated with the perpetual unease, such as thought blocking, agitation, tremor, headache, restlessness, sleeplessness, nightmares, loss of appetite and sometimes nausea and vomiting. It is important that clients reporting these symptoms are initially referred to their own doctor to ensure that these are manifested entirely from a mental source, as some of these symptoms could also be created by adrenal gland tumours, endocrine disorders such as thyrotoxicosis or cardiac conditions.

Counselling can be highly beneficial for clients experiencing anxiety states, and although tranquillising agents are often the first course of action taken by medical practitioners, many now see that some form of counselling/psychotherapy as a complement or alternative is possible once initial symptoms of panic are controlled. Indeed it is commonplace for general practitioner (GP) surgeries to employ a counsellor.

Prolonged use of tranquillisers is discouraged, as this may result in dependency. Once again cognitive therapy has been found to be most useful in anxiety states, especially techniques such as thought-stopping and thought-changing strategies: equally neuro-linguistic-programming[3] approaches have been shown to make rapid improvements in individuals, though they are less typically used. Once again, as pragmatists our approach would be to use the best-suited approach for our client, and probably more than one approach simultaneously. Sometimes, some of the quickest techniques that help clients are sufficient. Naturally this does not preclude continuing with more traditional counselling sessions if the client can see the benefits.

## Phobias

Phobias are intense irrational fears or panic attacks derived from a specific focus of attention. Many of us have fears, even intense fears, of various creatures, situations or potential events in our lives: this does not necessarily mean we are phobic. Common 'normal' fears often feature spiders, heights, mice, rats, snakes: we even knew someone who was terrified of worms and wouldn't go out after it had recently rained in case she came across one! Irrational fears which are so intense that they disrupt or interfere significantly with an individual's life are diagnosed as phobic, and are considered to require treatment.

As a practising community psychiatric nurse Graham used to joke that it was always a joy to visit an agoraphobic client because you could be sure they were always in when you got there – if they weren't then you didn't need to make a further appointment! Joking aside, many people are completely paralysed by irrational fears. There are two types of phobias: those that are simple and those that are complex. For the former, a technique known as 'desensitisation *in vivo'* has been the quick and easy psychological 'cure' for aeons. This involves introducing the client gradually to their fear in small doses, until, with familiarity, the physiological response of anxiety begins to reduce: exposure is made incrementally until the client can be calm in the presence of their fear. This can be done live with an actual object – a spider, for instance – or using photographs or other symbols which represent the object of fear. With people who are agoraphobic, for example, introducing short walks, either real or imaginary, with constant reassurance and pauses so that anxiety reduces, is the most obvious method for desensitisation.

Bandler suggests a cure for phobias using Neuro Linguistic Programming (NLP) approaches, through accessing and changing the individual's current response to the fear by using their sensory modalities.[4] However, with complex phobias the desensitisation of one particular phobia may simply result in the phobia switching to another focus – this is known as symptom substitution. When this occurs it is symptomatic of the sufferer having some deeper mental conflict which is manifesting itself as a phobic reaction. For example, someone who has a phobia of going outside may be desensitised by a therapist only to discover the next day that they have developed an irrational fear of touching a doorknob.

When situations such as this occur it is likely that the client is in fact manifesting symptoms in order to obtain some relief from an unpleasant prospect (please note these are real symptoms – this is not about malingering). This would generally point to the client having some psychological problem other than a simple phobia. In this sort of situation, counselling/therapy is probably the best approach to the problem. It may turn out that the client is having relationship problems and the subconscious fear of their partner abandoning them may be what is precipitating the symptom. Counselling/therapy in such cases can help the client to look carefully at their lives, make realistic adjustments, and deal with issues more productively: once this has happened, the phobia will 'miraculously' disappear.

## Substance abuse

Dependency or abuse of drugs, including alcohol, are not in themselves indicative of 'mental illness'. In fact 'categories' of people placed by professionals under the umbrella term 'mentally ill' changes from decade to decade. 'Moral defectives', chronic masturbators, homosexuals and alcoholics have all been labelled mentally ill since the inception of the term in Victorian times, and many people were admitted to psychiatric hospitals compulsorily, and detained for many years, with such diagnoses. Unmarried mothers, and sometimes illegitimate and unwanted children ended up in mental hospitals for no more than the whim of the family.

Although this has now changed, and diagnoses and labels are more carefully considered it is still not easy to clarify at what point substance abuse can be placed in the category of mental illness. Individuals who excess to the extent that the substance takes over their lives could certainly be said to have mental health issues – whether or when this is amenable, susceptible or advantageous to be 'treated' by psychological or chemical means is by no means clear. So where does this leave the counsellor or therapist when a client presents with some form of substance abuse?

We are of the opinion that clients dependent on drugs or alcohol can be helped by counselling and therapy, though not convinced that it should be 'compulsory' in rehabilitation programmes. We would underake the following considerations when counselling someone who is substance dependent.

Firstly, substance dependency of any description can induce identifiable mental disorders. The prolonged use of alcohol, amphetamines, narcotics and 'recreational drugs' such as 'ecstasy' or cannabis are considered to be associated with 'paranoid' psychosis, memory loss and diminished cognitive function. Many studies have shown strong links between the use of recreational drugs and psychosis.[5] The abusive use of alcohol and drugs is also associated with clinical depression and suicidal ideas, as well as the more obvious physiological disorders. Clients in acute withdrawal are also vulnerable to psychotic episodes, and the counsellor must tread carefully – we have seen on more than one occasion complete personality change in people who are desperate for narcotic relief, resulting in violence to self or others.

The onset of mental disorders can also, on the other hand, be the precursor of substance abuse: a depressive illness (either bipolar disorder or reactive) may precipitate the unwise overuse of alcohol and other mind-altering substances. Life events such as bereavement, divorce, separation, childbirth, menopause or retirement may lead to depressive mood which in turn leads to excessive alcohol or substance abuse. It is our view that counsellors and therapists can be helpful *unless the client exhibits signs of psychosis*. At this point help should be sought from psychiatric services and advice taken. It is desirable that concurrent psychological help is continued: whether that remains with the original therapist, someone in the 'psychiatric services' may be a process of negotiation between the client, counsellor and doctor. Psychiatric treatment for substance abuse in all its forms will often be a combination of medication and psychological approaches, so it is not inconceivable that a co-operative approach to helping is initiated.

What is very clear to us is that clients who have problems with substance abuse are not readily helped by counselling and therapeutic approaches either while under the influence of the substance, in acute withdrawal from the substance or suffering psychotic symptoms. Seek assistance as soon as possible for your own well-being as well as for the well-being of your client.

## Drugs used in psychiatry

Drugs used for the treatment of psychoses are mostly derived from the phenothiazine group of drugs. Possible side effects may include Parkinson's-type symptoms, such as tremor, mask-like facial features, jaw chewing (*tardive dyskinesia*) and 'jittery' legs.

More recently new antipsychotic drugs have been introduced for people who are resistant to phenothiazines and these are said to have fewer side effects. These are categorised as 'atypical' antipsychotic drugs. Drugs commonly used for neurotic illnesses are generally antidepressants and anti-anxiety (anxiolytic) drugs. Mood-stabilising drugs are sometimes used, especially in the long-term treatment of bipolar disorders. There are various side effects of such drugs, which may need to be researched and/or discussed with the client.[6]

## So what does it all mean?

Counselling is not the panacea of all ills: some mental disorders can be well dealt with by counsellors and therapists, others are not really appropriate or amenable to this approach. The psychoses generally are a minefield which most counsellors are well advised to avoid. Some skilled counsellors and therapists have achieved very good results when working extensively with clients with psychotic illnesses. Don Bannister and his team used Personal Construct Therapy with notable outcomes. Bandler reported some significant success in using NLP to help clients with delusions and hallucinations to restore some order to their thoughts, and indeed we have both used NLP in conjunction with other approaches to help delusional clients regain thought management. Taking an empathic, unconditional, warm and genuine approach to any one, whether or not they are suffering from a serious mental disorder, is not beyond any of us. However, counsellors and therapists do need to take care to avoid complicating an otherwise complex situation.

*example*

My client Mohamed had previously been diagnosed with a paranoid 'schizoid' disorder. Although controlled on a weekly injection of Depixol – a long lasting phenothiazine drug – during the course of the counselling he demonstrated some bizarre ideas. One of these was that the medication was poisoning him. A classic counselling empathic response would be 'you sound suspicious that the medication is harming you'.

While this is fine theoretically for the mentally healthy client, this response would be likely to reinforce Mohamed's faulty thinking and confirm for him that he is right to be suspicious. A better response would be 'I can see that you are feeling anxious', followed by a gentle challenge such as 'what are the consequences of not having the medication?', 'Do you remember what happened last time you felt like this and stopped taking your medication?'

A less gentle challenge to a client diagnosed as paranoid schizoid may run the risk of him losing trust in you. Worse, it might begin the process of him interweaving you into his distorted ideas.

Having said this, it is of course possible that his medication does have side effects that are affecting him adversely, and on this occasion, we were able to sort these out without radical rejection of treatment. Many clients on major tranquilisers do suffer lethargy, and Parkinson's-type side effects, which may lead them to discontinue their medication. In such cases it is important to support the client in their enquiries into their dosages, and to receive medication that can help with the side effects. Drug interactions can be intricate, and potentially hazardous, so you may be safer referring the client to a more knowledgeable or specialised professional. Medication is often quite complexly calibrated to afford the client the best quality of life without risking relapse in psychoses. Such knife edge balances are well beyond the expertise of most counsellors, and should lead us to refer.

Similarly, serious neuroses such as profound depressive states can be helped with counselling. However, it should be remembered that lifting depressive symptoms can reveal other traumatic states.

*example*

A client of ours who is a refugee from eastern Europe presented with extreme anxiety associated with intense flash backs, which induced panic and depression. Treating the debilitating symptoms with some Neuro Linguistic Programming (NLP) techniques was exceptionally helpful. We worked carefully here as the rapid relief of the panic symptoms led the client to uncover the deep sense of guilt and anger that was creating the serious threat to her mood state, and her likelihood to self harm. While one of us worked with reducing the anxiety state, the other provided intensive counselling to help her to understand and resolve her strong feelings.

Jorge had been referred to us with severe depression, having been diagnosed as schizophrenic for many years. Following some counselling sessions in which we listened very carefully to his rather rambling and often incoherent conversation, it emerged that his recent increase of medication had, in his own words 'sent my friend away'. He was referring to the fact that an increase of medication had been effective at removing his auditory hallucinations. Superficially this was a good thing, but it left this particular client lonely and isolated without his 'friend' to talk and listen to. This required some negotiation with Jorge's psychiatrist in order to reduce his medication in order for his 'friend' to return.

We have to remember that the recovery period from severe depression can be the point at which the client recovers sufficient motivation to act suicidally. This leaves the counsellor with the dilemma of whether to counsel or not to counsel. Once again this is a balancing trick which is best done in co-operation with a mental health professional.

So, there are three very different scenarios here. Most clients with mental health issues or disorders can be helped to some extent with the careful application of counselling and counselling skills, and it is not our wish to deter counsellors from using their expertise to help this group of people. However, the point of this chapter is to remind you that working with mental health issues is an area requiring knowledge and expertise. Working in an interdisciplinary forum can be a way forward to acquire the experience and expertise should this be an area of counselling that appeals to you.

## Glossary of key terms

* *Delusion*: A delusion is a 'false belief' that cannot be shaken by reason or argument and is outside of the cultural norm of the individual.
* *Paranoid*: The primary delusion – usually now ascribed to mean delusions of persecution.
* *Grandiose*: A belief that you are all-powerful, omnipotent, with special powers, rich, invulnerable, related to royalty, famous, etc.
* *Ideas of reference*: The belief that everything or certain things are specifically relating to yourself, hoardings have special significance only to you, television transmissions are directed to you, radio waves or television signals are affecting or controlling you.

- *Nihilistic*: A belief that you don't exist, or some part of you doesn't exist, that someone or something has ceased to exist etc.
- *Symptom substitution*: When a primary symptom is alleviated, another symptom replaces it.
- *Desensitisation*: A technique employed to treat phobias. By introducing the subject gradually to the source of the phobia until their fear subsides.
- *Incongruity of affect*: The inability to respond emotionally to situations, people or events in a way which matches 'normal' response – e.g. to be upset by good news, sad when receiving good news, or similar inappropriate emotional responses.
- *Emotional blunting or flatness*: The inability to respond appropriately in emotional terms to events, situations or people. Low responsiveness to intense situations, the inability to feel or express emotion.
- *Psycho-motor retardation*: The reduction of all physical activity, an inability to physically respond at 'normal' pace to stimuli.
- *Psycho-motor excitability*: Increased physical activity, rapid, often random, physiological responses to minor stimuli, often resulting in agitated inappropriate behaviour.
- *Pre-morbid behaviour*: The 'normal' or 'baseline' behaviour in existence before the onset of the illness.
- *Pre-morbid personality*: The personality previously in place before the onset of the illness.
- *Hallucinations*: Hallucinations are false perceptions created from internal stimuli. These can be visual, auditory, tactile, olfactory (of smell), gustatory (of taste). Some specific types such as Lilliputian (small creatures or people) seen in toxic states, dementias or alcohol and drug withdrawal.
- *Obsession*: A recurring thought of which the sufferer is unable to rid themselves, and is often only alleviated by conforming to some behavioural ritual – hence –
- *Compulsion*: A behaviour or ritual required to be performed in order to achieve relief from a recurring oppressive thought.

# Notes

1  Aidan Shingler was diagnosed as schizophrenic at the age of 19. His account of his personal journey, and an exposition of his art, can be found in his book *Beyond Reason*, and is well worth a read.
2  *The Seven Faces of Eve* was an acclaimed portrayal of a woman whose multiple personalities derived from an abusive childhood.
3  Bandler and Grinder, who wrote advant-garde books such as *Frogs into Princes* in the 1970s, have found some lasting proponents of their ideas. Many counsellors and psychotherapists now use some of their techniques in conjunction with more traditional approaches for their clients' benefit.
4  Bandler suggests that the sensory modalities of visual, auditory, smell, touch and taste, can be accessed in light hypnosis or relaxed state and changed.

For example, to access the current phobic state and see how it is visualised by the client – then have them change it to seeing it as if from the seat of a cinema – being able to zoom in and out, change the colour to black and white, run the scene backwards, add music – inappropriate circus music perhaps, dim the contrast, decrease the volume, add smells, add texture etc. All these devices then rather change the phobic imagination to something more manageable by the client by diluting its fear response.

5   A full review of research can be found in Moore et al. (2007).

6   A useful website for more information on 'psychiatric' drugs, their use, side effects, interactions, and other valuable professionals and clients alike, is www.nice.org.uk.

# 7

## let's get all this counselling stuff into perspective: we can only do what we can do!

**Abstract:** In this chapter we explore the context of counselling and how it affects the activity itself. We discuss and analyse a number of issues which provoke dilemmas and potential blank minds. Firstly, we look at some of the complexities and contradictions of professional and agency ethics and goals. Secondly, we have some points to make on some of the conflicts which can occur between the rights of clients to a useful and professional service, and the rights of counsellors to a useful and professional life – indeed to a life!

## Introduction

So far we have offered some principles and strategies for dealing with blank minds and sticky moments. Now we explore some specific issues which recognise that the practice of counselling, although always determined by the individual practitioner, is influenced by its context. Practitioners working within organisations are sometime constrained and find themselves frustrated or helpless because of conflicting professional codes, goals or directives. On some occasions this conflict, and the challenge that it can provoke, can be a good thing. Yet sometimes agencies that have been set up to help people can seem to be counterproductive to helping. This may be particularly true when the organisation has grown to the extent that it has forgotten or dislocated from its original purpose. In this situation practitioners are often left in a position where they are restrained by policy or procedure from optimising their potential.

Many helpers working for health trusts or social services will identify with this comment, when government policies or targets prohibit flexibility or effectiveness. Similarly, non-statutory agencies and organisations may have goals which are inconsistent or which are mutually incompatible. For example, counselling associations may have espoused aims of promoting counselling, supporting counsellors and protecting the public, yet forget to support its counsellors.

## Ethics and agency goals

### The state and the counsellor

It could be argued that the state may avoid responsibility of care for its citizens by employing counselling programmes as an alternative to active intervention. For example, redundancy counselling became more used over the decades of the 1980s and 1990s while industrial action became more fragmented: once seen as a political or social issue, redundancy became viewed as a personal problem. If it is possible to convince the average person that they are entirely responsible for their situation, and that counselling is the panacea to enable people to marshal their resources and take self-responsibility, then it may also be used as a device for maintaining the status quo. This enables those actually responsible for social conditions and resourcing active interventions, such as medical research, housing programmes or employment initiatives, to avoid their absolute responsibilities. If social problems can be redefined by engaging counsellors and counselling programmes instead of by other means, then this may signal that counselling has become another 'opium of the masses'.

It is easy to see how enthusiastic new counsellors embrace the activity with gusto. Counselling is presented as something very special; its training groups have an exclusiveness for 'safety' reasons: closed groups encourage greater levels of disclosure. Having taught extensively to Master's level across the social sciences, we note that only within the discipline of counselling have students been able to submit Master's dissertations which may be seen only by tutors and examiners.

Ostensibly, counselling demands 'of ourselves'. It is easy to feel delighted in the first flush of success with clients. Thus the larger cultural and social consequences can be easily missed. Ideally, we would see philosophy and sociology taught as components of any higher-degree counselling course. An awareness, at least, that counselling can be an agency of social control must surely be integral to the discipline. These perspectives cause us to believe that it is

**I know you think you've been treated in a sexist way, but do you not realise that if you hadn't been a woman, it would never have happened?**

hard to assert that the social practice of counselling is or should be 'value free'.

It can be useful to ask ourselves some key questions:

* Are my responses to the client enabling them to take action and change their life for the better, **or** am I placating or suppressing the appropriate anger and injustice that they feel towards a society that treats them unfairly?
* Do I encourage the client to 'take ownership' of everything that happens to them, **or** do I challenge the client to clarify for themselves and accept only what is appropriate responsibility for their situation?

Such questions invite self-challenge. Counselling is best considered to be an occupation that operates in a context: when transposed to another context, for example war zones, it becomes more difficult to justify in terms of either need or usefulness. Some 'politically aware' practitioners might feel that they have lost faith in counselling; by this, we mean that they can see no good reason for doing such a trivial thing, when people are starving, being tortured, slaughtered, and so on, in other parts of the world. Closer to home people in distress, such as the homeless or those with addiction problems, require more active help than just counselling. We can all recognise this uncertainty, and indeed can see the argument that, ultimately, counselling is an inappropriate and even counterproductive activity.

We were faced very sharply with the challenge of considering our own contribution when, in conjunction with the University of Hull, we delivered a Master's degree in Counselling to Muslim refugees from the former Yugoslavia. We worked hard, were invited to share extremely traumatic accounts and experiences, and became increasingly frustrated with what we were doing. The counsellors had come, but where the heck were the UN troops? Every time we flew back to Britain, we were incensed, wanted to chain ourselves to railings to make the world listen and act, and really felt that we were doing nothing.

True, we were not stopping the war, we could not explain humankind's destructive violence to itself and we could not give people back their homeland. Our students, however, let us know very clearly what contribution we had made to their lives in emotional and pragmatic terms, and to the possible choices that they now had. In a strange way, our very natural helplessness could have become a form of arrogance, by defining what is useful and wanting 'big' results. And in the end, it became fine and valuable to be two counselling trainers who offered a different kind of approach to a group of people who found it of value. We learned a lot in the process, including a humility which we would like to keep.

---

*Principle:* eat humble pills: help in the way you can, when you can, in a way which is appropriate to the circumstance and the context in which you are offering help

---

## Report writing and recommendations

We have both been asked on numerous occasions to write reports on, or recommendations for, clients. These are often requested by agencies such as social services, the courts, or even on occasion the church. These may cause some concern to the counsellor, but can generally be 'negotiated' with the parties concerned with a little honesty and immediacy. One question is whether this service is part of the negotiated contract, or if it is reasonable to ask for it at this point in the relationship? Does the counsellor feel 'pressured' or 'coerced' into providing this service? Is it antithetical to provide a report which has within its scope 'assessment' when the relationship has been based on an ethic of being non-judgemental?

For example, a client asked if we would submit a report to the court for the purpose of supporting a lenient sentence. It was explained to the client that if such a report was to be contemplated then it would be written without prejudice. This meant that the report would be written honestly and without any intent to influence the court outcome one way or another. Once written it was handed to the client who was free to choose whether to submit it or not. Furthermore, it was explained to the client that the request to write such a report raised some issues, and some questions may need answering if counselling was to continue:

- How long have you been thinking about asking for this report, and has it influenced your honesty of disclosure?
- Does the content of the report change the relationship we had established?
- Have you any other surprises up your sleeve, oh dear client?

You may sometimes be asked to write references for employment, or to submit in a law suit. We would strongly advise that in these circumstances you remain objective and stay strictly within your proven professional competence. If necessary, take legal advice on your position before submitting any reports or recommendations to a court (written or oral); this may be done through contact with your professional association or organisation such as the British Association for Counselling and Psychotherapy (BACP) or the British Psychological Society (BPS), as written client waivers may be necessary for your own protection. Reports about current clients by similar agencies will almost certainly require the client's informed consent in writing to avoid recriminations at a later date.[1]

## Working for specifically focused agencies

Perhaps the most important question to consider when working for specialised agencies is whether the specialist nature will affect the way we view and work with clients. The answer is invariably 'Yes' in some shape or form. 'Can I live with that?' is the second question it begs for us all. Undoubtedly, agencies with specific objectives make great impact into people's lives and mostly this seems to be beneficial; our caution is that as a counsellor, you should only have one client, and it is that client that has the right to determine the outcome. Hence, if you find yourself working for an organisation primarily concerned with helping people with drug or alcohol problems, for example, it is useful to check out if there are any underlying policies which constrain the client, and whether you wish to co-operate in this constraint.

Some such agencies may dictate that all clients must have the goal of giving up the substance to participate in the programme. Although this may be both realistic and practical, we also have to acknowledge that it is one less option for the client to choose from. Would you consider working for a 'pro-life' agency that would only help pregnant women who chose to reject termination as an option? And if so, could you consider your contribution as non-directive counselling?

The question of pregnancy counselling in all its forms raises some extremely contentious issues (Russell, 1997). Counselling in agencies where the given brief is to offer voluntary counselling to a woman who is unsure what she wants poses little problem, as it is possible to maintain the general ethos of counselling. More contentious, however, is the issue of counselling within the decision-making process regarding termination.

Under the current Abortion Act (1967), women who choose to have terminations have to prove, within the definitions laid down, that to continue with the pregnancy would be detrimental to their welfare. In order to do this, agencies insist that the woman see a 'counsellor'. This raises serious discrepancies:

- The counselling is non-voluntary – can it be called counselling?
- The objective of the session is to determine the woman's 'eligibility' in some way, in the terms of the Act – can this be called counselling?
- The woman is now being seen as non-autonomous – what implications does this have? It can be argued that the institutionalisation of counselling is instrumental in diverting the termination issue from a political issue into an individual one. The edict 'a woman's right to choose' has been manipulated; termination is seen as the woman's problem, but she does not yet have the right to choose – she must do psychological somersaults in order to get the assent of a doctor. Should counselling be involved in this?

Our view is that anyone has the right to counselling, and a woman may decide this will be helpful to her decision making. However, it is a misnomer to call an enforced consultation on termination, whose purpose is specifically to ensure that the termination can take place, counselling: it is a different activity. It may include elements of support, it will hopefully be facilitated with the use of counselling skills, it may even be part of a larger counselling contract. But it is essentially a necessary step in a legal procedure whose underlying tenets are antithetical to the spirit of counselling, to the autonomy of women: it is not counselling.

Pregnancy is not the only issue where counselling has become a requirement. Counselling is positioned as integral to IVF treatment, as part of the assessment procedure.[2] It is also common for drug rehabilitation programmes to include a counselling element.[3] And while we believe that often this is useful, the point is that as soon as we make the activity compulsory, then we are on sticky ground. Unfortunately, this rather institutionalised use of the term remains a weakness of the profession. We still take a strong stance on this issue, and would welcome clearer definitions in order to prevent collusion with oppressive practice and to dissociate from it.

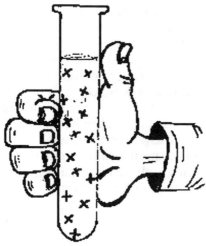

**Now that we've found your test is positive, you must realise that you are incapable of making any further decisions on your own.**

## Pride and prejudice

Then there are agencies which overtly expect that their staff absolutely share values and personal criteria in order to be involved with the agency's work, for example in women's refuges, or some religious organisations. This is complex: because you are what the organisation wants does not exempt you from considering the ethics of exclusive policies. When it comes to counselling, various questions need to be addressed in deciding whether only women be involved in helping in women's refuges, and only those sharing the religious values of the church be employed to help those requesting counselling. There are undoubtedly issues of safety concerned with refuges, and there is an argument as to the special

137

sensitivity of counsellors who are in some way identified with the client group.

However, if counselling is indeed a credible activity, then we need to recognise that each person is dealing with their experience, their responses, even where a practice is universal. If you are a woman who has been raped, you might decide that all men are bastards; if I am a woman who has been raped, I might decide that one man I know was a bastard, and as the mother of a son, have an agenda to negotiate and communicate with men. Even if we have exactly the same view, it should be irrelevant unless identification is seen as particularly helpful; as documented in Chapter 2, identification can be extremely unhelpful, and group identification carries some weaknesses as well as the obvious strengths of support.

Furthermore, identity is somewhat more complex than merely a celebration of my religion, my sexual preference, or my gender. Working with a particular women's organisation not too long ago, we heard the statement that any woman was welcome to become involved on the management group, but no men. The facilitator pushed the point – so, if a very right-wing woman wanted to be on the management group, would that be all right. The resounding answer was no. Ultimately, any policy on segregation or specific cultural criteria for exclusivity needs to be carefully examined in the light of the purpose of the organisation and in terms of the interest of the client group.

## Ethical codes: counselling, therapy, counselling skills?

Although we believe that the current ethical codes set out by the BACP and BPS do an admirable job, we would draw the reader's attention to the potential of ethical codes to clash. For example, a professional nurse may discover that the disclosure she/he is hearing from another nurse during a counselling session is something which she/he is obliged to act upon according to the nurse's professional code of ethics, but not from the counselling code.

For example: Judith is a qualified health visitor who has competed a diploma course in counselling and has been accredited by the BACP. She is therefore obliged to accept and observe both her health visiting and counselling codes of practice. One of her clients is a registered nurse who discloses that she is stealing sleeping tablets from the ward stock because she has had great difficulty sleeping during her traumatic divorce. She offers the explanation that her GP has refused her a prescription because he is concerned that she might become dependent on them. Judith now has a dilemma. Her health visiting ethic decrees that she must disclose this information to the health authority which employs her client. Under the BACP code of ethics, however, such action might be seen as breaching the client's confidentiality. Would informing the health authority also be seen as betraying the client's trust, and would Judith be seen as judgemental, disrespectful to the right of self-determination and lacking warmth? The BACP go even further, suggesting that their ethical principles may even conflict within themselves occasionally![4]

**To tell or not to tell, that is the question ...**

Similar situations will occur for other counsellors who have professional codes which determine professional behaviour. Under the Children Act professionals have a statutory obligation to report any incident of child abuse. On occasion, however, independent counsellors might hear such disclosures within a confidential contract. They might have real personal and professional dilemmas about whether the client's interest would be served by disclosing the information concerned. The worker may feel that they have very good reasons, connected to the maintenance of rapport and trust, and the long-term safety of the client, that prohibit them from taking action.

Those professionals who are using counselling skills to augment their role are not necessarily bound by any code other than that of their own profession. The BACP suggest that workers using counselling skills should follow the ethos of the counsellor, and lay this out clearly for those intent on using counselling skills.

Ethical codes are only developed because people transgress them; in other words, if people always had the wherewithal and motivation to act with total integrity all of the time, then there would be no need to devise such codes. Currently, we are both at liberty to use the BACP ethical framework of ethics as our primary guide, although even that demands unique judgement calls, of course. We have developed strategies and skilled responses to forestall some of the potential difficulties, and each set a great deal of store by clear and careful contracting. This is so helpful as a baseline for avoiding clashes of interest and divided loyalties, because it allows for exceptions and conflicts to be identified before the counselling begins. Examples of what might go into a contract to minimise conflict and to set the limitations of the counselling might be as follows:

- My confidentiality is limited to, or boundaried by:
  - the law of the land;
  - disclosure of endangerment to yourself or others;
  - disclosure of exploitation of vulnerable others;
  - my need to sleep at night.
- I have to keep within the ethical codes of (nursing, social work, police, etc.).
- I would have to act if ...........
- I would have to say if ...........
- I would ...........
- I will not ...........

Counsellors, whether or not they are constrained by other codes, need to consider very carefully exactly what they can and can't hear about, or be party to, before entering into counselling with any client. We need to create contracts which seem to serve the interests of the client while maintaining the personal comfort and safety of the counsellor, and part of the nature of the work is that facets are always evolving – for example, the aspect of contracting which allows us to talk about our work more freely, albeit with anonymity and discretion, developed after we had experienced isolation. Ultimately, the more that counsellors can consider these issues from the outset, the better. Each individual will still have to examine their own conscience and decide what they believe they should negotiate on, and what are their bottom lines. The professional codes and frameworks only provide the crucible within which each counsellor will determine their own contracts.

## I would if I could, but I can't so I won't, so you'll have to do what you can

People who have impaired or limited abilities for judgement may benefit immensely from helping activities which incorporate the use of counselling skills. However, it is unrealistic to imagine that everyone can benefit optimally from counselling, and individuals who have impaired or restricted judgement, for whatever reason, may be put at risk if they are left to self-determine without support or guidance. We know that this is an immensely tricky area – who determines who has impaired judgement? However, if we're honest, we do all operate some criteria – would we let our best friend, when completely drunk, do something drastic that we know they would regret in the cold light of day, and which would have severely detrimental consequences? To use counselling as an excuse to allow cavalier attitudes with others is not really acceptable. And although we would caution, as we guess you would, before determining that someone's judgement is impaired, we do believe that at times some people would benefit more from guidance, suggestion, persuasion and occasional restraint, than from a counselling approach. We would certainly advocate the use of high-level communication skills such as active listening, reflecting and the use of a focused problem-solving model, but believe that it is folly to commend all of counselling's philosophy and interventions to every situation.

For example, the bereft woman, depressed and suicidal following the tragic death of her son, about to jump out of a 40-storey window, would not much benefit from any of the following:

- It's up to you, pet, you need to decide for yourself.
- I can see that you are upset; your son is dead, you have no one left and no, you don't have anything worthwhile to stay alive for.
- So tell me, what would it look like if it were a little bit better?
- You feel sad and depressed because your son has died, and you feel that there is little point in carrying on.

We would suggest that empathic understanding and challenge, the urge to self-determination, and future goal setting might not be quite so appropriate as persuasion, distraction, calling emergency services or hanging onto a leg.

So who has impaired or restricted judgement? Well, people in drug-induced states, children, people with learning difficulties, people in extreme reactive states, and people with mental health problems – perhaps even Søren Kierkegaard, if assessed in today's culture. If you are up in arms about such untrendy categorisation, we urge you to stay with us just a little longer. We want to make it very clear that we do not believe that anyone in these categories should always be told what to do, that their judgement is never useful, or that they should never have any influence over their lives. Neither are we saying that 'the rest of us' always have full and good judgement. But we do believe that there is a matter of degree of the probability of judgement being impaired, and that some factors, such as those mentioned above, will create a more likely tendency to such impairment than others. Having said that, decisions about people's lives should only be made in the interest of increasing the potential for quality of life as far as we can best discern, and compulsion of any degree would ideally be reserved for issues of safety, either of the person themselves or those around them.

Life is not simple, and there are many blurred edges here. Children, for instance, may have difficulty making a choice between something yielding immediate gratification that has long-term difficult consequences, and something which has long-term benefits yet which is immediately unpleasant or irksome, or whose value cannot be seen. Going to school might fall into this category. Yet few adults would support the decision of a seven-year-old to abandon school because they were a bit fed up that week; some employ varying degrees of coercion and compulsion to get children to school. Yet children must be listened to, and there may be some underlying cause. Further, if the same child was unhappy at school at age 12, and was interested to find other ways of pursuing education, then they would probably find more adult support, and their decision be given more credibility as perhaps better thought out.

Controversy has raged over the years over adults with learning difficulties or with some serious mental impairment, and whether or not they should be able to make choices about marriage, spending an inheritance or deciding to have children. Some tactics used have seemed abhorrent and disrespectful of the people concerned. In terms of helping, however, we have found that most people who we have encountered with mental limitations can, with careful listening and with effort, explain likes, dislikes and preferences, which should influence any decisions which might have to be made on their behalf. Using some of the principles and adapting some of the techniques in this book, for example, it should not be beyond a counsellor's ability to identify abstract goals, determine a person's values, and find some understanding of a person's emotional world. If any communication is possible, then *this* communication is possible. These are sticky areas, and we can only do our best.

## Informed consent

The argument regarding whether someone has 'impaired judgement' is linked to that of whether a person can give informed consent. The idea of informed consent may be applied to processes that lead to change and where the outcomes are likely to have implications for the well-being or quality of life of the individual affected.

Conventionally, this is applied to treatments such as surgery or the prescription of medication or physical treatments of psychiatric disorders which involve serious, or irreversible change. The law requiring such consent is very specific and clear, especially when addressed to patients who may suffer diminished judgement.

It is perhaps easy to see that counselling may lead to change; clients are not only aware of this implication but, indeed, desire change of some kind. However, if the nature and extent of change is difficult to see at the onset, then it could be argued that informed consent is required. One view may be that in counselling there is always an implicit prescription for self-reflection and this in turn will produce change. Even if that change is perceived by the client as 'good', and has been freely chosen, there is still an exhortation to become more 'self-aware'. It could be argued that prescribing 'self-awareness' is the riskiest of prescriptions, for, logically, informed consent cannot have been given, since the client may not yet know precisely what they might uncover.

Prescription of any kind carries with it, for the prescriber, some responsibility for the outcome. For example, general practitioners carry both legal and moral responsibility for any drugs that are prescribed for their patients, and an investment consultant carries some responsibility when their advice leads to financial losses rather than profit. The equation, it would seem, is that the narrower the choices and the greater the degree of directiveness, the more responsibility is carried. Responsibility can be seen as being mediated by the awareness of risk and the influence which the prescriber exerts over the choice. When therapists of any description prescribe anything for their clients, they do so with considerable responsibility, and should always seek informed consent by offering clear explanations of the likely outcomes of the work.

## Rights and duties

Ultimately, much of the above discussion is arguing firmly for the limitations of counsellling, and for a realistic approach towards the objective of counselling for client, agency, society and indeed the counsellor. For the last section of this chapter, we would like to focus on the world of the counsellor and to suggest some limitations to how far they might take their role. Counsellors can easily take the view that they are more than mere mortals, that they are able to turn round in a telephone box and suddenly turn into SuperCarl, with their knickers over their tights and a nice line in Lycra. It is therefore quite important to look at some of the more absurd expectations which counsellors either accept or provoke and to debunk some of the myths surrounding this.

## I have to be there for them – day or night

Yes, this is absolutely true. Once you become a counsellor, you have no right to any social life, any independent happiness or any human autonomy. Such luxuries are only fit for your client. Much like entering a holy order, you must make yourself available day and night, consider your client's needs before your own, and allow any intrusion. You have total responsibility for all your clients' lives; if anything goes wrong then not only is it your fault, but you should have foreseen it and helped them to avoid it. Now that you didn't, however, and they're in this mess, you must immediately rescue them!

Although this may look ridiculous when written in black and white, it is amazing how these or similar beliefs can creep in. Of course, we do have responsibilities to our clients; one of these is to discourage dependency. We have already mentioned how Janice spent three weeks responding to suicide notes pushed through the letter-box of her home on a Saturday, before realising that this was not helping the client. We also know various tales of counsellors putting up with a mild version of 'stalking', outside houses or in shops, and even being publicly verbally assaulted, under the guise of the 'therapeutic relationship'. In our opinion not very therapeutic for either the client or counsellor.

The social activity of counselling is not all about the client: counsellors have rights too. We have a right to privacy, respect, free time and our own lives. Each of us must decide where our boundaries and preferences lie, what impact our work has on our private relationships, and what messages we are giving out to clients. This may mean that we are not always 'there' for someone. In our first edition, we relayed how one of us had a phone call on a Sunday lunchtime. We'd just had a 'family' meal (and don't those families taste delicious!) and a couple of glasses of red wine. The phone went. It was a prospective client to whom we had been recommended. Immediately, our response was that yes, it was the right number, but could she possibly call us in office hours. She began to tell her tale of distress. Again, we reiterated that we thought we could be really helpful – tomorrow. We also drew attention to emergency numbers. This client never rang back. For some counsellors, this would be untenable. For us, it was important to our own health and privacy that we were persistent with not having our private world intruded upon, and we had no belief that this person's welfare was our responsibility. Everyone must make the realistic choices that they think serve their own rights and well-being, as well as their duties.

## *My clients are small, fragile and precious flowers*
## *If I say something wrong, they will be scarred forever*

Students of counselling can be terrified that if they say the wrong thing it may have some dreadfully dire consequences for their clients. It has been our experience that clients wanting help are already proving just how hardy humans can be. Clients are not some hothouse plant which will crumple and die at the first frost; they are hardy annuals that have already been through a lot; often they have survived more than we care to think about. To treat them as so fragile is both patronising and nonsensical. Counsellors will make mistakes, they will say the wrong thing and their clients will survive. Counsellors should respect and trust their clients enough to treat them at least as equals.

## *If I open this can of worms ...?*

The fear of opening the can of worms can prevent counsellors moving their clients forward, or exploring the 'real' issues of the client's problems. Some counsellors confess to fearing the consequences of facilitating strong emotion. Will it make things worse? Perhaps one of the fears here is that although the emotions belong to the client, they are like a genie being released from the bottle – once out maybe things will get out of control. Supposing once faced with all of these emotions, the client can't cope, becomes more and more distressed and ends up committing suicide – I mean, it is possible, isn't it?!

Yes, sometimes, although we believe rarely, clients opening up to their own emotions and becoming distressed can be problematic – yes, true. However, sometimes, again rarely, a client may self-harm, and yes it just may be because you helped them get in touch with their feelings. But let's get real – the practice of any psychological technique has its risks. Be aware that this is not about counselling being risky, it is about some individuals being at risk from themselves. Having willingly elected to get to know themselves better, it remains their right to self-determine from their self-knowledge. The practice of counselling deliberately avoids diagnosis. Assessing 'can this client be trusted to be confronted with their own deeper emotions?', once we have already negotiated the contract and agreed suitability and informed consent, is not within our remit. We then need to assume with trust and confidence that clients can deal with their own emotions.

Okay, but what if things *do* get sticky – what can be done? Over our years of experience we would have to say that all of our clients survived exposure to their deeper feelings. Although we have experienced our clients self-harming on occasions, as far as can be established, this has not been as a direct result of exposure to their deeper feeling, rather a repeat of an existing pattern which subsequently changes. If clients get upset, and more rarely deeply distressed, our antidote (if one is actually needed) is to allow time and quiet; to challenge their strengths; and if appropriate to move them briefly into their goals. This latter strategy hardly ever fails, providing it is done skilfully, moving the client into the arena of hope by simple prompts – 'So what would you like to be feeling instead?', or 'What would you like the situation to change to?' But beware, this would not work if it were appropriate for the client to stay with their distress such as in acute bereavement, for here we would reinforce our belief that the client needs to ventilate their emotion, not escape from it.

Remember also when avoiding the can of worms, it is the client's worms, and they have probably come to counselling for help to open it! They may well need to open up before they can move on. Let's not waste their time simply because of our anxieties: help them get moving again as quickly as possible.

## Summary

To summarise, we are suggesting that there is a limitation to counselling as a social practice. Part of our objective is to state the obvious and put a little common sense back into the sometimes esoteric tripe that can be found in counselling culture:

- Change is voluntary. Unless the client is assisting this process, any change is unlikely.
- Not everyone is helped by counselling, some clients require different approaches and some clients cannot be helped!
- We can only do what we can do. Do your best: it is probably better than what is otherwise on offer.
- Agencies exist to serve clients, not to serve themselves.
- Know your ethical codes, limitations and areas of conflict.
- Counsellors have rights to a life too. Know your own boundaries and limitations.

146

# Notes

1 Bond and Sandhu (2005) provide an excellent overview of issues regarding counsellor involvement in court and law suits.

2 CARE Fertility, which proudly ranks in the UK top 10 for private 'assisted conception' clinics, boasts, 'By coming to **CARE**, you are placing your trust in us. And it's not just in our medical and technical skills, but in our understanding of your emotional as well as your physical needs. It is a responsibility we don't take lightly. ALL of our staff are committed to your wellbeing. We understand the emotional intensity of trying to have a child and we will support you with guidance and counselling every step of the way' (carefertilityweb.co.uk, 2007).

3 A web trawl on drugs counselling produced **1,350,000** possible sites. I know of no drug rehabilitation programmes which do not insist on counselling, and while counselling is probably extremely useful to full rehabilitation and recovery, we cannot assume that some people might not require something different.

4 'Ethical decisions that are strongly supported by one or more of these principles without any contradiction from others may be regarded as reasonably well founded. However, practitioners will encounter circumstances in which it is impossible to reconcile all the applicable principles and choosing between principles may be required. A decision or course of action does not necessarily become unethical merely because it is contentious or other practitioners would have reached different conclusions in similar circumstances' (BACP, 2002).

# 8

## they seek it here, they seek it there, they seek for counselling everywhere...

**Abstract:** This chapter advances the discussion regarding the context of counselling to a more theoretical base, seeking to contextualise counselling as a social practice to date. It is largely unchanged, though there are some additions, and our intent is to aid your thinking regarding the limitations of counselling. We begin by exploring the ubiquitous nature of counselling and its culture-specific context. We ask 'who wants counselling?', and no doubt those of us whose income depends on clients will be relieved to hear the answer ... everyone! We then suggest some functions of counselling in twenty-first-century society. Finally, we urge you to consider the status of counsellors and how this can lead to some dangerous and narrow assumptions. We believe that it is important to have a wide view on counselling. This helps us to remember that counselling relies on theories which only represent one way of looking at human behaviour: it is only one option. It is good to remind ourselves of the myriad expectations which clients might have: our hope is that this helps the practitioner to understand and to feel freer about what could be done in counselling. Hence, it becomes important to consider counselling from the point of view of how the practice of counselling informs behaviours, norms and expectations.

## Consider this somewhat tongue-in-cheek introduction to a public lecture

I woke first of all at seven o'clock feeling slightly nervous about this event, so I had to spend 20 minutes doing some relaxation as advised by my stress counsellor. I felt instantly calmer, and after showering and having a light breakfast, as suggested by my dietary consultant, I weighed myself. I had lost a stone in a month, what with combining the diet with a series of exercises exclusively designed for me by my customer-centred fitness consultant. I was shocked. Half a stone, yes, that's what I'd targeted. But a stone – what a tremendous loss. I made a quick call to my bereavement counsellor to help me come to terms with the actual and hidden loss which I knew that this change would entail.

Then it was time to dress. I hovered a little. I had had a fairly recent appointment with an image consultant, who had colour coded me to make the best of the gifts which nature has bestowed on me (I feel confident to say that now, after a few counselling sessions to boost my self-esteem). I chose this outfit with little hesitation.

Just as I was about to set out to my consulting rooms, my son reminded me that he had an appointment with the educational psychologist. He's been underachieving in modern languages, and the school feels that he has some resistance to the teaching methods. They're trying to unblock him so that he can be more open to their student-centred approach ...

I wished him good luck, and just managed to see my husband who couldn't quite make it tonight. We had an appointment with our marriage guidance counsellor. We had some communication problems several years ago – I was on the pill for six months before I realised that he had had a vasectomy – and we found this marvellous counsellor who really helped our communication patterns while simultaneously releasing our animus and anima respectively. We're much better now, and so we go along every three months for maintenance counselling. As I couldn't go, dearest one decided to go anyway so as not to hurt the counsellor's feelings. We think she may be becoming dependent on us, so he's going to gently try to recommend her to a colleague of ours who works a lot with separation anxiety. (Russell, 2000)

**How many counsellors does it take to change a light bulb? An infinite amount, but the light bulb really has to want to change ...**

And so on and so forth: in this introduction, Russell manages to name more than 10 types of counselling or counsellor. Although the excerpt is somewhat over the top, all the professional roles referred to exist.

Sometimes, when we hear people talk about counselling as a remedy for all ills, we step back and wonder at the narrow vision that this can create. It can be salutory to remember that the professional practice of counselling is comparatively new to the world; we existed for a very long time without it, and do well to retain some humility about its potential for humankind. Counselling has emerged from diverse sources, with various roots which may be traced to practices of magic, religion, medicine, psychiatry and experimental psychology. Not surprising, then, that there are many different 'versions' of counselling which both complement and compete with each other.

It is still difficult to describe what it is we counsellors 'do'. If an alien were to ask us, then it is much more difficult to describe than the job of a doctor, a bricklayer, a technologist, a teacher. How many counsellors have tried describing their activity to children in a way which makes sense? Indeed, to potential clients who know nothing about it. We help people – to do what? To feel better – how? By helping them understand themselves better – what do we do to enable this? We use techniques and qualities to help them explore their minds. How do we know it works? We don't. Is there a tangible end product? No, no wall, no feat of engineering. Is there research done into counselling? Yes. What does it tell us? Nothing tangible. Why do we do it? Because we believe it works.

Not only do counsellors believe that counselling is worthwhile, but, increasingly, so does society. The number of agencies offering counselling continues to grow, although the shape of that growth is changing, as many agencies now integrate counselling as a given and even necessary part of various life routes.[1] More integration may mean a slower rate of actual agency growth, but still indicates counselling as a growth area.

Counselling, then, is firmly accepted as a valid intervention to social problems. You may think it extraordinary that counselling has exploded onto the scene, despite the fact that it has no quality assurance measures, no proven cost-effectiveness and no one can agree even on a universal definition of what it is and what it is supposed to do! However, part of the success of counselling may lie in its ability to be in the right place at the right time, i.e. in a society which has now firmly embraced individualism. Over 20 years ago, in 1984, then cabinet minister Nigel Lawson spoke of 'fighting and changing the culture and psychology of two generations', and that although 'this cannot be achieved overnight ... let there be no doubt that this is our goal'.[2] The direction of the desired change was one of individualism, 'every man for himself'. We would say that this goal has been well achieved and sustained into the twenty-first century. Our culture and psychology have been greatly influenced away from social care and community, towards extreme capitalism. The practice of counselling has been part of this movement. One of the great social responses to HIV, for example, was counselling; counselling as a response to political and economic redundancies has become well established; and counselling for 'post-traumatic stress disorder', which covers anything from long-term consequences of abuse or shock, to sudden and critical incidents such as the tragedy of the 2004 tsunami, is entrenched. The 2007 BACP conference agenda notes, in a tone of some pride, that now counselling for trauma has 'gone global'. Counselling, as we suggested in the introduction to this edition, can be championed as a response to virtually any life experience ranging from traumatic sexual abuse to your numbers coming up on the lottery the week you didn't put your pound on.

Counselling ideologies and theories are also demonstrated in 'folklore' understandings. It is widely accepted and understood at some level, for example, that the bereaved need to mourn psychologically rather than (or as well as) ritualistically. Many people have some concept that there is a grief cycle and while in Britain this is becoming increasingly acknowledged in terms and conditions of some work contracts, in the United States some private health insurance covers for a finite number of grief counselling sessions.[3] Many stages of human development are accepted as transitional within the life cycle, and expressions like 'finding myself' or 'working through' are common to everyday discourse.

## From agony aunt to doctor of divinity

Not too many years ago, people who saw themselves as needing help turned to the agony aunt in the local or national press for consolation. They were helped with advice and guidance, and periodically they would receive some minor admonishment for their immoral or deviant behaviour. Not so now; advice, guidance and admonishments are no longer acceptable; never again are we to be told that if we just put it all behind us, and get a new dress, my dear, it will all be allright. Instead we must have warmth, genuineness and empathy with large helpings of non-judgementalness.

We also now think that we know how to teach counselling. A record number of training courses are now available in counselling, and if it's difficult to attend, well, there are always distance-learning packages. 'In-house' training has peaked, within social services, health trusts, industry, voluntary agencies and the church. Where it declines, it is more for want of money to pay for it than a changing ethos. Counselling bodies have undergone a transformation of professionalisation, with courses and individuals vying for accreditation from recognised organisations, largely the BACP with some competing input from the British Psychological Society. Moreover, the teaching of counselling and counselling skills has been increasingly recognised as an academic discipline: many universities have well-established departments of counselling, with Chairs in counselling being increasingly established. Counselling can be studied to Master's level, and indeed to PhD level, at most universities. An extraordinary and extremely rapid achievement for a discipline so much in its infancy.

## ... and when they've found it, what's it do?
## The functions of counselling

By and large, the counselling movement sees itself as a 'good thing'. This of course might not necessarily be the case, and some of the assumptions which underpin counselling will be challenged later in the book. What is clear, however, is that counselling is being used to fulfil a number of different functions, some of which might previously have been served through magic, religion and medicine. Enumerating and understanding these functions may help to explain why counselling has become such a prevalent social practice, and yet why it seems so difficult to pin down precisely.

## *From here to eternity ... the quest for the meaning of life*

Sometimes, people who ask for counselling are grappling with philosophical and theological issues, and they see counselling as offering a method to help them make sense of what is happening in their everyday lives. Such issues are often to do with the meaning of life, the distinction between right and wrong, questions around how much of life is under individual control, and personal questions which go along the 'why' lines:

- 'Why do I get so depressed?'
- 'Why did this awful thing happen to me?'
- 'Why do my relationships not work?'

Such questions embody several fundamental issues for the individual: the search for causal explanation; the question of morality and values; the dilemmas of naturalistic man; spirituality and self-determination.[4] Counselling may also be seen as helping the individual in their quest for existential meaning, providing answers about the very state of being. Not only is the meaning of life up for exploration, but the meaning of *my* life. Sometimes people feel that they are uncertain in their existence, and that they want to 'get in touch' with their 'real selves'. Feelings of frustration that they are not living life authentically and to the full may influence their decision to seek counselling. Much humanist and existential counselling depends on a 'layer of the onion' version of self; wherein the 'real' person is found to be within those layers, waiting to be peeled. It is thought that counselling can offer the arena for the client to discover themselves in this sense.

Such questions would at one time have been answered through different media. 'Why me', for example, might have invited an answer which had to do with astrological forces, or curses from external sources. Questions of selfhood might have been answered through religious discourse.[5] We need to remember, then, that the language and metaphors of counselling psychology are more than a method of treatment; they are a whole system of ideas which pervade society at every level: they present a socially and culturally specific paradigm of understanding and explanation to both ordinary and extraordinary events.[6]

By way of illustration, consider eating disorders. There are many accounts of young women not eating in centuries gone by, one such being the tale of two women, Sarah Wright and Anna Trapnel. In the 1650s, both Sarah and Anna fasted for over 10 weeks while in

their early teens. One ate and repeatedly vomited and made suicide attempts, the other simply stopped eating. While delirious in their beds, each were visited by strangers and their words listened to for wisdom and guidance. Both were hailed as prophets, later to be accused of witchcraft. In the 1650s, the condition was interpreted and understood within a frame of reference revolving around the idea of the saving of souls and within a system of religious politics. Today, it would likely be construed as anorexia nervosa, which is seen as a psychological disorder associated with issues of power, control and self-esteem.

## Change is here to stay – with gusto!

Counselling is ambitious. In a rapidly changing world order, its theories and practices seek to explain phenomena which would previously have been explained in terms of other social practices. Within this context, counselling is also seen to offer a cure for the malaises from which individuals and society suffer. In individualist terms, malaise might originally be equated with Freud's idea of neurosis, where the focus is on the idiosyncratic circumstances of the client's development and life. In wider terms, however, it is commonly suggested that modern living has entailed a loss of purpose to life, a loss of freedom, loss of tradition, loss of morality, loss of norms and security of social relations[7] resulting in a fragmentation or loss of a sense of self.

The notion of the experience of loss as a significant part of the individual's development is increasingly common within counselling approaches. While loss as an experience is an obvious enough focus where experiences of bereavement and separation are involved, the more vague sense of loss experienced by some clients is most clearly signified by the idea of hidden loss,[8] a concept increasingly used to inform counselling practice. A survivor of child abuse, for example, is commonly conceptualised as having lost aspects of childhood and self. Members of culturally diverse families may describe feelings of alienation from each other, loss of control, or loss of role. Such issues refer to cultural as well as individual malaise.

## Mary, Mary, quite contrary, how does your story flow?

Within this context, counselling is also increasingly seen as offering a means of understanding our life narrative, or life journey. In the complexities of everyday life, some clients want to take the time and effort to review not only their identity, but to make sense of their past and present and to feel that they have some control over their future. It can be suggested that many critical life experiences are separated out from public life, leaving the individual with a sense of lack of continuity and security. Death, for example, once a very public and open experience, is largely sanitised and dealt with behind closed doors. We now know that there are many experiences of abuse which are hidden away, sometimes for many years. Issues of sexuality are also relegated to the private sphere of life, with many partners feeling sexually cold or exploited, and with many individuals keeping sexual preference a secret for fear of repercussion. The narrative of the self is the assembly of sequential life events and moments in a way that provides some sense of order, security and continuity. This idea is especially relevant to any kind of counselling which conceptualises the world as 'constructed'. Through sharing the details of one's life within a counselling relationship, it is deemed possible to reconstruct a narrative which makes sense of events.[9]

Within the 'narrative of self' purpose to counselling, it may also be seen that counselling psychology offers a means of making sense of life stages and transitional periods, through infancy, childhood, adolescence, adulthood, 'mid-life crisis' and old age, stages which were once known as 'rites of passage'. This idea has been widely taken up, with books like Gail Sheehy's *Passages* (2006) being major bestsellers in the Western world.[10] Indeed, it is now difficult to imagine the Western world without conceptualisations of life stages, so prevalent are terms like adolescence and mid-life crisis.

## Okay, so now I know who I am, where I've come from, and what's happening to me, ... what's next?

Counselling does not end with making sense of the past and the present. It embodies a decidedly future-oriented aspect to it in terms of the individual being encouraged to make choices and envisage what they would like in their life. This is seen as a part of 'life planning'. It is partly illusory, inasmuch as it is clearly impossible to predict or to control the future, and partly a recognition of the fact that, given this limitation, the individual may benefit from taking responsibility for those choices which are under their control. This process becomes a part of identity. We use visions of the future to make sense of current situations, feelings and decisions; strategies involving the amount of work we undertake, for example, are influenced by desired outcomes for next year, five years on, retirement, or whatever. We also use visions of the future to create an inner goal to the identity one would like to become.[11]

## I've hurt my psyche, can you make it better?

Counselling is, of course, often embarked upon at periods of distress or disturbance. Individuals may want to break behavioural patterns, such as drug addiction, or violent outbursts to self or others. Events might have occurred which have caused sudden distress such as separation or bereavement or coming to terms with serious illness. Or a series of events might occur which 'accumulate' to produce intolerable levels of stress or depression. Relationship problems might lead to couple counselling, sex therapy or family therapy.

In these instances, people want very varied kinds of help. One woman we know who chose to have bereavement counselling following the death of her father describes the main benefit, which she valued highly, as that of support. Another friend describes the preferred route of changing her excessive drug habit as one of management and behavioural programmes. Some people discover that, on facing loss, they rekindle other experiences of loss and choose to explore their past to help resolve the present. Still others wish to commit themselves to long-term therapy in order to make new meaning of their lives in the belief that this will aid the current feelings and processes.

## Prevention: the best cure?

Since the last edition of this book, counselling has been increasingly offered for prevention purposes: pre-empt the problems by having counselling before they occur. The organisation Relate has become proactive in this respect. They now advertise themselves as an organisation that 'can help families, parents and young people in their family life'. To this end, they offer much more than counselling, having developed a whole series of workshops on how to stay in love through to being new parents through to being parents of 'difficult' teenagers. Their website points to courses 'as featured in *Cosmo!*' (*Cosmopolitan* magazine), as well as the latest article in *Brides* magazine.

Counselling has also developed as a means of training people to help others. For example, in a move which may be seen as a logical and inevitable extension of family therapy, filial therapy is an innovation, in terms of its acceptability and use (Rye, 2006). Filial therapy 'empowers' the parent of a child with problems to offer that child some of the same responses and interventions that a therapist might, with the idea of being able to more effectively parent that child. While this is not a purely preventive strategy, it has a preventive aspect as its usage educates the parent to pre-empt future therapeutic needs. In a sense, this is a logical progression from both family therapy, where all members of a family are encouraged to take responsibility for their 'part' in problem situations, and of the 'empowering' ethos of therapy. Gerard Egan (1975), whose *Skilled Helper* model provided the basis for many a counselling course, has always maintained that helping should be an educative process, truly empowering the client to become their own reliable source of problem solving. This aspect of counselling has, in our view, been one of the least understood at any depth, that the counsellor should be, in the end, concerned with educating clients in a broad and deep sense. Perhaps then it is no surprise that trained counsellors are now part of an army of practitioners trying to hand out preventive medicine, or that prevention should be a motivating force for some clients.

# That hat looked good on her, why doesn't it suit me?

We can see that there are several functions, then, which counselling fulfils. Coping with loss and transition, specific or general, searching for meaning, making sense of the past, resolving painful feelings, and taking some charge of the future. Does this then mean that every counsellor can help every client, at any time? Not quite! When we remember that there are many different reasons which propel people to become clients, and a whole range of counselling and psychother-apies available, this should make us and our clients very selective about our work. Counselling is a purposeful activity, and it is well worth spending a considerable time understanding the purpose of each counselling contract before agreeing to and beginning the work.[12] The counsellor who has only one way of conceptualising what is 'really going on' is at risk of imposing a journey which might not have been requested, or which may not be appropriate.

It is important then to consider whether our own particular form of counselling is appropriate to the client and their purpose. This is not always easy. For example, few counsellors receive mental health train-ing within their courses, so may practise with very little knowledge of this area unless they are already trained in psychiatric nursing or social work.[13] Although we have advocated that clients can by and large handle their own emotions, we have also identified that there are mental states where this is not necessarily helpful.

Counselling covers a lot of ground, and serves many functions, but let us not get overambitious. It is good to help, but not everyone needs our help in our way. Even more serious is the realisation that not everyone will benefit from counselling. The cynic in us may see some of its practice as self-serving. In its most helpful mode coun-selling may be seen as a humane response to personal distress, which demonstrates a social understanding of the trauma experienced. But it must also be appreciated that bringing in the 'experts' can also have the effect, or contribute to the 'sequestration', or cordoning off, of life events. For example, dealing with grief in counselling might limit the form in which grief is dealt with within families and communities.[14] Little is yet really known about such consequences.

## Counsellor or God, that is the question

So where does all this leave the status of counsellors? The heading to this section is flippant, but sometimes we wonder just how omnipo-tent counsellors can believe themselves to be! At this point perhaps

**Well, I can't understand it ... it worked on the gorilla.**

we can highlight an important principle of counselling which we have previously introduced but whose importance cannot be overstated.

> *Principle:* never travel without your humble pills

It is apparent that the discourse of counselling addresses some fundamental philosophical questions about the self, particularly in terms of identity and purpose, as well as offering a forum for dealing with personal distress or unhappiness. If we accept that there are many different reasons why people come for counselling, we will know that to decide that we know the way to help clients after an hour's airing of their story is a decision that needs to be taken with respect and caution.

We once heard the tale of the counsellor who saw her (female) client for the first time accompanied by her (the client's) father. Within minutes, she had 'diagnosed' suspected sexual abuse. An extreme example, but how often do we think we know what the work is going to be from the briefest of introductions? There are complex reasons why people approach counselling, and there are always consequences to embarking on a counselling relationship. We do our best, and our best is enhanced by humility.

If, like us, you don't feel too godly yet, then the question of status may not arise for you. However, beware, for it has got us in the past and it has this nasty habit of sneaking up on you when you're not looking. We allude here to the tendency of counsellors to grade the problem or the work. It is quite common to hear a certain tone of distaste at the notion of 'problem solving', as if it is in some way superficial, or not as meaningful as 'proper' (and for 'proper' you may read long-term) counselling. Yet we find this bewildering. For some people, a problem consists of having to make a choice about whether or not to change jobs. This may be surprisingly straightforward; or it may uncover all sorts of dilemmas about upheaval, relationship, loss or self-esteem. For some people, a problem consists of their fear that if they don't get something changed soon, then they are going to become violent towards their children. For some people, a problem hinges around identity, or depression.

All of these occurrences are problems – they are problematic to the person experiencing them. It is not the role of the counsellor to make a hierarchy in terms of importance of issue, or 'depth' of work. Who is anyone to say that, for instance, working with young adults who are sexually abused, working with a woman terrified of molesting her daughter, in short intense contracted counselling, is any less 'deep' than working in a counselling relationship that spans months or years. Not everyone has months or years; not everyone wants to spend that much time on counselling; some people are as incapacitated by the prospect of changing jobs as others are by the prospect of living with a life-threatening illness. To scorn 'problem solving' is to narrow our choices considerably, and shows a misunderstanding of the term. It is all too easy to become the superior expert and to begin to assess the worth of counselling purely from a quasi-professional viewpoint, and not that of the client.

Every person is different, with the attributes, abilities and qualities which make them who they are. Just as there may be a difference in learning styles and abilities in conventional educational settings, so in counselling which, after all, is a process of self-education. One or two sessions may be enough for some people, others might want much more. We learn and process at different rates, and of course much goes on outside the counselling session. Therefore, people's needs are different, and the means of fulfilling them really should not be exposed to a rating of 'depth' or 'significance' by the counsellor.

Finally, there is the rating scale which has been covertly developed to grade the 'realness' and 'depth' of cognitive versus 'emotional' counselling. When we first wrote this book, we asserted that many counsellors saw the cognitive as lacking depth and status, and, despite developments, there remains some resistance to cognitive behavioural methodology (Wills, 2006). There is a cultural tendency to focus on the role of thought in self-empowerment, with an exponential creation of resources which urge us to think 'positively', and to challenge self-defeating patterns and behaviours. The film *The Secret* (2006) claims the release to the world of the secrets of happiness using 'the law of attraction'. While some of the focus of such works may be seen as superficial, with an emphasis on material riches, authors such as Robbins (2003) does branch out into areas of health and personal fulfilment, and overall such works at least foster the belief that the secrets of change and success lie in our thoughts, and that our thoughts can be changed.

In our understanding of personhood, cognition, emotion and behaviour are all interlinked. There can be as much value in identifying and changing cognitive processes as in experiencing emotion – actually, we don't really believe that either occurs without the other, it's just that counsellors sometimes seem to feel more self-satisfied if they can release the emotion first, and indeed, many counsellors lack competence in cognitive challenge. The effect of cognitive challenge has a tremendous range and potential depth. There is a danger that the counsellor puts such incredible value on the expression of emotion that other forms of being and expression are devalued. Snobbery is apparent between, say, 'professional' counsellors and psychiatric nurses. The psychiatric nurse may help people through suicidal, depressive and destructive episodes with the help of cognitive and behavioural approaches, yet they are usually seen as not doing 'proper counselling'.

## So, what's on the menu from here?

So where does this leave us? With something of a professional haggle over what can and can't be used in counselling, not always to the benefit of the client. Part of the reason for this is that the counselling movement has problematised the fact that we do not really know how the human mind works. In other words, rather than simply accepting this, counselling is part of an approach to the world which seeks to explain human behaviour in all its forms, when actually such explanations are not really forthcoming. This is not to say that we don't have observations, ideas, information. But it is well to remember another principle which is rarely admitted:

---

*Principle:* counselling psychology is no more than informed speculation

---

We don't have answers, we cannot make blanket statements, and we tread a challenging tightrope between applying what is known without excluding ourselves to new possibilities. One of the errors which the counselling movement makes is to try to monopolise a knowledge which it doesn't really have. It would be helpful to say, we don't know how the mind works, we have some ideas, we constantly test them. Some things work in counselling and we can't always extrapolate reasons or universally held theories.

But the profession chooses otherwise. Consider this next argument, presented to us by a senior figure within the counselling profession when we first mooted this book:

> The authors will need to be clear about whether they are being pragmatically eclectic or whether there is some overarching integration. Current trends in counselling are towards integration rather than syncretism. This is particularly important for the trainee counsellor or the counsellor seeking accreditation/registration. A pragmatic eclecticism would not be considered acceptable to most of the existing schemes.

Note that the priority here is for counselling to fulfil an academic standard rather than serve an effective function. Integration helps to make sense and order of things and demands theoretical understanding, whereas pragmatism allows some ad hoc interventions. It also admits of not knowing. Professions don't like not knowing. Living with not knowing, however, can be immensely liberating, and leads us to a further principle which we believe to be in the interests of the client:

---

*Principle:* within the context of a counselling philosophy ... if it works, and it's ethical, then use it

---

Ultimately, we believe that counselling has developed through different modes and orders of human communication. We believe that it is a mistake to become precious or territorial then about what will be counted as acceptable on the basis of what the profession demands. If people are to be excluded from accreditation or recognition on academic rather than pragmatic grounds, then we embark on an extremely precarious route. In other words, if proficiency is determined more by knowledge of limited theory, than by measuring counsellor competence, we are in trouble, and have lost client focus. This does not mean that we advocate an entirely 'ends justify the means' approach. And perhaps we need to answer the question:

So it's okay to do anything that works, is it?

This isn't quite what we said or quite what we meant! Before we can have some concept of what's expedient in relation to counselling, we have to have some conceptual notion of what counselling is. We will elucidate this point as a means of concluding this chapter. A key concept in most definitions of counselling is that of facilitation, which is seen as a central technique of self-development. Facilitation is used to describe a particular type of help to the individual, specifically without influencing, directing or subjectively contaminating through the values or advice of the counsellor. Through this process, the client is helped to develop a new perspective on themselves or their situation, hence to be able to experience self and events in a different way, and thus to make decisions about their present and their future.[15]

Technically, facilitation entails the use of a range of skills which are essentially reflective in nature. It is hypothesised that such skills are non-contaminative communication skills, i.e. the counsellor's thoughts, views, wishes or anxieties will not be expressed to the client. Reflection is thought to offer a summary 'mirror' of what the client seems to be saying and an opportunity for them to vent the accompanying emotions. Through such expression, the client is helped to develop insights and an opportunity to craft a considered and clearly goal-oriented future, within their own value system. Hence, the client is thought to reach their own solutions, rather than those suggested by the counsellor.

This emphasis reflects a cultural shift to the meaning of counselling, which may be seen as having changed from telling someone how to solve their problems, to listening and reflecting in order to help them solve their own problems. As an activity associated with mental health and well-being, it invariably refers to a process wherein people are helped not only to solve problems, but to develop insight, in order ultimately to shape their lives in a less stressed or more fulfilling way. Insight is assumed to be a desirable attribution, as is fulfilment. The concept of fulfilment is grounded in the client's own value system. Thus, any activity to help clients to shift attitude, thinking, feelings or behaviour needs to be both purposeful and facilitative to stay within the ethos of counselling.

## Summary

If you've got this far then we have at least caught your attention. We believe that counselling is grounded in purpose and principles, not in theoretical definition or pure skill delineation. Counselling also operates within a cultural context, and has implications for that culture. Although it is difficult to put our views and questions in a nutshell, key points of this chapter have revolved around the following:

- Counselling has infiltrated just about every pore of our society ... is this a good or a bad thing ... not sure yet, it's probably both.
- It used to be okay to give advice, but now it's a definite 'no no'. Even advice agencies seem to frown on advice. Although advice is not a good idea in counselling, has counselling infiltrated too far into advice?
- If we (society) can't solve a problem, or it's inconvenient or too expensive to try, then we can throw counselling at it: is this really what we want?
- Clients, clients everywhere ... did we need so much counselling ever before? Does this indicate we are transforming into a society of namby-pamby wimpy-wallies?
- In this age of quality assurance, performance indicators and essential empirical research, how on earth has something as nebulous as counselling thrived so well ... could it be magic, or is it?
- The functions of counselling are amazing ... to know who you are, to narrate your present, identify where you've come from, to support you in crisis, and to solve your problems. How did we manage before?
- Does everyone need counselling? In whose interest is all this proliferation of counselling activity serve? The clients, we hope!
- Do counsellors consider enough whether their method best suits the client's needs?
- The status of the counsellor needs to remain humble and egalitarian. There is a lot that we don't know; counselling psychology is mere informed speculation. Spare us from more gods.
- Counselling should be helpful, let us beware of becoming too precious. If it works for the client then let us use whatever is available with the proviso of the professional ethic.

# Notes

1 For example, doctors' surgeries, IVF clinics, abortion clinics, addiction units, holistic detox retreats, all have counselling on tap, rather than referring people to specific organisations. The BACP offers specialist divisions to reflect contextual counselling: there are currently six.

2 See Heelas (1991) for an interesting exposition of the relationships between individualism and the human growth industry.

3 Morgan-Jones (1993) and Worden (1993) provide classic texts on the subject.

4 See Bridger and Atkinson (1994: 18–19) for elaboration on this list. Carl Rogers conceptualises the question which he believes is fundamental to clients in therapy thus: 'It seems to me that at bottom each person is asking, "Who am I really? How can I get in touch with this real self, underlying all my surface behaviour? How can I become myself?"' (Rogers, 1961).

5 The interested reader may appreciate the work of Thomas (1974) for his historical documentation of changing social discourse to address questions of meaning. The work of Smail (1987) relates such change to the counselling culture.

6 See Smith (1989: 45–53).

7 See Giddens (1991: 49–51), Smail (1987) and Taylor (1991).

8 This is said to be characterised by a loss of sense of self, of security, of continuity, of trust, of safety and of freedom, a milder version of the ontological uncertainty described by Laing (1969) in his existentialist approach to mental health.

9 MacIntyre (1981) queries whether it is 'rationally justifiable' to conceptualise the self as such a unity, 'which resides in the unity of a narrative which links birth to life to death as a narrative beginning to middle to end' (1981: 189–91). Such sequestration is described in more detail by Clark (1993) and Giddens (1991).

10 Sheehy has published several editions of *Passages*, the last in 2006, as well as copious other books on life transition including *New Passages* (1995) and the somewhat unfortunately named *Understanding Men's Passages* (1999). Meanwhile, books on ageing continue to grow exponentially in number: over 6,000 books on the subject are currently available at Amazon at the time of writing.

11 See Berger (1973: 72).

12 We are constantly surprised at how contracts are seen as a somewhat perfunctory or superficial part of counselling. Perhaps it is the language which inhibits people from addressing it more thoroughly. From our perspective, however, a well-negotiated contract is the first foundation block for effective and ethical counselling.

13 See Chapter 5 for more discussion of this point. It is worth mentioning also that the BPS Counselling division puts more emphasis on this need currently than does the BACP, reflecting the different origins of the organisations.

14 See Sennett (1977, 1988).

15 The process is undoubtedly informed by the view that the self has several aspects, e.g. self-esteem (how one experiences oneself in terms of value), self-awareness (how one perceives oneself acting and the effects of their actions), and self-actualisation (the notion coined by Maslow, 1987: 66, meaning 'the intrinsic growth of what is already in the organism, or more accurately of what *is* the organism itself').

# 9

## talk, talk, talk: what is all this about?

**Abstract:** In this chapter, we will review the professional debate as to what counselling actually is, and the difficulties of definition. We will then offer our own definition which underpins this work, and offer a means of differentiating counselling from psychotherapy. Counselling will then be contextualised alongside other 'interpersonal activities', and, finally, we will introduce some issues regarding the exclusive consequences of the current push to professionalisation of counselling.

It would seem that whatever the social consequences of counselling, it is well embedded as a social practice on an increasingly global level. There is no doubt that there are a number of activities which constitute some form of counselling. There are also a number of arguments: who should control it, who should accredit it, and who should make money out of it? One fundamental principle which must influence all of these arguments is that:

> *Principle:* counselling is for the client

You may be wondering why this even needs saying – after all, we're all client-centred – aren't we? We all respect our clients – don't we? We always have the client's interest at heart – don't we? We never overestimate our own importance – do we?

Most counsellors would say that they are client-centred, although most would also admit that there are times when they forget this and become preoccupied with other matters. However, it is worth keeping an ear or an eye on just who we think counselling is for as we follow some of the professional issues regarding definition.

## So what is counselling?

The central British body committed to the professionalisation of counselling, which has provided an excellent forum for the exchange of ideas and practices, is the British Association for Counselling and Psychotherapy (BACP). The BACP was established, in the mid-1970s, in order to associate and co-ordinate diverse bodies of people concerned with the development of counselling, and to further the profession. The British Psychological Society has established a counselling division, and has instituted a charter system for counselling psychologists in order to retain professional identity and status. Likewise, the United Kingdom Council for Psychotherapy also stands in negotiation with the BACP. There is now a national register for counsellors, developed 'in the interests of the public', although there is as yet no evidence that such a register will achieve higher quality or more competent counselling, in either an ethical or a practical sense.[1]

Over the years since the first edition of this book, much has changed in the development of professional organisations. Most notably is the aforementioned development of the British Association for Counselling to the British Association for Counselling and Psychotherapy. This 'marriage' is convenient, and recognises some overlaps between activities. However, from our point of view, it also sidesteps the issue of defining precisely what differentiates the services that practitioners offer to clients. We still feel that there are an awful lot of activities subsumed under the heading of counselling and psychotherapy, and it is worth exploring some of the differences – just in case a client ever asks us what choices they have!

In 1992, the Code of Ethics of the then BAC stated:

> The overall aim of counselling is to provide an opportunity for the client to work towards living in a more satisfying and resourceful way. The term 'counselling' includes work with individuals, pairs or groups of people, often, but not always, referred to as clients. The objectives of particular counselling relationships will vary according to the client's needs. Counselling may be concerned with developmental issues, addressing and resolving specific problems, making decisions, coping with crisis, developing personal insight and knowledge, working through feelings of inner conflict or improving relationships with others. The counsellor's role is to facilitate the client's work in ways which respect the client's values, personal resources and capacity for self-determination. (BAC *Code of Ethics*, 1992: 2)

While this seems straightforward, complications can arise because of the advisory meaning to the word 'counsel'. 'Counsel' originates from the Latin *consilium*, meaning consultation, advice, judgement or deliberating body. The advisory aspect of counselling is perhaps its oldest and most traditional meaning, a tradition still evidenced in legal, medical and, to some extent, religious circles. The term 'counselling', however has undergone an expansion in meaning over the last 300 years, as counselling has developed as a practice of psychosocial intervention. The *Oxford English Dictionary* recognises such a shift, and defines counselling as both advice *and* as a form of psychotherapy in which the counsellor is supportive and permissive of the client in their own problem solving.

Yet there are difficulties in defining counselling as an activity independent of any advisory meaning. Firstly, there are historical factors in which advice is very strongly linked to counselling, as mentioned; barristers are still referred to as Queen's Counsel, financial experts are still seen as offering wise counsel on pecuniary affairs, and more recently, a whole host of beauty counsellors, fitness counsellors, have developed (although some of these are now changing to coaches, a term which we will mention later). In the public arena, then, the advisory meaning is not only located in the past.

Secondly, there is no doubt that the counselling profession wants to define its terms in order to identify areas of exclusive expertise. This may or may not be helpful to the client in the long run; it is certainly seen as necessary if counselling is to be a fully fledged profession. However, since there are different professional bodies at work, definitions inevitably become part of the game. Take counselling psychology, for example. We used the term counselling 'psychology' to refer to the theoretical underpinnings of counselling practice: but according to the BPS, only graduate psychologists can be counselling psychologists. Whose interests are being served here?

There is another reason why counselling is difficult to define, and this is that individuals have unique reactions to particular language.[2] Some counsellors, for example, despise the phrase 'problem solving'; some understand 'goal' as a useful concept which is flexible and may be abstract, whereas some understand it as a rigid constrainer. There is a tendency for the individual to associate the meaning of an activity with an emotional reaction to the words used to describe it. Those for whom counselling has a comfortable 'feel' to it because of it being described as non-directive will understand the activity differently from those who feel uncomfortable with a lack of clearly defined steps within the activity. In the end, it may not be possible to reach a consensual definition of counselling. So where do we go from here?

There is a group of 'helping' activities which overlap – advice, guidance, befriending, counselling and using counselling skills. A study commissioned to differentiate between these activities found that practitioners in all five found the notion of giving the client direction to be undesirable and incompatible with helping them make appropriate choices and decisions.[3]

It is likely that there is a process of mutual influence between these activities. It is noteworthy that they are all seen as being fuelled by high-level communication skills, known as counselling skills, when they are used within the values and ethics ostensibly associated with counselling. The notion of interpersonal skills as being a set of activities which individuals can learn, and then apply in the interests of desired outcomes, introduces factors to relationships which are perhaps specific to modern life. Interpersonal relationships become a reflexive venture, with individuals consciously considering their utterances before making them, and relating them to what effects they wish to stimulate. What is more, they become a subject, a topic to be learned, to be graded and improved through the use of feedback, itself a reflexive process. This is a move which is quite unique culturally and historically.

Our own belief, based on our experience and research, is that there is an identifiable difference between counselling and other activities. Our definition is as follows:

> Counselling is the process by which the client is helped to develop insight into themselves, identify their goals, and construct realistic and appropriate strategies to achieve them. This is done using whatever skills are useful; without offering advice, suggestions or guidance; with respect for the client's self-determination; and using whatever challenge is required to ensure that the client moves towards their valued outcomes.

## Counselling and psychotherapy: won't anyone tell me which is which?

While some professional disagreement is evident in distinguishing between the activities of counselling and the uses of counselling skills, the argument is generally settled to some extent by the notion of how the activity is contracted.[4] More controversy is evident in the clinical distinction between counselling and psychotherapy, and while the dictionary (and perhaps even the layperson) might be content to see them as forms of each other, the professionals have no clear distinctions between the two, claiming substantial similarities and differences within a rather vague context of no committal. There are paradoxes: the BACP has moved to merge the two activities as being part of the same profession: yet over 90 per cent of training courses offer either one activity or the other, and seem to be able to distinguish perfectly well between theoretical orientations and practical requirements. Generally speaking, psychotherapy trainings last for more years than counselling trainings, and require different demands (Aldridge and Pollard, 2005).

Rogers' fundamental principles have formed the main exemplar of what has become understood as 'counselling'. This term is now used to indicate a therapeutic process which for the most part does not include advice, prescription or direction. Rogers[5] reported that therapists taking his non-directive approach changed their responses from interpretive, diagnostic, questioning, reassuring, encouraging and making suggestions, to responses that demonstrated understanding of their clients' feelings and attitudes.

From the original idea of counselling as a replacement for medicalised therapy and to today's multiple approaches,[6] which flourish and prosper under the umbrella term 'counselling', the differences between counselling and psychotherapy have become blurred. It is now the case that many students and practitioners find the whole business of sorting out counselling from psychotherapy both confusing and tiresome. It would almost seem that the profession (if we are yet that) has given up on trying to distinguish the two and instead has decided, much like Rogers, to use the two interchangeably.

Even the more obvious distinctions between counselling and psychotherapy seem to have lost their definition. At one time the simplest contrast might have been that counsellors dealt with the more practical everyday problems of people and their relationships, and psychotherapists dealt with the more esoteric, 'intrapsychic' dimensions of the human condition. Today, with counsellors increasingly experimenting with techniques to elicit deeper understanding and to help reconstruct identity, and with psychotherapists becoming increasingly concerned to incorporate skills models into their therapeutics, there appears to be little or no consensus amongst practitioners on definitive distinctions.

It is possible, however, that this move to not distinguish between the two activities is premature, and misses some extremely important distinctions between counselling and psychotherapy which might, just, be of great interest to potential clients. It is also our sense that such a move is more easily acceptable to counsellors than to trained psychotherapists. It is true that both have in common the expressed intention to aid the client's capacity to self-determination and to self-understanding, or insight. Both claim to abstain from advice-giving by the counsellor or therapist. Both claim a facilitative aspect in terms of the process required. They are rendered distinctive, however, both by their method and the theories and philosophies which inform them. The clinical debate will no doubt continue, and may be seen as representing issues and arguments of professionalism within expert systems. In the meantime, however, clients may suffer from not having a clear idea of the range of options open to them, and the demands of any one approach. Each professional body will make its differentiations when setting out its credentials and examining its own brand of product, and in selling it to the client group.

It seems that either the profession really believes that there is no difference, or else it has given up because the issue is so complex. If the latter is the case, then shame on us! Surely it is imperative that the client has some understanding that the type of help they receive might demand quite different things of them, especially with the deep intrapsychic exploration and potential change that some psychotherapies insist upon. Moreover, we might recognise that the motivation of clients to enter any kind of therapeutic activity may be very diverse. And, as we mentioned earlier, some people want help with a specific issue, some wish to confront issues of identity or existentialism. It would seem helpful if they could have some information as to whether they are in the right place!

## Directive and non-directive

*Will you tell them what to do or will they do what they want?*

However, we recognise that it is not surprising that the terms counselling and psychotherapy are used interchangeably, for counselling is certainly about 'a person's well-being' which when liberally interpreted could be described as 'therapy'. Also the work is usually focused upon 'self awareness and insight' which is, of course, a mental process – thus in line with the prefix 'psycho'. However, the difficulty may be in the therapy part, which carries with it so many connotations of 'doing to' someone, rather than some process that has an egalitarian ethos. It can, of course, be argued that therapy, or the process of therapeutic change, can be done by oneself to oneself, and undoubtedly this is the way Rogers perceived it. Rogers' view[7] was that although there was a therapist present who 'facilitated' the process, it was the clients who, given the necessary conditions, developed their own insight, healed themselves, solved their own problems and became fully functioning. Despite counterclaims arguing that even Rogers himself was directive,[8] it is clear that it was his intention to be non-directive.

One way out of this confusion may be to think of counselling as a process of helping which could be categorised as 'non-directive' or 'directive'. But this sits very ill at ease because when Rogers coined the term 'counselling' as a means of professional demarcation, he used it to specifically exclude directiveness. Another alternative might be to see psychotherapy as the umbrella term and simply have 'non-directive psychotherapy' and 'directive psychotherapy', and our hunch is that currently, implicitly, this is what we already have!

## Will you tell them where to go or just how to get there?

Another factor, just to make the complicated more complex, is that there are both degrees and different types of directiveness. One type of directiveness refers to the advisory role of the therapist who will suggest a specific technique to try, such as fixed role therapy in Kelly's Personal Construct Theory.[9] The direction of the fixed role therapy will be dictated by the client, and there is no directive from the therapist or client to discover why the client is faced with particular problems. Another type of directiveness is linked to advice, in terms of the therapist suggesting strategies, or ideas of what might be done.

Other psychotherapies follow a cause-and-effect model of psychic development, and seek to explain behaviour. Such therapies are directive through their insistence on the theoretical framework driving which developmental issues need attention; moreover, such theory also directs the focus of the relationship between therapist and client. Hence, the directiveness is channelled through the theoretical framework.

In all types of directiveness, there is a range of degree. The therapist who is directive of strategies or techniques might impose their view through the raised eyebrow which shows some disapproval, or an encouraging nod, to the fully frank 'no you mustn't', or 'that sounds really good'. The theoretically rigid therapist will make sure that the client makes specific intrapsychic explorations, e.g. the relationship with a particular significant other, whereas the theoretically flexible will be more experimental.

'Pure counselling', on the other hand, claims to be non-directive in both senses. No single model of human development underpins the process, though various skills are recognised as essential for its conduct; listening, attending, empathic understanding, focusing, challenging, summarising.[10] Additionally, counsellors espouse a philosophy wherein particular personal qualities are seen as essential to the counselling process, as are the adoption of specific attitudes.[11] The counsellor is seen as having to be genuine and respectful, to offer a 'congruence of self'. She/he is expected to suspend judgement of the counsellee, to adopt an attitude of unconditional positive regard, no matter what the behaviour of the client. Moreover, she/he must be able to convey such personal attitudes and qualities to the client.

Such complexity makes it difficult to be clear. An added complication is the reluctance of some professionals to define counselling at all, as each counselling relationship is 'unique' as a human interaction.[12] However, we believe that counselling can be defined in terms of purpose and principles, and in the spirit of inquiry, we propose the following differentiation between counselling and psychotherapy.

## I can see clearly now the fog has gone!

Firstly, let us take 'counselling' to mean something close to Rogers' proposition of meaning 'non-advice', 'non-directive', 'non-interpretive', 'non-suggestive', 'non-reassuring', 'non-prescriptive', 'non-diagnostic', but for absolute clarity we label this type of psychotherapist a 'non-directive, person-centred counsellor'. And we take something approximating the opposite type of practitioner who is 'directive', 'advisory', 'diagnostic', 'controlling', 'prescriptive' and 'interpretive' and for absolute clarity we call this person a 'directive psychotherapist'; we can then compose an axis which would be helpful to measure where we fit on it, help us describe our preferred way of working and therefore how we intend to work. Again, we would suggest that this is useful to the client.

Whereas counselling embraces eclecticism, psychotherapy often embraces a 'cause-and-effect' theoretical model of human development. The therapist has access to the theory being applied and offers interpretations of the client's feelings, experiences, thoughts or behaviour, in direct correlation to the specific ideology. For example, a therapist who embraces feminist versions of psychotherapy might suggest that her female client is depressed because of the patriarchal system in which she has been placed by society. A Freudian psychotherapist may interpret dreams about trains and tunnels in direct association to sexuality.

The traditional psycho-analytical model of psychotherapy is a lengthy and intense process wherein the client is encouraged to relate present-day feelings to past influences and relationships, notably those within the family. The therapeutic relationship is seen as central to the process, and is used systematically to explore relationships, express 'repressed' feelings and produce changes in ways of relating.[13] Here it is clear that the therapeutic relationship is analysed in terms of transference and countertransference, projection and projective identification. Within this theoretical framework concepts such as stages of bonding, dependency, confrontation, integration and separation may also be identified, speculated upon, and suggestions for change made.

# Why ... psychotherapy? What ... counselling?

In crude terms, then, it could be suggested that the major distinction between the two activities is that while psychotherapy is concerned with the question why, with definite notions of cause and effect being inherent in the theory, counselling may be seen as addressing the question what; for example:

> What are you experiencing, what are you feeling, thinking and doing, what do you want instead, and what is your best way of achieving it?

Although we believe that this is helpful in underlining one of the biggest distinctions, we are only too aware that all the distinctions are not as clearly silhouetted. For us, however, counselling and psychotherapy need to be clearly differentiated in order for the client to receive a better service, to provide the client with a clearer choice, and to help the practitioner to work more purposefully. To this end, we have developed a practical axial model of differentiating from psychotherapy which we hope will be helpful to the reader, or at least prompt some further thought.

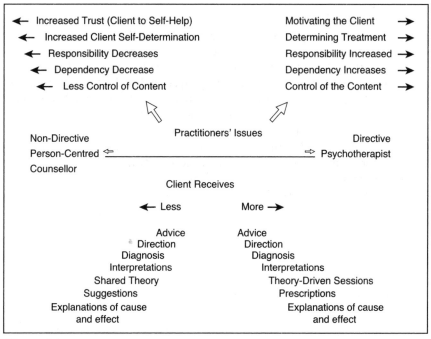

**Figure 9.1**

The diagram reflects some of the central concepts which we believe fundamentally separate the two extremes of counselling and psychotherapy. In addition to the diagram we would add notes on the following issues.

## Responsibility

Issues of responsibility have been discussed in Chapter 6. Basically, we are suggesting that prescription of any kind carries with it, for the prescriber, some responsibility for the outcome. When choices of which issues to explore, what strategies to take, are limited in any way by the practitioner, then the greater the degree of directiveness and the more responsibility is carried. The counsellor should always seek informed consent by offering clear explanations of the likely outcomes of the work.

## Dependency

My client's very wealthy, she comes to see me eight days a week!

Prescription and advice, inherent in some of the approaches labelled psychotherapy, carry with them the greater possibility of dependency. Some approaches even embrace dependency as an inevitable and helpful part of the therapy, by some it is considered in much the same light as transference, i.e. to be employed gainfully in the helping process. We have no doubt that the majority of clients who experience dependency are initially undaunted by it and indeed welcome it; after all, to be given clear direction and answers to questions that have previously eluded one, is a relief. However, it is our view that, in the longer term, dependency can be debilitating to the individuals' prospect for self-determination, for the client has only learned to be thankful for the therapist's good suggestions and blame them for the ones that didn't work!

## Control

Let's move on, or tell me about your sex life.

Another way of distingusihing between counselling and psychotherapy is to examine how much and what type of control is exerted over the client by the therapist. It would seem to us that when the therapist takes complete charge of both the process and the content of the client's session, then considerable control over the therapy has been exerted – this we would consider to be at the 'directive therapy' end of the continuum. Towards the counselling end of the continuum, it would seem that the control of the process would be more evident, but hardly ever the content. For example, using Egan's framework, the counsellor might ask the question, in stage 2 'So what would you like instead?', or in stage 3 'How many ways can you think of that would enable you to achieve your goal?', but never 'Tell me about your sex life'. There is still inherent expertise here, in terms of the counsellor being able to understand and apply any framework, but it is an expertise in helping the client find their own solutions via their own routes. It is never telling someone what to do, or which areas it would be useful to explore.

## Counselling and other interpersonal activities

Oh my God, there's more!

The debate and distinctions between counselling, psychotherapy and other activities is deeply enshrined within the establishment of professional boundaries and the development of systems of expertise. There is another set of distinctions and similarities which bear a brief visit: namely, those between the activities of counselling and relationships of friendship.

Friendship is apparently very little discussed within most clinical and counselling literature, although it is frequently posited that loneliness and isolation, or lack of intimacy, are common reasons for entering into counselling. Friendship and counselling enjoy a complex and paradoxical relationship. On the one hand, counselling claims some of the qualities we might normally associate with friendship, such as unquestioning support and acceptance, genuineness and empathy,[14] to be available to the client all the time, although whether or not this is actually possible is of course a debatable point. On the other hand, it is also seen as very definitely different from friendship in its contractual nature, and it is ethically required that counsellors makes it explicit that they will not transgress their own boundaries by becoming friends with their clients, although in practice we know a substantial number of counsellors, ourselves included, who will use their skills and understanding with friends within a contracted period.[15]

**Yes, but will you still respect me after the session is over?**

There are identifiable similarities and differences between counselling and friendship. For example, it is commonly supposed that the
counsellor has more power than the friend, in a specific kind of way;
the counsellor works to a professionally, and sometimes legally,
enforceable contract; the counsellor offers promises of virtue and reli-
ability; and the counsellor is especially employed to foster the client's
self-esteem. The friend, however, although offering some similar qualities of warmth and acceptance, is likely to have a more equal relationship in terms of power and status, and will expect a mutuality in
quality and activity in a two-way process. Friends might offer advice,
be judgemental, share their flaws as well as their insights, and negotiate their relationship in an ongoing way which recognises that it does
not have predetermined, or specifically anticipated, outcomes.

There are activities which seek to transgress the differences between
contracted helping activities and benevolent helping relationships,
the most prominent being befriending and co-counselling. References
to befriending go back to 1879, when missionaries 'befriended'
offenders and their families.[16] In the last decades of the twentieth century, befriending was commonly associated with the Samaritans, and

with agencies dealing with HIV and AIDS, such as the Terrence Higgins Trust. Befriending schemes in this context are often referred to as 'buddying'. Befriending is defined by practitioners as providing a high-quality level of support to individuals in periods of distress, its purpose being both to help the befriended (friend? client?) to develop appropriate coping skills, and to lessen the person's sense of social or personal isolation. Befrienders might also take on an advocacy role at times, in order to help the client-friend to have access to all available resources.

Befriending is specifically associated with countering social isolation, and befrienders actively resist the move to make it a profession. This becomes more difficult as the activity takes on more and more the use of counselling skills. There is an inherent paradox being highlighted in this resistance, which hinges around the apparent incompatibility between human closeness as an informal and 'natural' activity, and as a 'skilled' activity, as detailed above. Countering isolation implies some sort of level of intimacy, perhaps, while there is suspicion as to whether this is genuinely possible if the emphasis is on skills.

## So after all of that, what is proper counselling?

So who does proper counselling? Apart from the disputes between counsellors and psychotherapists, three main arguments exist over this question. One is over the status of the problem of the client, and another the intervention style of the counsellor (cognitive versus emotional, for example), both of which have been addressed in Chapter 7. The third regards the battle of the barefoot counsellor versus the mighty shod, which deserves brief mention.

> I'm terribly distressed, but first show me your certificate.

The barefoot counsellor is usually highly experienced and counsels in situations where all that stuff we're taught on our training courses to Master's level doesn't apply. The barefoot counsellor counsels through letter-boxes when women are not allowed out for either personal or cultural reasons: she/he counsels in corridors and crowded rooms, with children running around; she/he counsels on the bus, in the car, on any moving object with wheels (well, they do say that counselling is like taking a personal journey!); she/he counsels people who are short of a fix, or about to get one; she/he counsels in situations of crisis, and has to deal with the unexpected. This is not the type of counselling where two people sit in a peaceful room and work solidly together for 50 minutes out of an hour. This is on-the-hoof work, rapid response work, with individuals often developing their skills alongside their nous; not everyone can afford to undergo the highly expensive training programmes which are currently cornering the market and defining counselling, and not everyone wants to. One of the consequences of the current training movement and the accreditation movement, which is not competence-based, is that it is producing a highly value-laden and culturally specific notion of what counsellors should do. As well-shod counsellors shout louder for their value, command higher fees and persuade organisations that their counsellors should be accredited/trained, so the value of the barefoot counsellor is reduced. Moreover, training courses become more and more expensive, and more and more academic, with insistence on an understanding of counselling theory which becomes exclusive and which may be quite unnecessary. The barefoot counsellor can, however, take some comfort from the fact that none of the distressed people we've helped have ever asked for a look at our certificates. Just as well, really! However, they have asked for and been offered information regarding our experience and our approach. Perhaps these are, after all, the most important aspects of our credibility.

## Coaching

Personal or 'life coaching' is growing significantly worldwide, often billed as one of the fastest-growing professions. Coaching is seen as an activity wherein an individual is supported to identify what they want in life and find ways to achieve it. Coaches motivate their client. They are seen to offer unconditional positive regard, a non-judgemental environment for personal growth and change.

Coaching is aligned to increased performance, skills enhancement and professional development. As such, it might be more likened to mentoring or the clinical understanding of supervision than counselling. It is fuelled by a skilled facilitator with a sense of 'process' (Parsloe, 1999). People do not recruit a coach because of problems – they recruit a coach to help them 'do better'. In a way, the coaching process resembles stages 2 and 3 of Egan's framework – what do you want more of, less of, where do you want to get to – and what do you need to do to get it? We would not include it in the axial model of helping as its primary goal is not therapeutic, although it might have the benefit of being a therapeutic process.

# Summary

In sum, then, we are suggesting that, currently, there is still much diversity within counselling about the activity on offer. However, we do not see much discussion now regarding this: it would seem that there is a gentle conspiracy to accept that all related activities have more in common than different. There is now an acceptable rather than controversial blur between what differentiates counselling and psychotherapy. Our own perspective remains that it is important to distinguish between counselling and psychotherapy as they are informed by different theoretical approaches, and therefore require different activities and commitments from the client. This differentiation seems much more important than the distinction between qualified/unqualified practitioners. However, it is the latter which currently grips the profession, and we will be interested to review the consequences of this focus in the future.

# Notes

1   It can be argued that the registration of practitioners is more for the good of the profession than the safety of the public, which is the usual justification. There is no evidence of standards of work being increased through such moves. See Pilgrim and Treacher (1992) and Russell and Dexter (1993).
2   This realisation was made during an exercise in differentiating counselling from other activites (Russell et al., 1992), and is also made eloquently by Feltham (1995: 6).
3   See Russell et al. (1992: 17).
4   The BAC *Code of Ethics and Practice* (1989) states that:

The term 'counselling skills' does not have a single definition which is universally accepted. For the purpose of this Code, 'counselling skills' are distinguished from 'listening skills' and from 'counselling'. Although the distinction is not always a clear one, because the term 'counselling skills' contains elements of these two other activities, it has its own place in the continuum between them. What distinguishes the use of counselling skills from these other two activities are the intentions of the user, which is to enhance the performance of their funtional role, as in line manager, nurse, tutor, social worker, personnel officer, voluntary worker, etc. The recipient will, in turn, perceive them in that role.

5   In his early book Rogers (1942) highlighted an entirely new way to offer help without taking an 'expert' position, and emphasised that there was no need for advice. His faith in the client's ability to help themselves if the right conditions existed was a theme he vigorously pursued throughout his lifetime.

6 Feltham (1995) and Karusu (1986) suggest somewhere between 300 and 400 approaches are currently operated under the guise of 'counselling or psychotherapy'.

7 Rogers' (1957) classic article setting out his 'necessary and sufficient conditions for change using a counselling approach' is well worth the effort to read first hand. Also available in Kirschenbaum and Henderson (1990).

8 Rogers and B.F. Skinner debate the possibility that the non-verbal prompts gestures and smiles may well be considered to be directive; see Kirschenbaum and Henderson (1990).

9 Kelly (1955a, 1955b) used many different approaches in his work with clients: very little could be inconsistent for him, as his consumate theory, from a cognitive frame, allows a refreshingly flexible approach without excessive directiveness.

10 See Carkhuff (1987), Culley (1991), and Egan (1994).

11 See Corey (1996), Egan (1975, 1990, 1994), Rogers (1951), Truax and Carkhuff (1967).

12 This seems to be rather a copout. Any 'helping' profession, including teachers, social workers, foster parents, nursery nurses and psychiatrists, all establish human relationships of a higher or lower calibre. Their professions can all be defined, though, in terms of what they are there to do.

13 One short description of psychotherapy is:

...the systematic use of a *relationship* between therapist and patient – as opposed to pharmacological or social methods – to produce changes in cognition, feelings and *behaviour*. (Holmes and Lindsey, 1991: 31)

14 See Feltham (1995: 19).

15 Feltham (1995: 20) makes the same point that although there may be hallowed rules which divorce counselling from friendships, in practice it is likely that some counsellors do contract counselling with friends much more commonly than is currently admitted.

16 See Hagard and Blickem (1987).

# 10

## Philosophy, psychology, faith and goodwill

**Abstract:** This chapter is left more or less as it was in the first edition. We contend that the underpinning philosophy and values of counselling are based on some rather flimsy and somewhat superficial consideration of debate on the nature of self. Despite the rich philosophies of self available to us from both Western and Eastern philosophies over hundreds of years, counselling has almost unquestioningly embraced that of Kierkegaard. In other words, it exhorts us to 'be that self who one truly is'. There is an increasing philosophical and sociological literature[1] challenging the wisdom or credibility of such exhortation, literature which argues that the metaphorical 'wearing of masks' is in fact both useful and necessary to 'healthy social relations'. In this chapter, we introduce some of those arguments through considering the core conditions.

## Aimless prattle or just common sense?

Counselling literature talks about self all of the time. Indeed, the wide range of counselling literature depends on all kinds of grand claims regarding selfhood; the self is tripartite (id, ego, superego), the self is in constant mental conflict, the self is ultimately good, the self exists as a self-contained [*sic*] unit, the self is an essential attribute, the self is layered, and so on. However, the legitimacy of these assertions seems somewhat taken for granted, rather than contextualised or questioned within relevant discourse. Therefore, the philosophical speculations which they represent are sometimes presented as truths. So once again, some humility and careful considerations would be much welcomed into the counselling world on these issues.

There is much theoretical exploration to be had here, and hopefully the next few years will see more of it in print. For issues of practice, it is useful to examine the philosophical foundations which currently inform the practice of counselling. These can be usefully summarised

**A rather gloomy man called Kierkegaard said we had to drop all masks, so I suppose we better had – even though it didn't seem to do him much good ...**

by looking at the assumptions which inform the 'core conditions' which have come to be accepted as legitimate principles of successful counselling. What beliefs underpin such conditions and are presented as truths within the counselling world? Consider the following:

- People are intrinsically good.
- People, given the right conditions, move toward 'self-actualisation'.
- There is such a thing as self-actualisation.
- Self-actualisation is intrinsically social.
- Counselling can provide the right environment for self-actualisation to occur.

Sometimes, these are presented as such absolute and unchallenge-able beliefs, so fiercely held, implicitly trusted and so assertively espoused as to render any doubt or scepticism almost sinful in some circles. However, *they are only beliefs*. This does not render them useless, but in order to enhance our understanding of the possibilities and limitations of counselling, it is necessary to analyse or deconstruct them. It is our view that a healthy dose of critical subjectivity, or scepticism, is of great value to the counsellor. We do not believe that students (and we use this term in its broadest sense) should accept without reservation all that they have been told. Good counsellors are social scientists, and as such should be able to step back a little from their discipline to critique it. So, in this chapter, we invite you to look carefully at some of the concepts which are perhaps too readily accepted in training courses, and to determine for yourself whether all of the ideas first adopted in your training still hold for you the same magical entrancement when they are demystified. Through offering a critical appraisal of the core conditions, we are also suggesting that some of the philosophical doctrine in counselling is not simply constructed from an altruistic stance, entirely for the benefit of the client. Indeed our conclusion is that many of the value bases of counselling have very pragmatic purposes.

## The core conditions and associated concepts

We are informed by the research that empathy, warmth and genuineness[2] are the necessary preconditions which must exist for the client to benefit from any form of therapy or counselling. Eminent authors[3] argue other essential counsellor attributes, i.e. non-judgementalness, unconditional positive regard and respect for self-determination, as enhancing the process of therapeutic personality change. These are widely, although not universally, accepted as central concepts of counselling. Indeed, it is mooted that these are the conditions which are so mighty that they can transform whole personalities, even interstate relationships. What are these conditions, then, which are claimed to make counsellors the 'strongmen' of the Western world?

### Empathy

Empathy is defined in most counselling texts as the listener's ability to thoroughly understand the client's world without contaminating that understanding with their own thoughts or feelings. Empathic listeners are said to be able to perceive the client's thoughts, feelings, behaviours and experiences 'as if' they were one's own.[4]

This would seem to represent a difficult task for any human being. There are four points which make it so. Firstly, this quality of understanding needs to be communicated effectively by the client either in the form of language, which in itself has its own limitations,[5] or by non-verbal messages which are open to interpretation.[6] Secondly, the negotiation of accuracy is mediated by the motivation of the client to allow such intimacy with the counsellor. The relationship between the counsellor and client will be a significant variable in this latter respect. Intimacy requires a relationship of trust which may not be in place immediately. This would rather point to empathy being a state that exists as a process rather than a moment-to-moment event. Thirdly, if this special understanding is possible, and all these difficulties can be surmounted, there still remains the potential for contamination in regard to the cultural contextualisation of the client's experiences which may not instantly be available to the counsellor. For instance, the class, status, education and race of the two people engaged in the interaction may have significant influence on the accuracy and depth of understanding between them.[7]

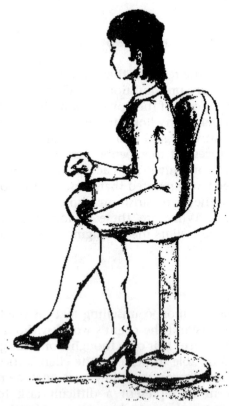

**I know that you believe you understand what you think I said but I'm not sure you realised that what you heard is not what I meant.**

Finally, feelings, and their interpretations, represent a formidable barrier to understanding. Precise understanding would require very skilful negotiation between client and counsellor to ensure accuracy, and this would rather preclude the *'moment-to-moment'* immediacy that some authors propose. After all, the counsellor has only his/her own perceptions of verbally labelled emotions to gauge the client's world. To elucidate further, it is only possible to understand what jealous, hateful or relaxed mean, in terms of one's own psychological and physiological state an individual has no way of knowing the intensity that is currently occurring for another. It is only possible to approximate from observations, and be corrected by the other. This will invariably take time, and therefore cannot be an instant or spontaneous event.

This does not logically mean that empathy cannot occur. It simply means that if, or when, it does, it is an uncertain event. Neither party can be sure that a state of empathy has existed. This assertion is in regard to the inability of any person to be positive of what is occurring in the other's world. Clients, for their part, may simply be unable to communicate their complex worlds adequately to the counsellor, either verbally or non-verbally, or they may withhold some private elements of their world from the counsellor, either consciously or unconsciously, deliberately or accidentally. Neither the client nor the counsellor can be absolutely certain. It is perhaps more sensible to look at empathy as a difficult skill which is evidenced by the development of understanding between two people.

Empathy as a skill, then, will also depend on the proficiency of the counsellor, and the way that they articulate their empathy will have different effects upon the client and the subsequent relationship. There is no doubt that empathy is understood variously, and practitioners think that they demonstrate empathy while relating their understanding in very different ways. For example, possible differences may take the following forms:

*Client*: Last night I had a heavy row with my lover and said some terrible things. (Sighs) And this morning I wish I hadn't.

At least three possible responses may occur here, for argument's sake, which might have different effects.

*C.1.* So last night it seems as if you were angry with your lover, and now it sounds as if you feel some regret.

*C.2.* (Nodding copiously) I feel the sadness in you.

*C.3.* I think you've done something which you wish you hadn't and I think it's brave of you to admit that. I think you've done really well.

The first response is purely reflective to help the client identify the emotion. It combines 'there and then' empathy along with 'here and now' empathy. There is no attempt to merge with the client or to offer opinion. The second attempts some kind of statement of 'altered selves' and some display of merger. The third offers 'empathic challenge', in noting the hidden strength of the client, but within the framework of the therapist's opinion and offer of approval. Each may have different consequences in the quality of the emergent relationship as perceived by both parties. While we would only call one of these responses empathic, we know full well that others might argue that the other two would create the state of empathy. A complex area then.

To summarise, empathy may or may not be possible, but it would seem that its existence is always doubtful in any interaction. The existence of empathy rests largely on the ability of the two parties to willingly negotiate complete understanding. Many factors play a potential part in making this difficult, i.e. language, and its intrinsic potential for misinterpretation; cultural, educational and individual incompatibilities; the motivation of the individual to communicate honestly and completely; the ability and willingness of the counsellor to hear accurately all of the client's disclosure and not to listen selectively; and the accurate understanding of non-verbal communication with its inherent cultural identity. We doubt that it is some God-given intrinsic ability or gift that only some of us can have, or some mysterious artistic magic that defies description. We believe that it would serve the interests of the profession to be very honest and describe empathy as hard work requiring full concentration, sensual acuity, rapid data collecting and plain common sense.

We might also note that there is sometimes a quality of empathy possible because two people have experienced a similar situation – surviving cancer, deaths of parents, war trauma. In this instance, it is possible for an accelerated rapport which paves the way for a very supportive quality of empathy which is almost intangible. Obviously, this must be tempered in counselling with caution not to overidentify, as specific nuances and emotions may be different for each party.

A key question arises: is empathy actually *necessary* to therapeutic change, to counselling? Do I actually have to be understood by the counsellor to feel respected by them enough to benefit from their expertise? While the automatic answer is yes, it could be argued that as long as the counsellor enables me *somehow* to better understand *myself*, then why do *they* need to understand me at all? What if I don't want you to understand me, but I desperately want to be challenged in my thinking to help me make an important decision – and I'm confident enough that we don't have to have an empathic relationship to achieve this? Empathy can only ever be instrumental to the counselling goal, so it is by no means *absolutely* certain that it is *per se* necessary to all counselling. However, from the evidence of our own experience and of available research, we do conclude that it is helpful for counselling to occur effectively.

*I'm telling you sincerely, folks, that what you see is what you get ...*

Genuineness is possibly one of the most abused terms in counselling discourse. It is used to incorporate congruence – is the counsellor acting in a way which demonstrates their immediate thoughts and feelings; transparency, can the client discern this; or authenticity, a concept which refers to the counsellor being that self who they truly are without masks or role. All these terms have been used to refer to the helper's effective avoidance of posturing, playing a role, or erecting a façade or a barrier between the client and her/himself. In essence, it is the counsellor being 'real'. Two common misinterpretations occur: one that the 'role' of counsellor demands nothing more or less than being how you usually are, and one that if you adopt postures of any kind, then you are erecting façades. There are some very tenuous links made in these equations which are not necessarily either true or helpful, and which have resulted in two weak developments. One is the extreme emphasis placed on counsellor self-development, and the other is on the spurious belief that the genuine nature of the relationship is more important than the level of skill or competence. Additionally, some authors[8] point to a lack of genuineness or authenticity as a source of client dissatisfaction and lack of effectiveness in therapy. So what is this really all about?

Firstly, let us examine whether genuineness is feasible. Is it possible to be completely genuine with clients whilst trying to establish a climate approximating the prerequisite core condition of warmth, which is discussed later in this chapter? Only, it would seem, if the individual can 'genuinely' feel warm towards the client. We may ask the reader: is it always possible or indeed prudent to express *genuine* warmth when clients disclose certain types of behaviour?

For example, where would the reader be warm and where would they be genuine when faced with the following:

- A woman who discloses her contempt for all men.
- A man who discloses his contempt for all women.
- The client who relates the actions involved when helping their sick mother with her suicide.

- A client's joy at the death of their partner.
- Indifference of a mother towards the welfare of her children.
- The racist comment of the client relating their acts of discrimination.
- The HIV+/hepatitis C client carelessly exposing others to infection.
- The therapist abusing their trust with their clients.

These situations can sometimes take the counsellor by surprise, when we guess genuineness will take care of itself; but what of a deliberately chosen response for the second time this situation is disclosed – what then? Genuineness, unconditional positive regard or warmth? Maybe such dilemmas herald a blank mind or sticky moment.

As this book seeks to inform as well as stimulate your thoughts, we'll answer these questions in this way. **We believe that to abandon your own values in order to be able to be genuinely warm towards a client holding values that would normally be abhorrent to you is not acceptable or helpful!** The price is too high, and the risk of colluding with offensive and antisocial behaviour is too great a risk. The philosophers and theorists who suggest that it is okay to remain warm towards the person and still condemn the behaviour are at odds with the practicalities of everyday life. The idea that the client, or the counsellor for that matter, can separate them'selves' and their behaviour, and thus make sense of this idea, is unrealistic. Most clients that we have worked with have a clear union of them'selves' and their behaviour. They are proud of, or down on, them'selves' because of their behaviour. Even if we are able to genuinely respect the person in front of us and separate her/him from their behaviour, doing so carries with it a great risk that the client will not be able to differentiate so easily.

To illustrate this we invite the reader to imagine what they would do if they had two clients, each of whom recounts a story about them losing their temper and hitting their partner. If client A relates this in a tone of deep regret and client B without any remorse, how do your responses differ? If, for example, both are responded to with empathic responses such as 'It seems as though when you remember hitting your partner you do so with deep regret' and 'You feel satisfied about hitting your partner because they irritated you', what might be the effect upon each client? We could suppose that in the worst-case scenario of each example client A would feel more guilty, and client B may feel that his behaviour was accepted as justifiable in the eyes of the counsellor. The way in which the empathic response is delivered may have immense potential for tonal innuendo; if the counsellor is extremely careful to avoid judgement in their voice, they may inadvertently produce a tone of assent. Too much sympathy in the tone may indicate an opinion that the behaviour was acceptable or they too might have been violent in these circumstances. It is because of the potential for inadvertent messages such as this that we would advocate clarification of the counsellor's position in any circumstances where there might be confusion. To place emphasis on the 'you' in 'you feel' in these circumstances is extremely important. This then carries with it the correct inflection indicating that this is the counsellor's *neutral* demonstration of understanding of the client's world and not the counsellor sharing an opinion about the behaviours or experiences disclosed.

On the other hand, we can only remain neutral if we really are. It can be argued that we should do our utmost to avoid inadvertently colluding with antisocial behaviour, malevolent thoughts, or in any way contaminating the client's ability to review and assess their own true feelings being related. We have no doubt that in the reality of the counselling situation your values will inform your natural warmth towards clients, and this will differ depending on the personality before you. We know that it is useful for the client to encounter warmth, and yet we can also see that on some occasions it is necessary for clients to see genuine reactions to their behaviour, their personalities and their physical presence. Indeed, feedback via the counsellor's personal responses to the client's behaviour, as in immediacy, is sometimes a part of helping the client see themselves more neatly. The counsellor may decide to use their own judgement in such circumstances, and choose to contextualise their reactions and inadvertent opinions disclosed. When this contextualisation is carefully implemented the fundamental underpinnings of the philosophy of client self-determination is more likely to be preserved.

More trivially perhaps but equally pertinent, can we always be genuinely at ease and display warmth when confronted with disfigurement, looks which we perceive as plain ugliness, or lack of charisma in our clients? Do any of these give rise to greater concern for you? Does the reader recognise themselves in any of the following examples?

- The sudden exposure to physical disfigurement stimulates an involuntary shudder or wince directed to the vision rather than the person exhibiting it.
- Counsellor finds eye contact and interest more difficult with the 'ugly' client?
- Lack of charisma is confirmed by the counsellor's excessive distraction and lack of concentration.

None of these appear to be particularly damaging to a relationship over a long term, but each in its turn demonstrates the absence of warmth – yet they are genuine. Equally, if we did feel warm towards a client and found them immensely attractive and charismatic, would we disclose this to the client?

We would assert that to recoil at the client who for the first time reveals their disfigurement, to be angry and disgusted by some recounted behaviour, or demonstrate your feelings towards some prejudiced remark can be both natural and helpful. (For more on this see Chapter 3.) We would be quick to qualify this by also saying that **the therapeutic process is only enhanced and pursued if the counsellor is able to contextualise their reaction**. The client has the benefit of knowing that her/his therapist is genuine, and that despite what was disclosed they want to be helpful. It is important that the counsellor finds a way of being able to demonstrate their feelings towards a disclosure and simultaneously inform the discloser that it is the *client's* feelings which are under review. They need to know that disclosure of themselves in any form will meet with some human reaction, but should that reaction be perceived as negative, it does not mean they they are judged to be a 'nasty' person without hope of help if they wish it. In this way the counsellor can remain genuine and real, whilst remaining supportive to the helping objective and accepting of the person as having potential for change.

So, we might conclude that genuineness is possible though complex. The second set of questions regarding genuineness are to do with its nature and its worth. Is it always a good thing, what impact might it have on the client, and is it the same as authenticity?

The counselling profession has almost automatically accepted that being genuine is a good thing. Although we as individuals have come to this conclusion ourselves, it has not been automatic and does rest on some pragmatic reasoning rather than idealism. Genuineness is important because it may have strong influential properties. One possibility is that genuineness is an instrumental agent in the client's change. The client's perception that the counsellor is genuine will have the tendency to validate the counsellor's skilled responses, whether they are attitudinal, i.e. demonstrating warmth, positive regard or whether they are skilled empathic responses or challenges. Because the *counsellor* is perceived as genuine their *responses* are also perceived as genuine. The client, then, may experience a powerful influence, in terms of feeling understood, valued or, if we were to be prescriptive, encouraged to take a particular direction or course of action. In other words, genuineness encourages credibility, apart from anything else.

Further, therapy is acknowledged as having the potential to be persuasive and powerful,[9] with potential for exploitation.[10] Moreover, the counsellor will, in behavioural terms, be modelling genuineness and thus, if the client is susceptible to this influence, it is possible that the client will move towards becoming more genuine her/himself. Taking this theme of genuineness even further, we are obliged to register what the behaviourist school of psychology adds to this debate. The effects of modelled behaviour described within social learning theory suggest clear possibilities that it is possible for clients to manifest a behaviour or behaviours that were first portrayed by the counsellor.[11] The likelihood of this occurring is enhanced by factors such as admiration or respect for the person exhibiting the behaviour.

It can be seen then that counsellor behaviour, especially if the counsellor is in some way charismatic, may well be mimicked by the client. Thus, behaviour observed in the client may have been originally instigated or 'modelled' for the client by the counsellor. This tends to suggest that there is potential for the process of counselling to be more directive than initially suspected or intentionally proposed. The reader at this point may want to consider the advantages to the counsellor of the client becoming more open and genuine and contemplate the practicalities of 'modelling genuineness'. We might also want to stop and explore the cultural ramifications of exalting genuineness as a *desirable* quality to emulate.

Finally, you will have gathered that we largely agree with the concept of genuineness as helpful, although we would stress that our agreement only holds when genuineness as a practice and a concept is purposeful and contextualised. We do not understand genuineness to necessarily mean the same as some understandings of authenticity. We feel free to consider our responses, and to not share all our thoughts and feelings with the client. Being genuine does not, for example, mean saying everything that occurs to one, voicing your opinions without thought for the reactions and impact upon others; although this may be genuine, it would seldom be either helpful, skilled or caring. A withholding of an opinion, reaction or thought, when motivated by regard for the client, does not make the counsellor ingenuine; simply more tactful and sensitive to potential adverse reactions. There needs to be a distinction acknowledged between genuine in terms of motive, choices made, responsibility taken, and genuine in terms of 'I make my every inner thought and feeling transparent to you'. A thorough knowledge of your own beliefs and clearly held values, congruent with what you espouse, would be closer to our contextualised definition of genuineness and therefore helpful in a therapeutic relationship.

In addition to the above qualities this genuine person would be someone who is not afraid to disclose facets of her/himself *when it is appropriate to helping,* but is capable of differentiating what is purposeful disclosure and what would be fruitless. This genuine person would know the difference between privacy and tact, and secrecy and indiscriminate comment. As a final note, it is perhaps important to make clear that these comments are not intended exclusively in regard to counsellors. The client may also have good reasons for avoiding certain disclosures which would not automatically indicate non-genuineness. For example, a client may avoid talking about essentially pertinent issues, simply because it involves talking 'disloyally' about someone they feel protective, supportive or lovingly towards. This does not mean that their desire for help is not genuine. 'Genuineness' does not exist in a vacuum – genuine for what end, within whose framework, and in what context? Such questions inform us to a more realistic quality rather than some ideal mumbo-jumbo.

In summary it can be argued that the therapist's genuineness can exert a considerable effect on the client in relationship to potential influence; that genuineness and warmth are unlikely to be consistently congruent unless the counsellor is accepting of others' values; genuinely displayed negative reactions, although not always associated with warmth are not only acceptable but helpful if contextualised; and genuineness is purposeful and thus should not be confused with tactlessness and indiscriminate comment.

*Even though you are a sleazy, greasy, slimeball with the morals of an alleycat and the manners of a pig, I prize your very being – or the myth of unconditional positive regard*

Carl Rogers described this concept as a warm caring and acceptance for a client which is not possessive, demands no personal gratification, and sets no conditions on the thoughts, feelings or behaviours of the client.[12] Clearly, his clients were more on the Gloria side of the human continuum than the Adolf Hitler side. In coining unconditional positive regard, Rogers merges three concepts already being used in the practice of 'client-centred therapy': warmth from the therapist, the unconditional basis for that warmth, and acceptance. It has to be noted that acceptance is not the same as unconditional positive regard, as it has a connotation of neutrality, i.e. I can tolerate or accept a person's behaviour; this does not mean I prize it, as unconditional positive regard implies.[13]

Rogers' ideal is the 'prizing' of the client's feelings irrespective of them being 'good' or 'bad'. This then goes beyond an acceptance or tolerance of the client as a person. The more pragmatic counsellor might read Rogers as reserving the concept to describe the feelings of the client, and this enables them to address the concept without appearing to condone antisocial or 'bad' behaviour of the client. However, this is not precisely what Rogers wrote. In his book *On Becoming a Person: A Therapist's View of Psychotherapy*, published in 1961, he is very clear that this regard for the client includes behaviour:

> By this I do not mean that he [the therapist] simply accept the client when he is behaving in certain ways. It means an outgoing positive feeling without reservation, without evaluations. (p. 62)

Without reading this with extreme care, it is easy to see how a counsellor may be misled into believing that they need to suspend all of their moral judgements during counselling. Implicit in Rogers' writing is the belief that people have the ability of being 'good', and his philosophy is one that prizes the person *despite* the behaviour; this does not necessarily mean that he would approve of some behaviours, as the last quote may indicate.

Another difficult question is whether adopting a position of unconditional positive regard is possible or valuable. Rogers' idea of 'a fully functioning person' is his description of a person 'potentiated' in personal growth. The use of this term enables him to describe a person fully potentiated without having to label that end point as 'good' or 'bad'. However, there is no doubt that it is seen as both individually desirable, and of a social nature. In other words, there is a checklist which is to do with whether we are fully functioning or not, so that there is a very clear and value-laden directive as to how and when personal growth is realised.

Moreover, Rogers does hold an implicit belief that all human beings are capable of becoming 'good'. In his writings there is the flavour of the evangelist, a fundamental belief that there is no innate evil, and if each infant was surrounded by the core conditions, i.e. they were cared for by real 'genuine' people, in a climate of warm regard, empathically understood, and prized for their feelings and behaviours, they would evolve into the inherently good person.

Taking Rogers' hypothesis to its furthest end, does he mean that if society accepts unconditionally any behaviour an individual manifests, and also prizes them for it, that each individual in society will develop into a 'fully functioning' person? Would society's 'problem behaviour' no longer exist? Without being too critical of this idea, the variables appear somewhat difficult to control. Although it can be argued that extinction of non-reinforced behaviour can be rapidly reversed in controlled conditions, these conditions would be hard to replicate in today's society, and within a person's cultural reality.

If society is to accept *any* behaviour and prize it, where would society's values stem from? The reality is of course that they derive from history and context. In countries such as Rwanda, where violence is a second-generation norm, the ability to be effectively violent might be prized. This does not differentiate the individuals concerned from the rest of the human race; it merely illustrates that society's terms of fully functioning may be wide and varied. Therefore 'fully functioning' *per se* is a questionable ideal. In Western society, the drive towards 'fully functioning' which idealises authenticity and self-fulfilment is perhaps really only helpful if it takes the individual to a point of understanding self, which includes a heightened awareness of their (social) values and morality. This in turn needs to be contexualised into their dialogue with others and society to prevent it becoming self-defeating for them. If the route to self-fulfilment does not take account of significant others and society, e.g. relationships are simply instrumental to self-actualisation, the ultimate result is a degeneration to selfishness without any intrinsic value for the individual.

If the counsellor then is relentlessly practising unconditional positive regard, in behaviourist terms this would be the ideal to be modelled to future generations as 'normal' learned behaviour. The difficulty then arises from the task of producing the *environment* which will establish 'fully functioning' people as counselling ideology decreases. If we adopt a Rogerian view, and simply take one case at a time, then the task is a great one, for it cannot easily be seen how, in periodic sessions with a client, the influences of peers, significant others and society in general can be reversed. Can the application of unconditional regard by a single therapist reverse the extremes of 'bad' behaviour where the formative roots are in childhood behaviour. The practical application of the idea appears to be seriously flawed.

This leaves only five logical explanations for believing that unconditional positive regard is helpful to clients in counselling. These are:

1 Counsellors only take clients that are already 'good' people that can have that 'goodness' enhanced.
2 Counsellors must operate some judgement as to the proposed outcome of change and influence this throughout the counselling process.
3 Counsellors dissociate the client as a person from their behaviour. This would give freedom to the counsellor to respond congruently to the behaviours from their own value orientation, whilst still maintaining unconditional regard for the person.
4 Counsellors begin by operating on a basis of unconditional positive regard, which changes to conditional positive regard in the light of relevant disclosure.
5 Combinations of all of the above.

If these conclusions are correct it may explain some of the other interpretations of unconditional positive regard in the literature. For example, Gerard Egan's preference for the term 'respect' allows the counsellor more scope to use their personal judgement of a client's behaviour, whilst still holding a neutral position in regard to their client's values.[14]

## Warmth

Warmth is itself difficult to define without contrasting it with cold-ness. Objective, logical and calculating individuals more concerned with fact than emotion are often perceived as cold. However, counsel-lors may need to have just such qualities in order to see the client's world without becoming subjectively engaged in it, and losing their effectiveness. Thus counselling appears to require the ability to stand back objectively and perceive rationally what is going on.

However, somehow, in some way, whilst operating this 'objectivity', the counsellor must be perceived by the client as being 'warm', i.e. as having some caring[15] towards them. How is this feat achieved? We would suggest that the non-verbal behaviour of the counsellor is 'read' by the client as warm, rather than the words spoken necessarily demonstrating agreement or a positive regard. This is really rather

**My counsellor is so warm and tropical I just melt ...**

**I envy you, darling, mine has all the sensitivity of a snowman!**

important, because we believe some counsellors perceive 'warmth' towards their clients to be conveyed by demonstrating that they are 'on their side', that they agree with them or by commiserating with them about their predicaments and problems. In this understanding, warmth is presented as a feeling rather than an attitude. We strongly disagree! If this were the case then a considerable amount of the criticisms levelled at counsellors in regard to them being prescriptive and directive would be confirmed. It is most important that counsellors do not collude with their client's view, but instead reflect back the stated view to the client for further contemplation.

An illustration of this may help here. Some time ago whilst working with a client who was regularly beaten by her husband, one of us (Graham), was confronted with the client's desire to be supported with regard to the way she felt towards her husband. This was easy to spot because her descriptions of events and her opinion about such behaviour was permeated with 'isn't he' and 'shouldn't he'. The client was not only seeking understanding of her situation and how it affected her, but reassurance that her perception of her husband was correct. The easiest course of action in this type of situation is to agree, to say 'Yes, your husband is a bastard; yes, I don't blame you for wanting to kill him; Yes, of course you should ...' but, of course, for those of us who respect the principle of self-determination, this would be falling into a very deep trap. On the other hand, to withhold some judgement of the husband's behaviour may leave this woman in confusion, or worse, confirm to her that her suspicions are correct – it really *is* her fault!!

So here we have a situation where the counsellor may feel outraged by what they are hearing, but cannot express this, for fear of influencing the client in which direction she takes. The counsellor's caring instincts may be a powerful desire to convey their personal warmth for her, to hug, comfort, protect or in some way make it better for this woman. All of these approaches are unacceptable to the counselling approach for reason of non-interference, yet to suppress these emotions and desires may lead to non-genuineness, another no-no. The professional who wants to be able to negotiate around all of these issues, stay client-focused, demonstrate warmth and genuineness, has a difficult job. Without wanting to sound trite or glib we suggest this possible way around this logical impasse:

- Remain empathic – 'As you are telling me about these events I notice you tremble; I guess even remembering makes you feel unsafe and upset.'
- Use appropriate self-disclosure – 'Simply listening to you recounting your story stirs a lot of emotion in me.'
- Contextualise the self-disclosure – 'However, what I may think and feel is unimportant; what I really want you to do is examine your thoughts and feelings about these events, so eventually you can decide what is best for *you*.'
- Challenge dependency and potentially distorted thinking – 'Rather than me tell you what I think, ask yourself this question: what is your part in perpetuating this situation?'
- Inappropriate or impulsive action plans (I want to kill him) can be avoided by challenging the client to identify her goals – 'What would you achieve by killing him? Are there other ways of achieving what you want?' or 'What would be the consequence of doing that?'

In this way the best hope for some critical distance is preserved and potential for influencing the client is minimised. The client should still perceive you as warm because it has been demonstrated that you are understanding, that you have feelings about her story but that you are consciously (some may say professionally) resisting superficial sympathy in exchange for a positive approach which promises to be centred on what it is she wants to achieve for herself.

One of the essential and different ingredients of this approach which is often undefined is that here we have warmth which is selfless. By this we mean that counsellors' ability to express regard towards the client in this way does not depend on the client reciprocating this regard. In other words, the counsellor does feel warm towards the client, and being pragmatic it would be helpful if the client knew this; however, the counsellor is not dependent on the client for self-worth or positive regard. It is often this absence of need in the counsellor that will allow the client to be open and give an honest expression of their thoughts and feelings.

Warmth is an issue that often bewilders students on counselling courses. The same non-verbal behaviours that are used to communicate warmth in close personal relationships and friendships are required to be differentiated in some way when used in helping relationships. Both Carl Rogers and Gerard Egan suggest that the helper should have no personal motive for communicating warmth, other than to facilitate the helping process. However, it can be envisaged that both counsellors and clients may have some difficulties operationalising this principle on occasions. It may be postulated that clients finding themselves listened to empathically, addressed with unconditional positive regard, and responded to positively and warmly, irrespective of their disclosures, may find this situation confusing. It may be argued that clients who disclose, for example, foolishness, criminality, selfishness or antisocial behaviour and so on, and meet warm responses, may be forgiven for believing that the counsellor has more than a professional interest in them.

## *To be non-judgemental*

The idea of a non-judgemental approach is connected to the ability to be warm and to adopt positions approximating unconditional positive regard. However, the idea is reviewed separately because it would appear that it often substitutes for the absolute condition of unconditional positive regard and non-possessive warmth. The concept of non-judgementalness can be seen as:

- A value orientation for practitioners.
- An exemplar of good practice.
- A measure to seduce clients to engage in an intimate climate of self-disclosure to further the purpose of counselling.

As a value orientation, it serves to advise counsellors that the client has a right or entitlement to his/her own view of the world, their own behaviour within it, and their choices for their own self-determined changes. For instance, the client who is currently considering an abortion; reducing their alcohol intake; giving up smoking; using drugs; taking out private health insurance; sending their children to private school, etc., will all have some impact on the value perspective of the counsellor. It would not be of particular relevance or serve a therapeutic end for the counsellor to make known their view on the subject. Most counsellors would probably have no difficulty seeing this as logical if they were pursuing a non-directive approach. This is not to be confused with making no judgements at all; clinical judgements, and judgements about how we communicate, operate throughout.

Where judgement is suspended, however, this does not amount to unconditional positive regard or non-possessive warmth. The absence of judgement is a neutral stance, not to adopt an affirming or prizing of the client's choices or values. This adoption of a non-judgemental approach is therefore a half-way house for the therapist, one which allows him/her to proceed with a client towards some degree of self-determination without having to either condone or challenge the client's perspective. This approach appears to be the safe moral ground for most, but breaks down when the value ascribed to by the client is diametrically opposed to the one adopted by the counsellor. This is especially the case in situations when the course of action, or the value attached to such ideas, are extreme, counter-cultural or in some way threatening to the value integrity of the counsellor. An example of this might be the client who reveals that they are intent on committing murder, rape or some act that contradicts the 'norm' of legal, moral or ethical behaviour. In these instances, the counsellor may be forced to resort to an evaluative stance based on their own value orientation in deciding whether they can continue to be non-judgemental, or indeed whether they must act independently to prevent the exploitation or endangerment of other people.[16]

Counsellors who purport to address the qualities of respect and caring for the human individual would be identifying a conflict of interest if they were confronted with a choice of encouraging self-determination and protection of the life or liberty of another human being. It is theoretically possible to dispute responsibility for client actions on the grounds that without the conditions of intimate disclosure, they would not be forearmed with the knowledge of such intent, but this serves little logical argument in terms of the contradiction of acting upon one's values in such situations. On a very practical note this situation can often be avoided by clearly demarcating the lines of confidentiality and potential 'post-disclosure interference' by specifically contracting these areas before counselling commences.

A further, more contentious, view of non-judgementalness takes the rationale that, when adopting this approach, it will have the effect of seducing the client into honest self-disclosure. As a device, it precludes the need for the client to fabricate or try to deceive the counsellor, as the counsellor will adopt a neutrality of evaluation in each subsequent disclosure. The counsellor adopting this approach does not respond in any moralising way to what the client discloses, so the client learns that it is their responsibility to evaluate who and what they do.

The counsellor simply becomes a passive recipient of the person's disclosure, so that to lie, elaborate or deceive is to do so to one's self. The latter position adopts a pragmatic view rather than a moral one. It is not adopted from any philosophical value orientation, but simply from the practical position that it is likely to further the aims of counselling.

There is a third possible outcome of such absence of judgement, which is that the client will, in fact, self-delude, and that the counsellor becomes party to such delusion. To put this simply, the client, in the absence of judgemental feedback, decides that the behaviour, thoughts or feelings disclosed are acceptable or appropriate. This is justified by the lack of negative feedback that the 'untrained' client may be expecting from the professional helper. Thus the false belief is affirmed as correct! It is logical to assume that this potential as described would occur more often in counselling than in the more overtly moral and prescriptive therapies which might analyse disclosures and make determinations about them.[17]

In sum, then, we regard non-judgementalness as a *temporary suspension* of opinion and moral values for as long as that is tenable in the context of the counselling. It seems that at one time counsellors accepted it as a quasi-value to be aspired to at all times, and that now, current (welcome) critiques make it an impossibility. We would argue that all human beings are capable of making a temporary suspension of judgement while they replace such activity with something else, such as a willingness to understand another perspective; if they weren't, then our arguments, morals and perspectives on life would never develop. However, in any context, including counselling, information might come our way from either external or internal sources which interrupts our ability for such suspension. This to us is the realistic view, and we have no doubt that the tendency towards purposeful non-judgementalism within counselling is both useful and feasible.

## Self-determination

Finally, a central philosophical belief underpinning counselling theory is self-determination. Although few authors write specifically about it, it is a condition connected to respect and unconditional positive regard. The belief that each client has an absolute right to choose which direction she/he wants to go; to select goals from his/her own value orientation, and to determine behaviours for her/himself is strongly held in counselling circles. The central precept of counselling hinges on this concept. The preferred stance of the counsellor is one of an egalitarian relationship; one which asserts the position that the client is just as able to solve problems and gain insight into themselves as the counsellor. This differs slightly in psychotherapy, where the therapist may suggest treatment programmes and regimes from their particular theoretical framework, from which the client will work.

The reality of self-determination as an achievable objective is perhaps debatable. Although within the practice of counselling it has become a valued aim, in practice it could be argued that the evidence for its existence is scarce. To elucidate further, it can be seen that to maintain self-determination, the client would have to be offered unconditional regard; be resistant or immune from the influence of the therapist; and fully understand and choose their own goals and behaviour. In the light of previous arguments, it would appear that all of these conditions are unlikely. Unconditional positive regard is likely to be positive regard from the counsellor's own value orientation; to be resistant or immune from the influence of the counsellor is hardly what most clients seek a counsellor for, nor would their awareness of the implications of influence prepare them for resistance. And if self-awareness is to be achieved through the counsellor's most often chosen strategy – empathy – then the difficulties highlighted earlier make this also a somewhat unlikely proposition.

Taking a less absolute approach to this issue, it is quite possible to see self-determination as a matter of degree rather than an

**Where there's a whale, there's a way ...**

unequivocal state. From the arguments presented so far, it would seem that counsellors probably do influence client outcomes to some extent, in either their intentional or unintentional interventions in the world of another person. This does not mean that the notion of self-determination has to be rejected. In some ways, it may be viewed in the same way as the other core conditions. The concept is powerful and conceived from an altruistic perspective, yet it may be impossible, and even undesirable, to achieve it in pure form. An acknowledgement of the practical difficulties, and an alertness to them, may be a better position for counsellors to adopt.

It can be argued that encouraging self-determination is a somewhat self-indulgent approach, and denies the existence of the greater aspects of 'self' within a society. The individual, at some point, may need to be reminded of the cost and consequences of reaching their goals. It is possible that in the process of striving for and attaining one's own fulfilment, others and society can be damaged. For example, individuals who express their 'smoking behaviour' may deny other individuals, in their presence, their right to a smoke-free environment. Taking a more global perspective, the individualistic society based on consumerism may be encouraged to possess such twentieth-century paraphernalia as the motor-car, at the expense of the damage to the environment that others have to live in. Every action has some kind of reaction, and one person's freedom may, as a reaction, create another's imprisonment. Over the past few decades in this country, the individual has been encouraged to be self-reliant, to be less dependent on the state. Specific examples of this phenomenon are not hard to identify; privatisation of healthcare, education and pensions are all pointers to the gradual withdrawal of central govern-ment's provision to the average person, and a trend for individuals to provide for themselves. This general attitude tends to have the effect of enhancing individuals' idea of self-identity, and individualism at the cost of a more moral awareness of the common well-being of the collective society.

When we look at the practice of counselling and its doctrine of self-determination in this context, then it can be viewed as an amoral or an antisocial activity. Although we would agree that self-fulfilment in itself is not a bad thing, and that its pursuit does not have to mean the dereliction of responsibility for the collective good, we would also want to highlight that any pursuit of self-indulgent goals without consideration of their effect upon others may eventually lead to a serious erosion of collective human values, and a limited perspective on the world.

If it is possible to convince the average person that they are entirely responsible for their situation, and that counselling is the panacea to enable people to marshal their resources and take self-responsibility, then it may also be used as a device for maintaining the status quo, and enabling those actually responsible for social conditions to avoid changing them. And we may ignore that, every now and then, people may be so low that they are unable to self-determine. It is not enough to say that every action is a full choice, that if people are motivated enough, they can make desired changes. If social problems can be consummately addressed by engaging counsellors and counselling programmes instead of by other means, then this may signal that counselling has become another *'opium of the masses'*. Counselling in this context could therefore be labelled amoral as it takes the virtue of 'unconditional positive regard' and of 'self-determination' without reference to the wider view of society's needs or the effect that the self-determining person will have on another.

In consideration of this latter position, it should be made clear that the position of counsellors can be attacked from either direction. If counselling takes the position of non-directiveness and an amoral approach it may be damned for colluding in an individualist society that may be damaging to the collective good. On the other hand, the counselling approach that 'selectively' attends and responds to the client from the value orientation of the counsellor could equally be attacked for perpetuating a biased approach from whatever position the counsellor holds. Equally this latter position suggests that, as counsellors are largely recruited from the educated, white middle class, this situation offers simply another agency of social control, supporting the status quo and perpetuating the trend towards an indi-vidualist society. Taking these views into account, it is hard to assert that the practice of counselling is or should be 'value free'. The prin-ciple of self-determination in counselling practice is therefore an ideal that may well be fatally flawed, even though on face value it would appear to be desirable.

## In sum

It can be seen that the study of the core conditions is somewhat complex. It would seem that counsellors need to develop self-awareness in order to be genuine; engage with clients in order to understand them intimately; offer acceptance without judgement; respect the client's right to self-determination; and be aware of their own prejudices and discard them. In addition, the counsellor has to develop these attributes and attitudes irrespective of any conflicting client values or behaviours that they may encounter. We wish you luck!

However, it is our belief that an acceptance of the complexities makes for better, rather than impossible, practice. Principles and values are guidelines which can help a lot of the time: do you remember learning to drive, and being told don't worry about getting on that motorway, people would let you in. This is true for 99 per cent of the time, but we always keep an eye out for when the principle doesn't operate. Because in practice, it can't operate a 100 per cent. Perhaps counselling is a bit like that – let's not make its principles sacrosanct, or mystical. They are an aid towards achieving our purpose, not some immutable ideals of themselves. Ultimately, we need to be in constant negotiation with our clients – *have* I understood you, I'm having difficulty with this bit and I *want* to understand, I find it difficult to work with this attitude, but I know I can suspend my difficulty, or I know that I just cannot accept this and so am not the person for this particular job. Core conditions are approximations and useful devices; it's only when we hold them up as rigid imperatives that we begin to make impossible and saintly claims that are no good for either the counsellor or the client.

## Notes

1   See, for example, Richard Sennett's masterly exposition of 'Destructive Gemeinschaft' 1988, in which he argues that the drive to maskless relations is producing a tyranny of self and emotion. Also, Alasdair MacIntyre's 1981work on 'emotivism', wherein moral judgement is replaced by the ethical preferences of the unmasked self, offers some provocative viewpoints on the role of the Therapist in modern society.

2   These are the three core conditions, identified by Truax and Carkhuff (1967), which are suggested to be an essential precursor for clients to perceive the therapy as a positive experience helping to resolve their problems. These conditions were asserted as necessary components of successful therapy, irrespective of whichever therapeutic approach was being used. It was postulated that when these conditions are not present any therapy has a greater chance of failure. This research helped explain the rather random results of success and failure across a range of therapeutic approaches and pointed to the relationship between therapist and client as being as important as the particular therapeutic approaches used by any therapist.

3   Carl Rogers is the most prestigious, prodigious and classic source of much of the common wisdom and beliefs held by counsellors today. His work (1957) suggests not only that the core conditions are *necessary*, but also that they are *sufficient* for successful therapeutic personality change. His writings span a period of over 40 years and have been criticised and applauded by generations of counsellors and psychotherapists from

all branches of the field of helping. Much of this chapter is informed by the studying of his works and his critics. See also Egan (1994), Feltham (1995), Gellner (1985), Krumboltz and Thoresen (1976) and Strong (1968).

4    Rogers' (1990) description of empathy is as follows:

> The ability of the therapist to perceive experiences and feelings accurately and sensitively, and to understand their meaning to the client during the moment to moment encounter of psychotherapy ... Accurate empathic understanding means that the therapist is completely at home in the universe of the client ... It is a sensing of the client's inner world of private personal meanings as if it were your own, while never forgetting it is not yours ... The ability and sensitivity required to communicate these inner meanings again to the client in a way that allows them to be 'his' experiences are the other major part of accurate empathic understanding. To sense the client's fear, his confusion, his anger, or his rage as if it were a feeling you might have (but which you are currently not having) is the essence of the perceptive aspect of accurate empathy. To communicate this perception in a language attuned to the client, which allows him more clearly to sense and formulate his fear, confusion, rage or anger, is the essence of the communicative aspect of accurate empathy. (pp. 15-16)

5    Extended and elaborated codes studied by Bernstein (1962) and many other sociologists, make the significant point that culture, social status and ethnicity will have a profound effect on mutual understanding. Bandler and Grinder (1979) also make the point that 'Neuro-linguistic' compatibility will have an important impact on meaningful communication between individuals, i.e. 'I *see* your point of view' can be framed 'I *hear* what you are saying, I'm in *touch* with your meaning, or I can *feel* your discomfort', or even 'that *smells* fishy to me'.

6    The interpretation of body language and non-verbal communication is the subject of continued study. The complex nuances and subtle variations of messages are determined by culture, ethnicity and specific societal influences, making universality of interpretation extremely difficult for the individual therapist. See Argyle (1975), Seigman and Feldstein (1987) and Sue (1990).

7    There is increasing interest in cross-cultural counselling and specifically whether there are particular differences in cultures that make counselling and psychotherapeutic approaches inappropriate. As already mentioned earlier in this book, certain cultures view empathy for an individual's emotions an 'intrusion' into their privacy. See Chapter 2 and also Sue (1990).

8    Truax and Carkhuff (1967) suggest this as a definition of genuineness:

> Genuineness implies most basically a direct personal encounter, a meeting on a person-to-person basis without defensiveness or a retreat into façades or roles, and so in this sense an openness to experience. (p. 32)

9 Research in the 1960s argues that it is impossible to have a strong supportive relationship without exerting some social influence. Whether this is inadvertent, unconscious, accidental or deliberate is not necessary to determine. It is argued that our opinion is frequently given in our non-verbal postures and language, even if there are no clues in our spoken words. See Frank (1961).

10 It is unfortunately the case that many incidents of exploitation in counselling and therapy have come to light. Some of these are unintentional errors of judgement and simple cases of a deep relationship being misinterpreted by both clients and therapists, but others are more malignant examples of deliberate exploitation for purposes of therapist gratification. See Russell (1993).

11 Bandura (1977) has amassed significant research evidence that observed behaviour may be mimicked or learned by others in everyday interactions and experience.

12 Rogers, building on the work of Fiedler (1950) and Standal (1954), first described the concept of unconditional positive regard thus:

... the therapist experiences a warm caring for the client – a caring which is not possessive, which demands no personal gratification. It is an atmosphere which simply demonstrates 'I care'; not 'I care for you if you behave thus and so' ... I have often used the term acceptance to describe this aspect of the therapeutic climate. (1951: p. 283)

13 Some might argue that Rogers' meaning here needs to be contextualised in relation to his own life and his experience of receiving highly conditional approval within family and educative institutions.

14 Egan's (1994) view of respect is perhaps exemplified best through these quotes from *The Skilled Helper*:

Your manner should indicate that you care in a down-to-earth, non-sentimental way. Respect is both gracious and tough minded. (p. 54)
Challenge clients to clarify their values and to make reasonable choices based on them. Be wary of using challenging, even indirectly, to force clients to accept your values. (p. 195)

15 We use this term advisedly. Caring does not have to mean that we personally have an investment in how the client's life turns out; it means that we care in this counselling that the client is treated both professionally and 'with care', with respect that is driven towards their attaining the changes they want.

16 Some attempt to give guidance on these issues are reviewed in Tim Bond's book and are addressed within the British Association for Counselling's *Code of Ethics*. See BAC (1992) and Bond (1993).

17 Gerard Egan, the great pragmatic genius in helping, offers a gem of common wisdom in regard to non-judgementalness:

> Suspend critical judgement. You are there to help clients, not to judge them. Nor are you there to shove your values down their throats. You are there, however, to help them identify, explore, and review the consequences of the values they have adopted. (1994: 53)

# 11

## getting in and out of counselling: professional issues

**Abstract:** This chapter provides an exploration of three areas of professionalisation. Firstly, what does it take to become a professional these days in the UK. Secondly, what does it mean to be one? And thirdly, what is happening within the professionalisation process itself as we move into a rapidly changing world order, both geographically and technologically? In this chapter, we raise questions as well as offering perspectives on the professionalisation process.

## Becoming a professional

The issue of the professionalisation of counselling has a long and thorny history. Basically, in the beginning was the word, and the word was either Sigmund Freud,[1] Carl Rogers[2] and/or, in a different way, Gerry Egan.[3] To propagate Freud's theories, you had probably to be trained as a medical doctor; with Rogers, you probably came from a pastoral background, or entered the women's movement, or have gone the California route with its T-group phenomenon, the urge to find yourself, and so on; to find Egan, you probably happened upon him as you trained for social work, teaching, nursing, or something similar. Egan is different from both Freud and Rogers: the latter two espoused theories of human personality, while Egan proposed a model for helping people change.

Towards the end of the 1960s, followers of the new psychologies developed myriad workshops for self-development and counselling: a new social movement was gestating. There was no governing body to regulate this growth, and disciples could practise without training, just as the founding fathers had. This situation has now changed beyond recognition. There has been huge investment in trying to make counselling an income-generating and professionally accountable enterprise. There has also been enormous energy invested in making it academically credible. Many questions around this development remain problematic. How much theory do you need to be a competent practitioner? How much should 'on the ground' experience count for? Can some people be excellent counsellors even though they are not good at learning theory? How many theoretically educated counsellors do you know to whom you wouldn't send your cat to have kittens?

Inevitably, professional bodies with a vested interest have been through a bit of a brouhaha about how the profession should be defined, regulated and, to a point, owned. The British Association for Counselling was founded in 1977, just 30 years ago, and over that time has developed a very strong grip on the development of the counselling profession. In 2000, it changed its name to the British Association for Counselling and Psychotherapy, a move which, on the one hand, acknowledges the common interests of both counsellors and psychotherapists and, on the other, accepts a sense of defeat in being able to differentiate the two activities.

Meanwhile, the British Psychological Society (BPS) has propagated a counselling division. This differs from the BACP, as it is founded from a clearly identifiable group of professional people, i.e. psychologists, who already had an academically and professionally credible base. The counselling division traditionally sets clearer and more rigorous criteria for membership and registration than the BACP, and has implicitly claimed a higher status.

Both organisations have clamped a very heavy hand on the development of counselling, for better or worse, and accreditation is clearly the name of the game. Most health trusts, general practitioners and many helping professions, will not employ a counsellor unless they are accredited by a governing body. The BACP is recognised as that major governing body. What does accreditation entail?

For accreditation with the BACP, candidates must first be a member, and second have professional indemnity insurance (counsellors with less than £200 to spend need not apply). They can then go via two different routes. The first involves qualifications from a BACP accredited training course, and proof of supervised practice for between three and six years: or it can mean successful completion of practitioner training, a specified amount of taught contact hours over particular periods of time, and a supervised placement which includes theory, skills, professional issues and personal development, *plus* supervised practice. More details are available on request [4] – the point is that these are very clearly demarked criteria.

The old lags can still take a 'unit route'. This entails demonstrating more piecemeal chunks of training and practice. They need to provide evidence of a combination of units of training and practice containing a minimum of two units of training and three units of practice. Submitted practice units must have included at least 150 hours of supervised practice, which must have been supervised to the level of one and a half hours per month. Training should reflect theory, skills, professional issues and personal development.

The accreditation process is a paper exercise. That is not to say that it does not demand a great deal of reflection, thought and contribution. We simply mean that no demonstration of competence is necessary, as it might be in, say, nursing or teaching. It is not impossible for the practitioner to make things up, despite a rather appealing declaration of honesty which is required. Proof of actual competence seems to rely on the assessment of tutors or supervisors at some points in the process.

Counselling psychologists are different. According to the BPS:

> Counselling psychologists are a relatively new breed of professional ... applied psychologists are concerned with the integration of psychological theory and research with therapeutic practice. The practice of Counselling Psychology requires a high level of self-awareness and competence in relating the skills and knowledge of personal and interpersonal dynamics to the therapeutic context.

There follows a very clear list of tasks which the counselling psychologist will need to perform, including assessment, risk assessment and psychometric testing; problem formulation; planning and implementation of therapy; record keeping, outcome evaluation, supervision and training of others, team work and team facilitation; service and organisational development; research and development; and management of services. This list is specifically outcome focused. To become a counselling psychologist, the individual must first be a graduate psychologist, or else build a personal training plan with the help of a training supervisor, which must include ... a BACP-accredited counselling course!

It seems that 95 per cent of counsellors and psychotherapists are now trained (Aldridge and Pollard, 2005), although over half of the training courses in the UK are not accredited, even though they might be validated within further or higher education processes. Indeed, particularly within psychotherapy, it seems that courses are entering the postgraduate field, amidst unresolved debate regarding the desirability of this move, a move which will inevitably cause training to become to some extent exclusive, at least on grounds of academic abilities and finance.

How do people get on to a training course – what do they need? The answer to this question seems to be a mix of education, experience, qualifications and qualities. A trawl of courses for certificate level produced expectations regarding age, 'personal suitability' and current work; for diploma courses, a certificate in counselling, with some courses saying that engagement in therapy is considered an advantage (Westminster Pastoral Foundation);[5] and Master's courses generally require education to diploma level or equivalent. It would seem that the university route is becoming more and more the orthodox one, and while it may ease regulation, we need also to remember that conformity must never preclude innovation.

Finally, a brief mention of the wonderful issue of 'qualities'. The counsellor, naturally, is required to work ethically. To this end they are required to 'aspire to' personal attributes which the BACP now refers to as 'moral qualities'. The BACP states that it has changed the formation of its ethical code to reflect the fact that clients are bringing a wider range of issues and concerns to counselling than previously (although we are not clear how this manifests); there is a greater degree of expertise out there now due to training provision; and the association, at the time of the rewriting of the code, now had almost 30 years of experience (BACP, 2002).

The interesting point for us is that the rewrite of the Code of Ethics suggests that

> The practitioner's personal moral qualities are of the utmost importance to clients. Many of the personal qualities considered important in the provision of services have an ethical or moral component and are therefore considered as virtues or good personal qualities. *It is inappropriate to prescribe that all practitioners possess these qualities, since it is fundamental that these personal qualities are deeply rooted in the person concerned and developed out of personal commitment rather than the requirement of an external authority.* (BACP, 2002: our italics)

This is a plausible yet questionable statement, and paradoxical. On the one hand, counselling is presented as ever more suited to being a profession which people can join through training: on the other, moral qualities are presented as apparently intrinsic to personhood (although not for every mere mortal) rather than influenced by an external authority. So, we aspire to be morally superior, as in MacIntyre's (1981) idea of the 'character' of post-modernity; and this aspiration will only be met from somewhere within our inner selves. Echoes of a 'calling' are embedded here. Moreover, as we have argued elsewhere (Russell, 1993), there would be no need for a code of ethics if people's ability to develop and live by certain principles and qualities was indeed only internal: codes of ethics discourage transgression and enforce discipline. We would also argue that qualities can develop from repeated conformity to an external authority.

The personal qualities to which counsellors and psychotherapists are encouraged to aspire include empathy, sincerity, integrity, resilience, respect, humility, competence (we would suggest that competence is an ability, while willingness to be competent might be a personal quality), fairness, wisdom and courage. This list is not dissimilar to that presented by Egan in all of his editions of *The Skilled Helper*, to some extent Rogers, and doubtless many other fathers of the profession. We note again with interest that here is this subtle claim to specialness which we do not find in the professions of nursing, social work, medicine, teaching, law, all of which are expected to work towards identifiable standards and within precise ethical codes.

## Being a professional

The demands on the professional are high, then, and we have already mentioned in this work what effects counselling can have on the practitioner. In this section, we want briefly to outline possible demands on the counsellor from the point of view of their own development. We would like to touch here on supervision as we suggest that counsellors move through stages which might demand different needs to ensure competence.

The scenarios referred to earlier in this book represent some examples of the kind of blank minds and sticky moments which we and others have experienced. Roughly speaking, they have clustered under the headings of intrapersonal issues, interpersonal issues, values, purpose and the art of challenging.

It is our experience that the type of difficulties encountered might change over a period of time and over a trajectory of counselling experience. The concept of counsellor development might have some use. This concept has previously been usefully identified in relation to supervision (Carroll, 1996). The developmental increments which are usually identified span a spectrum where concern with the client's story or issues are at one end, with heightened self-awareness and focus on the internal world of the supervisee at the other.

There is also work available on counsellors' general development, and what influences them. As we all know, counsellor training, whether in-house or on a course, is often only the beginning of a career, not the end. A lot happens between training and death – we hope! And of course not all counsellors are formally trained. There are still a few of us who wend a winding road of personal and professional development which has not included three years in a classroom.

The nature of blank minds and sticky moments might change over time in relation to the experience and the developmental stage of the counsellor. As we develop, our ideas and values regarding issues such as sexuality, abuse, death, punishment or politics may change radically, alongside our skill level. It would be naïve of us to ignore the influence of such development. We would like to offer then some observations on a six-stage framework of practitioner development which highlights professional issues which might occur at different stages.

## Enthusiastic: bright-eyed, bushy-tailed and lamps burning brightly

Many of us begin to study counselling and psychotherapy with an enthusiasm not dissimilar to converts to a new religion. We have discovered 'therapy' through having it, seeing it done successfully, reading about it or through going on a course. The enthusiasm is often excessive, either because we have grown disillusioned by our current profession or because we are seeking newer, fresher antidotes for the ailing world we live in. Unsurprisingly, the new recruit passes through this stage avidly reading, practising and debating. Finding and attending all possible workshops is symptomatic of this phase, as is practising skills on unsuspecting friends and family; relationship problems take a high profile here! The lamp shining so brightly does not, however, always make for the best therapy, and blank minds and sticky moments are often concerned with 'What do I do now I've tried an approach?'

Let's take a hybrid figure from our experience, and call her Empathina. Empathina has always wanted to 'help people': young, idealistic and radical, she had dreams of saving people, of changing the world. She believed her motivation to be altruistic: and her insight into her own needs or her passionate concern for the underdog was near the zilch end of the continuum. Some social work training and a basic counselling course had equipped her with an introduction to some therapeutic techniques.

We use the word 'techniques' advisedly – they are different from skills. For example, Empathina was particularly keen to help a family with serious problems regarding care, communication and control: she had learned family sculpting in class, and was keen to try it. Every Thursday night, for six weeks, she visited the family, sculpted them and left. Sculpting seemed a good idea at the time; it was a technique. She went part-way to debriefing the sculpting, but did not have the skill to integrate it into a purposeful therapeutic trajectory. She has wondered from time to time what that family thought of her;

she remembers one of her favourite cartoons, which shows a couple sitting on the sofa, with the doorbell ringing, and the husband saying, 'Try to be non-judgemental, Doris, that'll be the social worker'. Empathina's lamp certainly shone brightly, but she had yet little or no idea of direction.

## Despondency: I'll never get the hang of this!

At some point the new recruit becomes a working practitioner. Whether this is simply working with other students on a course, or working with 'real' clients under supervision, a lack of clarity, concern not to harm and partially developed skills may lead the student into a potentially depressive phase. The overt symptoms of this phase include anxiety and panic attacks, especially before sessions. Use of observers or camera on courses might only add to the emotional concern. It is not uncommon to feel stuck, or to feel blank. Questions range from 'What should I do now', and 'Are you sure that I'll ever be able to do that' to 'Why do I have to do that at all'. Occasionally within this stage students will be overheard to remark, 'I'm sure this is the same as I was doing it before' or 'I can't see why this is better than the way I was doing it'. Other positions adopted by students are the 'Can't I just hint at what they (the client) should do' or 'If they (the client) can't think of a strategy can I tell them what I would do?'

All of these overt expressions of discouragement, frustration and mistrust are symptomatic of covert feelings of self-doubt. Inside the exploding mind of the student, the effort to paraphrase, reflect, empathise, summarise, clarify and challenge, as well as developing a sense of purpose and direction, *while* practising self-awareness, is overwhelming. The student is like the learner driver, feeling that they will never get the hang of changing gear, declutching, steering, looking in the mirror, indicating and manoeuvring simultaneously, even though they can do each bit on their own – and as for following a route into the bargain, well!

At this point, Empathina will be wondering whether counselling is for her. She may well be finding her own self-concept floundering – she always thought she was a 'good listener', but now it seems that she's not. She might be feeling exposed with the demands to self-awareness – there are many possibilities. The point is that this is a time of self-questioning, where incompetences are brought into sharp relief, and self-consciousness abounds.

## Competent and restless: this is okay but let's gets on with the sexy stuff!

Almost imperceptibly, the transition from despondent inconsistency changes almost overnight to 'Yes, now I've got it–what's next?' It is almost as if the 'therapy' fairy calls during the night and sprinkles competency dust over the student. There is no doubt that they have come a long way in a short space of time, but it always surprises us just how quickly the 'now competent' student wants to move on to the 'sexy stuff'.

It seems to us, that just as some of the hard work of learning skills, adjusting attitudes and operationalising the values and philosophy of therapy could begin to pay off, the student becomes bored and wants to move on. Zealous searches for magic, not dissimilar to stage one, are heralded by the typical question–'How does Personal Construct Theory (or Neuro-Linguistic Programming, or Jungian Psychology, or Hypnotherapy, or Transactional Analysis, or whatever the current "in" approach is) fit in to counselling?' Foundation skills are experienced as mundane.

Such searching may take months or years, and for some it never ends. Some practitioners never pass through this stage, and are always looking for the 'new' way, the way that will be 'easier', 'quicker', 'more interesting', 'deeper', 'better', 'cheaper', 'posher', 'slicker' and so on. This is both useful and healthy to some degree, and learning and developing should be a lifelong activity for all practitioners. However, it is perhaps not too useful when it becomes a substitute for using what skills you do have to be helpful. Sticky moments and blank minds might then occur when the practitioner is more bound up with trying to fit what they are hearing into their theoretical framework, rather than really listening with an open mind. It is likely that all approaches will have some merit, and all need to be employed gainfully and responsively with clients before consolidation of learning can occur.

Empathina got through her frustrations and developed more insights. She read Egan and Rogers more thoroughly, liked them, and integrated them into her counselling approach. She consciously acquired more active skills, and her unconditional positive regard was an asset to be proud of! The next few years saw her take a flit round the theories. She already knew about ideas of functional and dysfunctional families and systems theory: in subsequent years, for various reasons, she focused on feminist theory. She became a member of a gestalt group for a year, and was keen to encourage her own clients to speak to empty chairs, and to express their anger in a way which she approved of. Her own personal life and history was under review.

She was able to blame much sexual abuse on 'the patriarchy'. She was hitting some intrapersonal issues which were stimulated through the work, and was attracted to the work through the intrapersonal issues. Blank minds and sticky moments occurred when her preferred theories did not quite do the trick, or when her intra- or interpersonal issues were impinging on the work; she didn't get on with a client, she felt angry at a client's story, she liked a client too much, a client didn't like her. Awareness changed again. She began to depend on the groundwork skills, the bedrocks, to look carefully at her intentionality in her interventions. She realised that 'basic' skills were key, not to be seen as simple, easy or superficial, but to be understood literally as the absolute basis of everything else.

## Cynical: yes but is this (middle-class bourgeois practice) any use to the starving millions in Africa?

Once the practitioner becomes competent, experienced and insightful, there often follows a phase of disenchantment, or discontent. They are inevitably going to be faced with some problems that may be considered trivial, and some which may seem overwhelming. The 'trivial' problems, although important to the client, may induce a feeling that some of the most powerful techniques are being 'wasted' on such simple issues, or conversely that the techniques available are of little benefit when faced with some immense social problems. A common complaint heard from counsellors who are going through this phase is 'Yes, counselling is okay but it doesn't really address some of the bigger issues. There are very few homeless, starving people in war zones asking for counselling – they're all too busy trying to find food and survive.'

Although we have some sympathy for this view, it is a little akin to saying the skills of a cardiovascular surgeon are pathetically inadequate when they are faced with the problem of an undug garden. Abraham Maslow's hierarchy of need[6] can help here. A person's problem will always be contextualised by their current situation, and where that individual is within the hierarchy will determine their priorities.

The baseline of the hierarchy is to take care of the physiological needs of the person. Thus a starving person will not be yet thinking about their safety or social needs until food is found. It is only when a person has secured their physiological and security needs that they may be interested in progressing further up the hierarchy and attempting to meet their social needs. As counselling and psychotherapy are largely concerned with even 'higher' needs such as self-esteem, and self-fulfilment, it is often the case that counselling will not be in great demand to individuals struggling to meet the baseline needs. Recognition of such differentials may lead us to devalue our work and to see counselling as an indulgence.

For Empathina, it was certainly the case that issues arose for her which were more concerned with challenges to values than to her skills. Feminist theories could lead to a sense of despair that unless patriarchal values were challenged, the work was useless. Counselling suddenly seemed a rather bourgeois individualist activity, which helped to make private troubles of public issues, such as homelessness, redundancies, the epidemic of drug addiction. Blank minds and sticky moments took another turn again, more to do with her own frustration regarding large issues.

## Arrogant: I'm so brilliant – how can I use my insights to help the world?

Perhaps an inevitable stage of development for most practitioners is the 'proud and ready for a fall' stage. We have worked with many experienced and creative practitioners who say that they are stuck, only to find the reason is that they have, once again, forgotten or neglected the basics. The use of good old-fashioned empathy has gone; there is no clear contract of what client and counsellor expect and can offer. Instead, there is the preferred fashionable process, technique or theory that is not working. Instead of asking what am I doing wrong, or why aren't I getting anywhere with this client (despite my brilliant supersonic skills), the practitioner often projects onto the client – the client is resistant, or not working hard enough, or doesn't really want to change. Although all of these are possibilities, it is often useful to explore our own potential for arrogance and laziness first. With experience and success it is easy to arrive at a view of yourself as infallible. So keep taking the humble pills – both we and our clients will be better off!

So what of Empathina? She emerged from her heady days of radicalism, having taken a break from counselling, and re-entered the profession from a different perspective again. She realised that her theories were flawed, did not and could not explain everything, and that her own agenda needed to be clearer. When she was frustrated with clients for not understanding her, she realised that it was likely that she was not understanding them. She developed her own framework for helping people, trying to retain a sense of purpose, of realism, of joint enterprise, and of a future orientation. She no longer wanted to be superwoman: she counselled less, and supported herself more. Simple genuineness, and enthusiasm, re-emerged as crucial assets. She became more adept at helping to challenge clients in the sense of helping them to find different and more helpful ways of experiencing their world and taking some control.

When blank or sticky moments occur, they are more likely to be a matter of her awareness and how she can increase her flexibility in how she works and what approaches she offers, a sort of ongoing and gentle self-monitoring. Her aspirations as a counsellor are humble. She has now reached what we would regard as the sixth stage of counsellor development.

*Outcome based and professional: I'd love to help, and it will take some time, some hard work and unless you really want to change you'd be better off spending your time and money somewhere else!*

Somewhere after the arrogant stage, but so close that it may sometimes be mistaken for it, is the end professional stage. This is the consummate professional who knows their limitations, what exactly they can do, what service they are providing, and exactly what the client and counsellor must have attitudinally and behaviourally to make the contract worthwhile for both parties. At this end stage it is still easy to slip back into arrogance or complacency, and thus continued supervision is very helpful, but there are no longer intrusive self-doubts, false modesty or unrealistic expectations of self or potential client outcomes.

This is the stage when the practitioner realises that they can only be at the service of the client if they are realistic, honest and upfront with their clients. Competence requires an ability to say – 'I can only help in certain ways, I can only help if you will work hard with me, there are no magic pills and very few secret recipes, but I have some skills, techniques and processes which I will share with you, and if we both work your life can change for the better. The amount of change, the specifics of the change, and the success of the change are all controlled by you, I take neither responsibility nor credit for any changes you make in your life, only for the way I practise my profession.'

This is a realistic place for Empathina to reach, no longer evangelical, neat with herself, responsible and ethical. Individuals will reach this place at different paces: not all will go through each stage, and perhaps development might emerge differently for those who study counselling piecemeal, and for those who take a linear development through official courses. Whatever the journey, we believe that good supervision is one of the keys to remaining an ethical and accountable practitioner, and we will briefly explore this to end this section.

## Supervision

Supervision has long been accepted as a key element of being a professional, and is important as a route of accountability. There is a great emphasis on supervision as a developmental tool, which we believe it to be, but the accountability aspect is also extremely important.[7] As we have seen, supervised practice is a key element to ensure eligibility for accreditation. Supervisors themselves have an accreditation process to go through if they want to practise mainstream. We have seen that counselling psychologists are expected to contribute to supervision and training of others.

Most supervisors will recognise that counsellors at different stages of development might need slightly different things from supervision. Empathina the altruist, for example, may need some gentle challenging regarding her goals, personal, professional and, crucially, for the client. Empathina the despondent may need some focus on her intrapersonal self, and much support. Empathina the competent but restricted may need help with training input. Skilled supervision should always have as its central goal the well-being of the client.

As we said, we support supervision as a professional adjunct to good practice, with one or two caveats to stimulate thinking. Firstly, we are not sure that a stipulated amount of supervision is of great value, as it is the quality of the work which is key, not its regularity. Yet there is no doubt that having some figure stipulated is a useful tool to ensure that supervision takes place. Regularity also helps the practitioner to discipline themselves into self-supervision. We note that when we have introduced clinical supervision in health settings, the failure of organisations to build in regular time for its practice has often sabotaged the whole initiative. Perhaps in order to demonstrate commitment to supervision, counsellors need to be able to justify their amount/frequency of supervision within the accreditation process, rather than have to conform to a set amount.

Secondly, we have to ask a question which will lead us to the third and final section of this chapter. Counselling is becoming more and more formally regulated, and is also continuing to develop. What are the paradoxes which the profession is generating for itself? And, with certain figures inevitably turning up time and time again, who supervises those who implement the guidelines for training, accreditation and supervision? Who is most influencing the profession, and what does this mean for the discourse of counselling?

## Issues of professionalisation

So, we will be leaving you with some questions, some prods to stimulate your thinking, to challenge the professionalisation process a little. We will briefly cover several points.

The nature of communications is changing rapidly, and one of the delightful and daring developments is the provision of online counselling. Online counselling includes internet chat counselling, videoconference counselling, telephone counselling or e-mail counselling (Steele, 2002). With the exception of videoconference counselling, all of these methods operate without the cues and clues of body language, just as telephone counselling has, although it would seem that at some point we might be able to have counselling with avatars, computer-generated images in our living room – and once we have this, why not have group therapy with avatars? (Gross and Anthony, 2002).

One online counselling organisation boasts that all their counsellors are BACP accredited, while offering prerecorded 'advice' lines to telephone on certain predetermined subjects, all calls being recorded for quality control (www.talktoacounsellor.co.uk, January 2006). This really does present some lovely conundrums: a counselling organisation offering advice; confidential disclosures being recorded. There exist of course many other online counselling organisations who do not boast registration of their counsellors, or accreditation. This demands a huge leap of faith from the client, and can of course be easily open to abuse or exploitation. One reporter investigating online counselling (*Observer*, 18 February 1981) was shocked to discover that her counsellor, Kim Smith, was male – she had been disclosing as if to a female, although, on balance, decided that this was okay. Would it be for everyone? It could be argued that there is more scope for the client to lie, although, as we might ask, why would they, when they have paid for the service?

Conversely, online counselling can facilitate some very creative, safe and effective work. The client can imagine their counsellor to be however they want them to be, which can be therapeutic. There is also something freeing about the distance and the anonymity of the online counselling relationship. We have all sent e-mails where we wouldn't write a letter or say things out loud. We can reach degrees of intimacy very rapidly via electronic communication. So it is not really a question of whether online counselling is good or bad, but we do need to acknowledge scope for paradoxical developments. In a way, it is very freeing ... for the barefoot (virtual) counsellor!

Then there is the question of theoretical bases of counselling and, indeed, of the discourse of professionalisation. A quick trawl of the 'received wisdom' text books will show that a number of figures seem to have many more publications than others within mainstream counselling literature. We explored the SAGE website as an appropriate example. Of 17 titles in the classic 'Counselling in Action' series, 12 are written by men; 6 are written by Windy Dryden, 2 by Dave Mearns. Looking at the whole SAGE directory, about 70 per cent of the authorship is male. Eleven out of 15 of the 'Professional Issues' series are written by men; both of the books pertaining to ethics are written by Tim Bond. We have nothing against men, you understand, or Messieurs Dryden, Bond or Mearns! We recognise that authors with expertise in an area will inevitably reappear – and my goodness, does Windy Dryden reappear!

We are saying, however, that discourses and professions are shaped. There is no doubt that within any profession a certain cluster of people will be the 'in-crowd' at any one time. They will invite and recommend others to form part of the reviews and formulations of knowledge. We have argued elsewhere, although unpopularly perhaps, that the mainstream counselling ethos in the UK is still predominantly white male generated. We still employ the theories of Rogers, Freud, Perls, Berne, Adler, Ellis, Kelly, and so on, as core to counselling courses. We still depend on male-generated philosophies, that dear old Kierkegaard, as suggested in Chapter 9. This is not to say that women are absent from the profession or its development: they are well acknowledged in 'specialisms', and women feature highly in publications and expertises around professional supervision. We are just saying let's keep our eyes open to any limitations that we might be propagating.

Interestingly, many counsellors are fans of 'alternative' or 'complementary' medicines, methods of dealing with physical and mental health which until very recently have not been well recognised in the West. Of course, as we become more and more fans of such interventions, we want to regulate the training, companies want to mass produce remedies, and off we go again into the enterprise zone. However, let's remember that many 'alternative' (which often means Eastern) therapists did not train on a UK-recognised course, nor have to register for practice. Let's make sure we leave space for innovation within our profession – broadly speaking, we revert to if it works, and it's ethical – bring it on. Let's not get so tightly drawn into regulation for its own sake that we curb the 'alternatives'.

We note that the BACP conference in 2007 was concerned to explore themes regarding the global reach of therapy, and we see this as a welcome move. It seems important to learn more about how other cultures conceptualise life, happiness, trauma. Presumably, as we learn more, we will open our understandings of 'human nature' and create more flexibility in what it is to be a person, and how a person might be helped at any one time in their life. At this point we might see that sometimes people can be helped through the medium of counselling, but counselling has limitations. Let us hope the profession uses the understandings of its limitations to free it up rather than increasingly batten it down.

## Notes

1   Freud is generally credited with being the instigator of the talking cure, and his theories of personality remain of significant influence.

2   Rogers is credited with developing the 'person-centred' approach which remains a key concept in counselling today, and indeed in much wider social practices.

3   Egan's model has been a huge influence on counselling courses, particularly at certificate level. It is key to remember that his major contribution to the development of counselling has been in acknowledging key principles of the process of helping; his emphasis on being active and insisting on understanding goals was way ahead of subsequent New Age theories, and is pivotal to the change process. Sometimes Egan is regarded as 'superficial' because he talks of problem solving but, from our perspective, his clear mapping of the change process is fundamental to effective counselling.

4   A full list of criteria is available from the BACP website, at www.bacp.org

5   At one point, it was required that counsellors in training should receive personal counselling, on some accredited courses. This stipulation has now been dropped, but it is interesting that unofficially it remains a favourable criterion.

6   Reference to Maslow (1987).

7   If the supervision contract is effective, the supervisor will be able to pick up signs of dangerous or unethical practice. Supervision contracts need to state clearly in what circumstances the supervisor will break confidentiality, and in what form. We have terminated contracts and taken further action in two circumstances, one being the determination of the counsellor to pursue a sexual relationship with the client, and one being inept practice when working with clients with psychotic tendencies. Naturally, the supervisor is only able to act when there is openness and honesty, and supervision is by no means failsafe.

# 12

# blank minds — hardly
# ever sticky moments —
# not any more!

**Abstract:** This final chapter is a short organisation of the important issues attended to in the previous chapters. It is designed to enable the whole story to be seen, in much the same way as the unveiling of a finished picture enables the importance of the component parts to be seen.

Principles, theory, philosophy, skills and techniques may provide some food for thought, and in themselves can provide significant help for the practitioner and subsequently the client. However, it is our strong belief that practitioners who are largely familiar and competent in these areas, yet still suffer from stuckness and experience blank minds from time to time, would benefit mostly from using an organising framework. Frameworks are never rigid: they should not serve to straitjacket or constrain the practitioner, simply prevent them from getting lost. The success of the framework depends on how flexibly it is used.

We believe a framework or system should act like a map, offering signposts, alternative routes and clearly marked destinations. It should not tell us how to travel or at what speed. This chapter offers such a framework. Version one is unsophisticated and rugged, easy to remember and instantly available. We repeat it in version two in a little more detail, referenced back to the appropriate chapters and sections.

## Using a framework – not counselling by numbers

We are, as you may have gleaned, advocates of Egan's problem-solving model. We believe that those practitioners who balk at Egan's work as simplistic, and counselling by numbers, are often those who have not been well taught it, with the complexities and intricacy that it deserves. Or maybe some antagonists refuse to employ it because it takes discipline to remember it properly whilst doing so many other things?

At any rate, we close with the Russell and Dexter *after Egan* framework, suggesting how the complex can be made easier, and the simple given depth. Although we are taking some liberties with another author's work, we do so with respect. We are proposing modifications to Egan's work, to be seen as additions and simplifications which have worked for us in practice. We know that Gerard Egan would be the first to recommend creativity, flexibility and enhancement at the service of the client. For the full unexpurgated and original work we commend all readers wholeheartedly to his comprehensive book *The Skilled Helper.*

## The simplest of models

For a simple model to prevent the practitioner getting lost, thus reducing at least one source of blank minds and sticky moments, we suggest the following simple formula to remember:

| Contract | Empathy | Challenge Goals | Strategies |
|---|---|---|---|
| Why are we here, and who's (not) doing what? | What's up, and what's really up? | What do you want instead then? | How are you going to get what you want? |

If you are stuck, then one of these requires more attention. Perhaps you need to check your contract – What did I agree I would do if I got stuck? Did we agree boundaries? What about honesty? Did we mention homework? Or check your goals – What is it I'm trying to achieve for my client, myself, my organisation? Am I remembering to use accurate empathy and challenge as a strategy to get moving again?

## The more complex version of the simple model

### Contract

During the course of this book we have been very clear that contracting with your client in the first instant is very important. We suggest the following as essential parts of the contract which will help you to stay clear and prevent you getting stuck:

- Contracts should remain flexible and open to renegotiation by each party.
- Say what service you are offering – counselling and what it is, psychotherapy and what speciality accompanies it, or a mixture which is proactive according to the clients' needs.
- How non-directive, non-judgemental, active or passive are you intending to be – the client may like to know that you will remain silent without explanation, or that (hopefully) you will be clarifying and challenging, before they agree to pay you!
- Do you have any boundaries to your respect for confidentiality – what are these? Ensure your client knows before you begin.
- How long is the session, and do you really mean 'x' minutes or is this just a rough guide. Will you break this boundary if something 'really' important or dangerous comes up at the last minute?
- How many sessions are you offering, is there some possibility of renegotiating the number of sessions later on, or is the number fixed? Is it an open-ended contract 'I'll be here for you whenever, forever?'
- What are the boundaries of contact? Can the client ring you at any time? Do you expect a friendship or love affair to develop? How will you respond if you meet socially?

## Empathy and challenge

The emphasis at this stage is to engage with the client in whatever ways that enable an advanced state of understanding (essentially one-way) to exist. The purpose of this is to permit the practitioner to know the relevant thoughts, feelings and general situation of the client in order to demonstrate their comprehensive understanding. With this display of uncontaminated perception into the client's world, the practitioner will create the necessary trust and rapport in order for the client to continue disclosing sufficiently to enable a clearer view of themselves to emerge. This usually will not require any questions, any opinions or any direction from the practitioner. The use of simple skills such as reflecting, paraphrasing, clarifying and summarising (or similar non-linguistic skills as employed by art or drama therapists) should be entirely sufficient.

If the client's world is not clearly visible after such simple empathy, then challenging skills will be required (see Chapter 4). All sorts of potential challenges may be helpful for different clients in different situations and no one particular approach appears to be uniquely advantageous in all situations. This is perhaps where the study of differing approaches may be helpful to practitioners. Taking a didactic approach and pointing out the blindingly obvious, or subtly inviting the client to reconsider some entrenched position that is unhelpful are interventions which develop from differing philosophical viewpoints, but both may be helpful for some clients on some occasions. It is the principle of being helpful to the client that should influence your choice of challenge, not some intractable philosophical dogma.

## Goals

Ubiquitously misunderstood, goals often provide the most powerful of levers of helpfulness. They are in the main the most positive of challenges that can be issued. They are looked at in more detail in Chapter 4, but for the purposes of this précis, they can be divided into the following:

### Abstract goals

The hidden goals and values of the person that need to be accessed in order for the client to be able to make more sense of their existence. The words extracted from clients in this work will be emotions and states such as: peace, excitement, independence, freedom, stimulation, challenge, control, choice, a sense I've done my best, contentment, happiness, fulfilment, satisfaction, justice or equality.

### Abstract behavioural pictured goals

The abstract goals have to be translated into portraits of what would be happening if the client's life was better. Slightly more tangible imaginings that have some connection with their ideal existence need to be elicited. It is important to remember that much of what has been fantasised can be realised, but in order to do so it has to be specified in more behavioural terms.

What do I really want from my life? If I could choose, how would I spend the rest of my life? If I had a magic wand what would I really like to be happening in my life? Who would be with me, what emotions would I be experiencing more of, instead of the ones I currently have? Where would I really like to be, what would I really like to be doing?

*Concrete behavioural goals*

Out of the picture created by the clients' imagination, what is worth trying for? And what is something that could be achieved? If the client could describe in realistic terms a day, an hour, or a situation where they would be achieving their goal, what would it look like? This sometimes will require a detailed description of what would be happening to others, what each person would be saying and doing. However, it is most important here to remember the practitioner is asking 'What would' not 'What will' to ensure the client remains clarifying what they want, not what they intend to do!

*Fitting goals in context*

Once the client has elicited their goals, a final check as to how they fit in with their personal environment and value system is desirable. What will be the consequence of my pursuing more peace/ revenge/more relaxation? Of leaving my partner and children? Of not leaving? Clients need to check this in relation to themselves or others; this stage acts as a safety-net on impulsive action.

## Strategy

Strategies are forms of action which help the client to achieve their preferred goals. Practitioners are often tempted to start at this point in the process instead of ending here. Why should this be? Basically, it seems that human beings can be so arrogant that they believe that if they listen to someone's problem for a few minutes they can automatically solve it for them – more quickly and more efficiently than the other person ever can. This involves an incredible amount of expertise, wisdom and, of course, conceit. What always amazes us is that we have known counsellors think that this can be achieved without ever ascertaining what it is that the client actually wants!

The most effective and respectful of practitioners will patiently negotiate through a thorough understanding of problems and wants before helping the client discover what resources, strategies and plans are needed to help them achieve their chosen goals.

So the strategy stage is important to ensure that goals are achieved, and we agree there are many ways of helping clients to get in touch with their best resources and strategies. We also believe that it is much better for the client to generate their own strategies, rather than be served with the practitioner's best suggestions. There are a number of ways that practitioners may proceed in engaging in the strategic stage with clients, for example:

*Prompting clients to explore their own resources such as:*

- Who might be helpful in achieving your goal?
- What ways can you think of that would help you to reach your goal?
- How many organisations, agencies or groups can you think of which might help?
- In your day-to-day life do you pass or visit any places such as parks, shops, libraries that might help you achieve your goal?
- Are there any things or places that might help you get to where you want to be?
- Think of as many wild or crazy ideas as possible that might be helpful in achieving your goal.
- How many people can you think of who have had your problems – what did they do?
- Can you think of any training or learning that would help you to achieve your goal?

*Some therapeutic approaches may stimulate clients into exploring their resources. Some examples such as:*

- Rehearsing through role playing and role reversal techniques. – Gestalt and Dramaturgical approaches.
- Conducting small and safe experiments such as those involved in Kelly's Fixed Role Therapy. – Personal Construct Therapy.
- Trying out different ways of behaving through sensory re-programming and seeing what different outcomes occur: are they better? – Neuro-Linguistic Programming.
- Identifying thoughts or ideas that prevent goal achievement and replacing them with more goal-conducive ones. – Cognitive Behavioural Therapy.
- Changing one's inappropriate 'ego' states during interpersonal exchanges. – Transactional Analysis.

All of these are possible ways of stimulating the client into exploring their own resources and discovering their own wealth of creativity. They are then simply a list of strategies themselves. Some are better than others in some situations; some are more directive or didactic than others. Some involve more exploratory work, of past or present; to achieve peace of mind, perhaps someone needs to work through some unresolved grief, or to confront (metaphorically or otherwise) an important figure in their lives. Strategies are not merely lists of superficial actions: **they are everything that the client does through the process of counselling**. So it is very helpful to have them directed to the client's goal, and to remember the principle that:

Strategies should always be 'directed to the service of the client'

What is more, and most importantly, the choice of therapeutic approach, ever macro- or micro-intervention, is a strategy!

## Summary

Summing up is therefore rather simple. Whether the client's problem is some deep-seated misery conceived in traumatic childhood history, some existential issue requiring engagement through a lengthy contemplation of the meaning of life, or a plea of desperation by someone who is unable to pay next week's rent, they all represent symptoms of the human condition, and all require the practitioner's unhampered assistance once the contract is accepted. The practitioner, no matter what approach is being used, is required to utilise all their skills with integrity, practise their arts and science ethically, and serve the clients' needs, not their own. To do this, it is important that they remain focused, that their perspectives remain grounded, and that their mind stays with the client; thus the process remains freed-up.

While counselling is an extremely useful social practice, it is not the be all and end all. It operates many paradoxes, which, once admitted, can aid rather than prevent realistic work. And, finally, practitioners are people too, who have their own needs and limitations.

We wish you all a concentrated mind and many unfettered Moments.

# bibliography

## Publications

Aldridge, S. and Pollard, J. (2005) *Interim Report to Department of Health on Initial Mapping for Psychotherapy and Counselling*. www.mcfaolz. fsnet.co.uk/therapy/reg/mapping-interim-report.pdf

Anonymous (1996) *Primary Colors*. London: Vintage.

Argyle, M. (1975) *Bodily Communication*. London: Methuen.

Argyle, M. (1987) *The Psychology of Happiness*. London: Routledge.

Axline, V. (1964) *Dibs: In Search of Self*. Harmondsworth: Penguin.

BAC (British Association for Counselling) (1989) *Code of Ethics and Practice for the Supervision of Counsellors*. Rugby: BAC.

BAC (British Association for Counselling) (1992) *Code of Ethics and Practice (3.3)*. Rugby: BAC.

BACP (British Association for Counselling and Psychotherapy) (2002) *Ethical Framework*. Lutterworth: BACP.

Bandler, A. and Grinder, J. (1979) *Frogs into Princes*. Moab, UT: Real People Press.

Bandura, A. (1977) *Social Learning Theory*. Englewood Cliffs, NJ: Prentice-Hall.

Bass, E. and Davis, L. (1988) *The Courage to Heal*. London: Cedar Press.

Bass, E. and Davis, L. (1993) *Beginning to Heal*. London: Cedar Press.

Beck, A.T. (1976) *Cognitive Therapy and the Emotional Disorders*. New York: New American Library.

Berger, P. (1973) *The Homeless Mind*. Harmondsworth: Penguin.

Berne, E. (1964) *Games People Play: The Psychology of Human Relationships*. Harmondsworth: Penguin.

Bernstein, B.B. (1962) 'Social class, linguistic codes and grammatical elements', *Language and Speech*, 5: 221–4.

Berry, C.R. (1991) *How to Escape the Messiah Trap: A Workbook for when Helping You is Hurting Me*. San Francisco: HarperCollins.

Bond, T. (1993) *Standards and Ethics for Counselling in Action*. London: Sage.

Bond, T. and Sandhu, A. (2005) *Therapists in Court: Providing Evidence and Supporting Witnesses*. London: SAGE.

BPS (2005) *Professional Practice Guidelines For Counselling Psychologists*. Leicester: BPS.

Bridger, F. and Atkinson, D. (1994) *Counselling in Context: Developing a Theological Framework*. London: HarperCollins.

Byren, R. (2006) *The Secret*. Chicago: Prime Time Productions.

Carkhuff, R. (1987) *The Art of Helping*, 6th edn. Amherst, MA: Human Resource Development Press.

Carroll, M. (1996) 'To the point', *Counselling News*, no. 24, December.

Clark, D. (ed.) (1993) *The Sociology of Death*, Sociological Review Monograph. Oxford: Blackwell.

Corey, G. (1996) *Theory and Practice of Counselling and Psychotherapy*, 5th edn. Belmont, CA: Brooks/Cole.

Culley, S. (1991) *Integrative Counselling Skills in Action*. London: SAGE.

Department of Health (DOH) (2006) *The Regulation of the Non-Medical Healthcare Professions*. London: DOH.

De Board, R. (1998) *Counselling for Toads*. London: Routledge.

Deurzen, E. van and Howard, A. (1996) *Challenges to Counselling and Psychotherapy*. London: Palgrave Macmillian.

Deurzen-Smith, E. van (1988) *Existential Counselling in Practice*. London: SAGE.

Deurzen-Smith, E. van (1994) 'Counselling and intimacy: monologue, duologue, dialogue', selected papers from the 2nd International Counselling Conference, School of Education, University of Durham.

Dexter, L.G. (1997) 'A critical review of the effect of counselling training on trainees', PhD thesis, University of Durham.

Dexter, L.G. (1999) 'Bad for your health?', *Counselling News*, January.

Dexter, G. and Wash, M. G. (1997) *Psychiatric Nursing Skills: A Patient Centred Approach*. London: Stanley Thorne.

Dryden, W. (ed.) (1989) *Key Issues for Counselling in Action*. London: SAGE.

Duck, S. (1988) *Relating to Others*. London: SAGE.

Duck, S. and Pond, C. (1989) 'Rhetoric and reality', in C. Hendrick (ed.) *Close Relationships*. London: SAGE.

Egan, G. (1975) *The Skilled Helper: A Model for Systematic Helping and Interpersonal Relating*. Belmont, CA: Brooks/Cole.

Egan, G. (1990) *The Skilled Helper: A Systematic Approach to Effective Helping*, 4th edn. Belmont, CA: Brooks/Cole.

Egan, G. (1994) *The Skilled Helper: A Problem-Management Approach to Helping*, 5th edn. Belmont, CA: Brooks/Cole.

Ehrenberg, D.B. (1992) *The Intimate Edge: Extending the Reach of Psychoanalytic Interaction.* New York: W.W. Norton.

Ellis, A. (1962) *Reason and Emotion in Psychotherapy.* New York: Lyle Stuart.

Falk, D. and Wagner, P.N. (1985) 'Intimacy of self-disclosure and response processes as factors affecting the development of interpersonal relationships', *Journal of Social Psychology,* 125: 557–70.

Feasey, D. (2005) *Therapy: Intimacy between Strangers.* London: Palgrave Macmillan.

Fee, A. (2006) 'Transgendered identities', *Therapy Today,* February.

Feltham, C. (1995) *What is Counselling?* London: SAGE.

Fieldler, F.E. (1950) 'The concept of an ideal therapeutic relationship', *Journal of Consulting Psychology,* 14: 239–45.

Foucault, M. (1981) *The History of Sexuality: An Introduction.* Harmondsworth: Penguin.

Foucault, M. (1987) *The Use of Pleasure: The History of Sexuality, Volume II.* Harmondsworth: Penguin.

Frank, J.D. (1961) *Persuasion and Healing: A Comparative Study of Psychotherapy.* Baltimore, MD: Johns Hopkins University Press.

Fromm, E. (1979) *To Have Or To Be?* London: Abacus.

Fromm, E. (1982) *Greatness and Limitations of Freud's Thoughts.* London: Abacus.

Fromm, E. (1984a) *The Fear of Freedom.* London: Routledge (Ark Paperbacks).

Fromm, E. (1984b) *On Disobedience and Other Essays.* London: Routledge.

Frost, G. (2006) 'Hot and bothered', *Therapy Today,* November.

Gellner, H. (1985) *The Psychoanalytic Movement.* London: Paladin.

Giddens, A. (1991) *Modernity and Self-Identity.* Cambridge: Polity Press.

Goffman, E. (1959) [1971] *The Presentation of Self in Everyday Life.* Harmondsworth: Penguin.

Grosch, W.N. and Olsen, D.C. (1994) *When Helping Starts To Hurt: A New Look at Burnout among Psychotherapists.* New York: W.W. Norton.

Gross, S. and Anthony, K. (2002) *Technology in Counselling and Psythotherapy: A Practitioner's Guide.* New York: Palgrave Macmillan.

Hagard, M. and Blickem, V. (1987) *Befriending–a Sociological Case History.* Cambridge: Oleander Press.

Heelas, P. (1991) 'Reforming the self: enterprise and the characters of Thatcherism', in R. Keat and N. Abercrombie (eds), *Enterprise Culture.* London: Routledge.

Holmes, J. and Lindley, R. (1991) *Values of Psychotherapy.* Milton Keynes: Open University Press.

Houston, G. (1982) *The Relative-Sized Red Book of Gestalt.* London: Rochester Foundation.

Howard, A. (1990) 'Counselling plc', *Counselling*, 1: 15–17.

Howard, A. (1996) *Challenging Counselling and Therapy*. London: Macmillan.

Ingram, D.H. (1991) 'Intimacy in the psychoanalytic relationship: a preliminary sketch', *American Journal of Psychoanalysis*, 51: 403–411.

Irving, J. and Williams, D. (2001) 'The path and price of personal development', *British Journal of Psychotherapy, Counselling and Health*, 4: 225–35.

James, L. (2007) *Tigger on the Couch*. London: HarperCollins.

Karusu, T.B. (1986) 'The specificity versus non-specificity dilemma: towards identifying therapeutic change agents', *American Journal of Psychiatry*, 143: 687–95.

Kelly, G.A. (1955a) *The Psychology of Personal Constructs. Volume 1: A Theory of Personality*. New York: W.W. Norton.

Kelly, G.A. (1955b) *The Psychology of Personal Constructs. Volume 2: Diagnosis and Psychotherapy*. New York: W.W. Norton.

Kirschenbaum, H. and Henderson, V. (eds) (1989) *Carl Rogers: Dialogues: Conversations with Martin Buber, Paul Tillich, B.F. Skinner, Gregory Bateson, Michael Polanyi, Rollo May, and others*. Boston, MA: Houghton Mifflin.

Kirschenbaum, H. and Henderson, V.L. (eds.) (1990) *The Carl Rogers Reader*. London: Constable.

Krumboltz, J. and Thoresen, C. (eds) (1976) *Counseling Methods*. New York: Holt, Rinehart & Winston.

Laing, R.D. (1969) *The Divided Self*. Harmondsworth: Penguin.

Lasch, C. (1989) *The Minimal Self: Psychic Survival in Troubled Times*. New York: W.W. Norton.

Lazarus, A. (1971) *Behaviour Therapy and Beyond*. New York: McGraw Hill.

Lerner, H.G. (1989) *The Dance of Intimacy*. London: Pandora Press.

Littlewood, R. and Lipsedge, M. (1997) *Aliens and Alienists*. London: Routledge.

MacIntyre, A. (1981) *After Virtue: A Study in Moral Theory*. London: Gerald Duckworth.

Martinovich, J. (2005) *Creative Expressive Activities and Asperger's Syndrome: Social and Emotional Skills and Positive Life Goals for Adolescents and Young Adults*. London: Jessica Kingsley.

Maslach, C. (1982) *Burnout: The Cost of Caring*. Englewood Cliffs, NJ: Prentice-Hall.

Maslow, A. (1987) *Motivation and Personality*, 3rd edn. New York: Harper & Row.

McNiff, S. (2004) *Art Heals: How Creativity Cures the Soul.*, Boston, MA: Shambhala Publications.

Mearns, D. and Dryden, W. (1991) *The Client's Experience of Counselling in Action*. London: SAGE.

Moore, T.H.M., Zammit, S., Lingford-Hughes, A., Barnes, T.R.E., Jones, P.B., Burke, M. and Lewis, G. (2007) 'Cannabis use and risk of psychotic or affective mental health outcomes: a systematic review'. *Lancet,* 370: 319–28.

Morgan-Jones, R. (1993) 'Social anthropology and counselling', in B. Thorne, and W. Dryden (eds), (1993) *Counselling: Interdisciplinary Perspectives.* Milton Keynes: Open University Press.

O'Connor, J. and Seymour, J. (1990) *Introducing Neuro-Linguistic Programming: Psychological Skills: For Understanding and Influencing People.* London: Thorsons.

Parsloe, E. (1999) *The Manager as Coach and Mentor.* London: Kogan Page.

Pilgrim, D. and Treacher, A. (1992) *Clinical Psychology Observed.* London: Routledge

Postle, D. (2007) *Regulating the Psychological Therapies: From Taxonomy to Taxidermy.* Ross-on-Wye: PCCS Books.

Rashid, H.M. (1992) 'Human development theory: Islamic vs Western perspective', *Muslim Education Quarterly,* 9: 4–13.

Reyes, A. (1995) *When You Love, You Must Depart.* London: Minerval Paperbacks.

Robbins, A. (2003) *Unlimited Power: The New Science of Personal Achievement.* New York: Simon and Schuster.

Rogers, C.R. (1942) *Counseling and Psychotherapy: New Concepts in Practice.* Boston, MA: Houghton Mifflin.

Rogers, C.R. (1951) *Client Centred Therapy.* London: Constable.

Rogers, C.R. (1957) 'The necessary and sufficient conditions of therapeutic personality change', *Journal of Consulting Psychology,* 21 (2): 95–103.

Rogers, C.R. (1961) *On Becoming a Person: A Therapist's View of Psychotherapy.* London: Constable.

Rogers, C.R. (1990) In H. Kirschenbaum, and V.L. Henderson (eds), *Carl Rogers Dialogues.* London: Constable.

Ross, P. and Lwanga, J. (1991) 'Counselling the bewitched: an exercise in cross-cultural eschatology', *Counselling,* 2: 17–19.

Rowe, D. (1991) *Wanting Everything.* London: Fontana.

Russell, J. (1993) *Out of Bounds: Sexual Exploitation in Counselling and Therapy.* London: SAGE.

Russell, J. (1996) 'Feminism and counselling', in R. Bayne (ed.), *New Directions in Counselling.* London: Routledge.

Russell, J. (1997) 'Pregnancy lecture, Oxford', in G. Holden, D. Russell and C. Patterson (eds) *Abortion Counselling: Issues and Approaches.* Oxford: Pro-Choice Forum.

Russell, J. (1998) *Keeping Abreast.* York: Insight Press.

Russell, J. (2000) *The Hartop Lecture.* Durham: Durham University Press.

Russell, J. and Dexter, G. (1993) 'Ménage à trios: accreditation, NVQ's and BAC', *Counselling*, 4: 266–9.

Russell, J.M., Dexter, G. and Bond, T. (1992) *Counselling, Advice, Guidance, Befriending and Counselling Skills: Differentiation Report.* London: Department of Employment.

Rutter, P. (1990) *Sex in the Forbidden Zone.* London: Mandala.

Rye, N. (2006) 'Empowering the parent', *Therapy Today*, September.

Seigman, A.W. and Feldstein, S. (eds) (1987) *Nonverbal Behavior and Communication*, 2nd. edn. Mahwah, NJ: Lawrence Erlbaum.

Sennett, R. (1977) *The Fall of Public Man.* Cambridge: Cambridge University Press.

Sennett, R. (1988) 'Destructive Gemeinschaft', in R. Bocock, P. Hamilton, K. Thompson, and A. Waton, (eds) *An Introduction to Sociology: A Reader.* Milton Keynes: Open University Press.

Sheehy, G. (1995) *New Passages: Mapping Your Life across Time.* New York: Bantam Books.

Sheehy, G. (1999) *Understanding Men's Passages: Discovering the New Map of Men's Lives.* New York: Bantam Books.

Sheehy, G. (2006) *Passages: Predictable Crises of Adult Life.* New York: Bantam Books.

Shingler, A. (1999) *Beyond Reason.* Northern Arts.

Silverstone, L. (1997) *Art Therapy: The Person Centred Way – Art and the Development of the Person.* London: Jessica Kingsley.

Simmons, L. (2006) *Interactive Art Therapy: No Talent Required.* Binghampton, NY: Haworth Press Inc.

Smail, D. (1987) *Taking Care: An Alternative to Therapy.* London: J.M. Dent.

Smith, N. (1989) *Perfection Proclaimed: Language and Literature in English Radical Religion.* Oxford: Clarendon Press.

Standal, S. (1954) 'The need for positive regard: a contribution to client-centred theory', PhD thesis, University of Chicago.

Steele, P. (2002) 'Online counselling training', *Therapy Today*, April.

Strong, S.R. (1968) 'Counseling: an interpersonal influence process', *Journal of Counseling Psychology*, 15: 215–24.

Sue, D.W. (1990) 'Culture-specific strategies in counseling: a conceptual framework', *Professional Psychology: Research and Practice*, 21: 424–33.

Swade, T., Bayne, R. and Horton, I. (2006) 'Touch me never?', *Therapy Today*, November.

Taylor, C. (1991) *The Ethics of Authenticity.* Cambridge, MA: Harvard University Press.

Thomas, K. (1974) *Religion and the Decline of Magic.* London: Peregrine Books.

Truax, C.B. and Carkhuff, R.R. (1967) *Towards Effective Counseling and Psychotherapy.* New York: Aldine Atherton.

Weeks, J. (1986) *Sexuality*. London: Tavistock/Ellis Horwood.

Weeks, J. (1990) 'The value of difference', in J. Rutherford (ed.), *Identity: Community, Culture, Difference*. London: Lawrence & Wishart.

Westbrook, D., Kennerley, H. and Kirk, J. (2007) *An Introduction to Cognitive Behaviour Therapy: Skills and Applications*. London: SAGE.

Williams, D. (1991) 'Rogers is a post-Freudian', *Counselling Psychology Review*, 6: 22–5.

Wills, F. (2006) 'Delivering CBT', *Therapy Today*, June.

Wilson, R. and Branch, R. (2005) *Cognitive Behavioural Therapy for Dummies*. Chichester: John Wiley.

Worden, J.W. (1993) *Grief Counselling and Grief Therapy*. London: Tavistock.

## Web-based sources

Carolyn Vincent (2004) 'Sub-personalities' (www.psychosynthesis. org.nz/articles/sub-personalities.html)

Graeme Wilson (2004) 'A personal perspective' (www.psychosynthesis. org.nz/articles/subpersonalities.html)

www.bacp.co.uk

www.bps.co.uk

www.carefertilityweb.co.uk

http://mentalhealth.samhsa.gov/resources/dictionary.aspx#M

www.relate.co.uk

www.talktoacounsellor.co.uk

www.who.int/mediacentre/factsheets/fs220/en/

## Film references

*The Secret* (2006) Directed by Drew Heriot: Global Secrets.

*The Three Faces of Eve* (1957) Directed by Nunnally Johnson: Twentieth Century Fox Motion Pictures.

# index

1994

# DATE DUE

|  |  |  |  |
|---|---|---|---|
|  |  |  |  |
|  |  |  |  |
|  |  |  |  |
|  |  |  |  |
|  |  |  |  |
|  |  |  |  |
|  |  |  |  |
|  |  |  |  |
|  |  |  |  |
|  |  |  |  |
|  |  |  |  |
|  |  |  |  |
|  |  |  |  |
|  |  |  |  |
|  |  |  |  |
|  |  |  |  |